Education, Equality and Human Rights

To what extent did the twentieth century create equality for all? What has been and what could be the role of education in this?

Education, Equality and Human Rights addresses the issue of human rights and their relationship to education in the twenty-first century. Each of the five equality issues of gender, 'race', sexuality, disability and social class are covered as areas in their own right as well as in relation to education. Written by experts in their particular field, the chapters trace the history of the various issues up to the present and enable readers to assess their continuing relevance in the future.

With a new Preface by leading educationist Peter McLaren, the thoroughly updated second edition of this comprehensive book provides an important educational perspective on world-wide equality issues for student teachers and teachers at all stages. It is an accessible and thought-provoking text for all those studying or interested in education, equality and human rights issues.

'*Education, Equality and Human Rights*, 2nd edition, is an urgent and important contribution to the social justice literature as it intersects with current educational debates and struggles.' Professor Peter McLaren, University of California, Los Angeles, USA.

Professor Mike Cole is Research Professor in Education and Equality at Bishop Grosseteste College, UK. He has published a number of books in the field of education and equality and is well known for his research into issues of Marxism and educational theory.

Education, Equality and Human Rights

Issues of gender, 'race', sexuality, disability and social class

Second edition

Edited by Mike Cole

Routledge
Taylor & Francis Group

LONDON AND NEW YORK

kH

First published 2006 by Routledge
2 Park Square, Milton Park, Abingdon, Oxfordshire, OX14 4RN

Simultaneously published in the USA and Canada
by Routledge
270 Madison Ave, New York, NY 10016

Routledge is an imprint of the Taylor & Francis Group, an informa business

Typeset in Times New Roman by
Keystroke, Jacaranda Lodge, Wolverhampton
Printed and bound in Great Britain by
Cromwell Press Ltd, Trowbridge, Wiltshire

British Library Cataloguing in Publication Data
A catalogue record for this book is available from the British Library

Library of Congress Cataloging in Publication Data
A catalog record for this book has been requested

ISBN10: 0–415–35659–8 (hbk)
ISBN10: 0–415–35660–1 (pbk)
ISBN10: 0–203–48716–8 (ebk)

ISBN13: 978–0–415–35659–6 (hbk)
ISBN13: 978–0–415–35660–2 (pbk)
ISBN13: 978–0–203–48716–7 (ebk)

7/20/06

Contents

List of illustrations

Figures

Tables

Contributors

Dr Maud Blair was a lecturer at the Open University from 1991–2002. She was based in the Faculty of Education and Language Studies. Her main areas of teaching and research are related to issues of race, ethnicity and gender. In 2001 she was seconded as an advisor on ethnicity to the Department for Education and Skills. She joined the DfES on a permanent basis and works in the School's Directorate on issues of ethnicity and education. She is co-author of the DfES report *Making the Difference: teaching and learning Strategies in Successful Multi-ethnic Schools* published in 1998. She has written and published widely on issues of gender and ethnicity.

Professor Mike Cole is Research Professor in Education and Equality at Bishop Grosseteste College, Lincoln, UK. He has written extensively on equality issues. Current books include a second, completely revised edition of the highly successful *Professional Values and Practice for Teachers and Student Teachers* (originally published in 2000; reprinted 2003; new edition: *Professional Values and Practice Meeting the Standards* David Fulton, 2005). He is the author of *Marxism, Postmodernism and Transmodernism in Educational Theory: Origins, Issues and Futures*, to be published by Routledge in 2007.

Viv Ellis is University Lecturer in Educational Studies at Oxford University and a Fellow of St Cross College. He was a teacher in comprehensive schools for nine years before moving into teacher education and educational research. His research and publications have been in the areas of sexuality and schooling, teacher education and development, and new technologies and literacies.

Simon Forrest is currently working at the Open University, Milton Keynes researching young people's experiences of love and romance. Previously he has directed the Sex Education Forum – an umbrella organisation involved in promoting sex education – and been a Research Fellow in the Department of Sexually Transmitted Diseases at University College London and Senior Lecturer in Adolescent Sexual Health at St George's Hospital Medical School where he now occupies an honorary position alongside a Visiting Fellowship at the Institute of Education in the University of London. He is also a consultant to Working With Men and Trustee of AVERT (the AIDS Education and

Research Trust). Simon has a special interest in researching and writing about gender, sex, sexuality and young people and has published widely on these issues.

Dr Richard Hatcher is director of research in the Faculty of Education at the University of Central England in Birmingham, UK. He has written widely on issues of education policy and social justice. He is also involved in activity on these issues within the National Union of Teachers and the European Social Forum movement. He is currently researching aspects of privatisation in school systems in England and other European countries.

Tom Hickey is a principal lecturer in Philosophy and Political Economy in the Faculty of Arts and Architecture at the University of Brighton. Course leader of the MA in Cultural and Critical Theory, he teaches courses on critical theory and continental philosophy, Marxism and social theory, and aesthetics and cultural theory in an age of globalisation. His research interests are in aesthetics and politics, British labour history, and the history of Marxism and of the socialist movement. He is currently working on a history of the struggle for democracy in the UK to be published by Continuum in 2006.

Jane Kelly taught Art History and Women's Studies at Kingston University until 2002. Now retired from teaching, her research interests include Surrealism, Feminist Theory and Marxism. She is editor of *Socialist Outlook*, the quarterly journal of the International Socialist Group. Jane is active in Respect: The Unity Coalition and in campaigns on asylum rights. She is chair of the management committee of Southwark Day Centre for Asylum Seekers.

Professor Peter McLaren is Professor in the Division of Urban Schooling, Graduate School of Education and Information Studies, University of California, Los Angeles. He is the author and editor of over 40 books in critical pedagogy, critical ethnography and the political sociology of education. Professor McLaren lectures worldwide, and his writings have been translated into 17 languages. He is the inaugural recipient of the Paulo Freire Social Justice Award at Chapman University. Recently scholars and activists in Tijuana, Mexico created la *Fundación McLaren de Pedagogía Crítica* as an institution to advance Professor McLaren's work throughout Mexico and the Americas as well as the work of critical educational scholars worldwide. Professor McLaren's most recent book is *Rage and Hope: Interviews with Peter McLaren on War, Imperialism, and Critical Pedagogy* (Peter Lang Publishers).

Dr Jane Martin is a senior lecturer in History of Education in the School of Foundations and Policy Studies at the Institute of Education, University of London. She has researched and published widely on historical, social and policy issues in education but with a particular interest in the interlinked inequalities of class and gender. The relationship between feminist thought and actions, and the question of how one defines feminism is a central concern. She is interested in biographical research methods and biographical theory as well as social network analysis. Publications include *Women and the Politics of Schooling in Victorian and Edwardian England* (Leicester University Press, 1999) that won the History of Education Society Book Prize for 2002 and *Women and Education, 1800–1980* (Palgrave, 2004) with Joyce Goodman. Joyce and she co-edited *Gender, Colonialism and the Experience of Education: An International Perspective* (Woburn Press, 2002), a collection that grew out of a shared enterprise generated at the annual conference of the History of Education Society in 1999.

Jane is co-editor of the international journal *History of Education* and is a member of the Editorial Board of the *Journal of Educational Administration and History*. She also serves on the executives of the Gender and Education Association and the UK History of Education Society. She is the Brian Simon Educational Research Fellow 2004–5 nominated by the British Educational Research Association for her on-going biographical project on the British socialist educator activist Mary Bridges Adams (1855–1939).

Richard Rieser is a disabled teacher who has taught for 26 years in higher, further, secondary, primary, and nursery education; and has also written widely on inclusion. He has been full-time director of Disability Equality in Education for the last three years. Prior to this, he was an advisory teacher for inclusion in Hackney. He also served for four years as a member of the National Advisory Group for SEN which advised the government on inclusion and SEN, and is Vice-Chair of the NUT Special Needs Advisory Committee and Working Party on Disability. He is also a member of the TUC Disability Committee, and Vice-Chair of the Council for Disabled Children. He is currently undertaking the Reasonable Adjustment project for the DfES.

Professor Satnam Virdee is Professor of Sociology at the University of Glasgow. His research interests lie in the historical and political sociology of racist and anti-racist collective action, the relationship between racism and nationalism, and class and stratification in relation to race, work, and employment. He is currently engaged on a number of projects including a two-year ESRC-funded study focusing on the relationship between racism and nationalism in contemporary Scotland and England and a study critiquing current theoretical orthodoxy regarding the causes of the changing position of racialised minorities in the English labour market. His book *Racism and Modernity* (jointly authored with R.D. Torres, University of California) is scheduled for publication with Polity Press (Cambridge) in 2006.

Preface

Fashioning a Bulwark against barbarism*

It is evident everywhere that progressive educators around the world are harboring an anticipatory regret at what the world will surely be like if unbridled capitalism has its way. Great swathes of the globe are imploding from the expansion of the world capitalist system. Already the juggernaut of neoliberal capitalism has left in its wake life-threatening poverty, ecological havoc, the amassing and concentration of wealth in fewer and fewer hands, a ceaseless advancement of insecurity and unemployment for already aggrieved communities, and worsening living standards and quality of life for the mass of the world's population. Globalization has meant a worldwide empowerment of the rich and devastation for the ranks of the poor as oligopolistic corporations swallow the globe and industry becomes dominated by new technologies. The transnational private sphere has been colonized by globalized capital, as corporations, financial institutions, and wealthy individuals seize more and more control of the production and distribution of surplus value. The creation of conditions favorable to private investment has increasingly become the cardinal function of the government. Deregulation, privatization of public service, and cutbacks in public spending for social welfare have been the natural outcomes of this process. The signal goal here is competitive return on investment capital. In effect, financial markets controlled by foreign investors regulate government policy and not the other way around since investment capital is for the most part outside all political control. Even citizens in the affluent West can no longer be offered any assurance that they will be able to find affordable housing, education for their children, or medical assistance. And it is the International Monetary Fund and the World Trade Organization who oversee regulatory functions outside the purview of democratic decision-making processes. It is these bureaucratic institutions – including the World Bank – that have set the rules and that arbitrate between the dominant economic powers, severely diminishing the power of governments to protect their citizens, and drastically undermining the democratic public sphere in the process.

We are now in the midst of 'epidemics of overproduction', and a massive explosion in the industrial reserve army of the dispossessed that now live in tent

*An expansion of some parts of this Preface can be found in Peter McLaren, *Capitalists and conquerors: a critical pedagogy against Empire* (Lanham, Md: Rowman & Littlefield 2005)

cities – or *casas de cartón* – in the heart of many of our metropolitan centers. As we recoil from the most vicious form of deregulated exploitation of the poor that history has witnessed during the last century, we continue to witness a re-feudalization of capitalism, as it refuels itself with the more barbarous characteristics of its robber baron and Dickensian-era past. As social 'actors' in the labor process, we have become fuel for the machines of capital accumulation, grist for the satanic post-industrial mills of the transnational capitalist class bloody system for the high-tech jaws of the corporate hyenas whose driving compulsion is to devour living labor; we are remodeled as the living dead, a personification of dead labor in the theater of the damned.

The left's struggle against what appears to be an intractable and immovable force reflects the world-historical agony between socialism or barbarism, only this time such a battle is occurring at a time of unparalleled advantage for capital in a world where a single superpower has set its military into furious motion as neo-liberalism's global enforcer. Efforts by the transnational ruling class that range from attempts at smashing unions, increasing utilities costs in townships such as Soweto, privatizing the water system in Bolivia's Cochabamba, to the marketing of antibiotics to pediatric patients by drug companies whose marketing researchers help them exploit the developmental vulnerabilities of children, have made it clear that they would sell the tears of the poor back to the poor themselves if it would result in a high enough profit margin. Here in the United States, it doesn't help the cause of patriotism much to learn that most US flags that have peppered the homes, storefronts and cars across the country since 9/11 are made in China, and that Steve Walton, the poster-boy for the phrase, 'Buy American', now watches the WalMart chain he founded import 60 percent of its merchandise from China. But does outsourcing to China really matter in a country where most of the apparel industry in the United States is made under similar sweatshop conditions, when even the Department of Defense buys some of its uniforms from sweatshop industries?

In recent years it has become much clearer to me how and why much of the work by progressive educators in the United States has largely failed to effect the urgent and necessary advances in educational equality and social justice that are urgently demanded by the organic crisis we are facing in our schools. It is not that I havè suddenly freed myself from the custody of progressive thought. Or developed an instant clarity of mind forged of the necessary revolutionary adamant to enable me to grasp ideas and do things that had previously orbited outside the precincts of my educational work. It is more the case that I have begun to take stock of the antedating achievements of the Marxist educational tradition in the United Kingdom and elsewhere, and have been engaging works that are clearly within – or at the very least indebted to – such a tradition. This is not to say that most of the educational reform movement in the United Kingdom has managed to escape the kind of despairing capitulation to the inevitability of the rule of capital and the regime of the commodity fetish that we have experienced among reform-minded educationalists here in the United States. Or that we need to misprize everything about the liberal tradition of educational reform. It has more to do with the fact that the critical tradition in the United Kingdom has begun to reemerge in important ways that its United States counterpart has not yet managed to achieve – namely, as a serious reengagement with Marxist analysis and the concept of social class.

But I would be remiss if I limited the rediscovery of Marx and Marxist analysis to leftist scholars in Great Britain. While the border that separates Marx from the academy remains, in the main, unbreached, the tradition of Marxist scholarship and the history of Marxist-driven class struggles is currently enjoying a spiked interest among some constituencies in the North American academy, including education, just as there appears to be a renewed interest in Marxism among grassroots activists, as evidenced by the various panels and sessions at the recent World Social Forums. But it is safe to say that the work being done by British educators such as Mike Cole, Dave Hill, Glenn Rikowski, Paula Allman and others has managed to stir a debate in the United Kingdom that has so far failed to heat up with a similar intensity among the educational left here in the United States. This state of affairs is likely to change as the crisis of capitalism intensifies and world conditions continue to deteriorate into further criminal misuse and state terrorism, and as more Marxist and Radical Left works such as Cole's edited collection begin to attract audiences here.

It is in this context that the most recent edition of Mike Cole's *Education, Equality and Human Rights* needs to be read with renewed appreciation. Addressing issues that include the challenge of disability discrimination in schooling, gender and equality, 'race' and racism, sexuality and social justice, and class analysis and knowledge formation, *Education, Equality and Human Rights* is an urgent and important contribution to the social justice literature as it intersects with current educational debates and struggles. From the date of its original pub-lication, this generous and luminous volume has deftly advanced the fecundating power of Marxist, neo-Marxist and Radical Left analysis in moving educational change beyond the precincts of currently enfeebled liberal reform efforts. Its impact has been impressive and continues to wield considerable influence among theorists, policy-makers, and activists. Released in this new edition that will make it more readily available to educators, social workers, and students of sociology and the social sciences in the United States, this collection of essays could not have come at a more opportune time.

In the United States, the strategy embedded in the mainstream lines of descent emanating from Freire and his exponents and commentators of critical pedagogy has been to make the very concept of class a contestable social concept and an occasion to circumvent serious debate over the causes of exploitation and dynamics of the rule of capital and to increase the plausibility of the liberal imperative of overcoming low 'social economic status', a notion that distantly mirrors the liberal mandate for advancing equal opportunity rather than fighting for social and economic equality. We would be grievously underestimating the degree to which critical pedagogy colludes with ruling class ideology if we ignore its political inertia, theoretical flabalanche and progressive domestication over the years.

Much (but of course not all) of the 'mainstreamed' critical educational work in the United States, along with work in related fields, now appears woefully detached from historical specificities and basic determinations of capitalist society to be of much serious use in generating the type of critique and practice that can move education reform past its log-jam of social amelioration and into the untapped waters of social transformation. What is not on offer is an alternative social vision of what the world should and could look like outside the value form of capital. The construction of a new vision of human sociality has never been more urgent in a world of reemerging rivalries between national bourgeoisies and cross-national class formations where the United States seeks unchallenged supremacy over all other nation states by controlling the regulatory regimes of supra-national institutions such as the World Bank and the International Monetary Fund.

It is a world where the working-class toil for longer hours to exact a minimum wage that amounts to pin money for the ruling elite. Even if the ruling class somehow felt compelled to reconfigure its tortured relationship with the working class, it could not do so and still extract the surplus value necessary to reproduce and maintain its own class formation built upon its historical legacy of class privilege and power.

It is also a world undergoing an organic crisis of capital as domestic class fractions within the United States not only struggle to avoid membership in Marx's reserve army of labor, but are thrust, *nolens volens*, into service as the new warrior class destined to serve as capital's imperial shock troops expected to fight wars of preemption and prevention declared by the US administration under the cover of the war on terrorism. When, as leader of the most powerful nation that has ever existed, you declare war not only on terrorists but also on those who *might* one day become terrorists, you are, in effect, declaring war on the structural unconscious of the nation that you are supposed to be serving, nourishing the psychic roots of national paranoia. It is a war of both direction and indirection, a war without limits and without end, a war that can never be won except on the Manichean battle-ground that exists not in the desert of the real but in the maniacal flights of fancy of religious fundamentalism. The powers and principalities that duke it out with flaming swords beyond the pale of our cynical reason can only be glimpsed in the reverse mirror image of our particular liberties and values that we attribute to the resilience and successes of free market capitalism. But the issue exceeds that of the role of the United States. The detritus of capitalist security states is growing more and more visible throughout the world, as the poor in numerous developed and developing countries continue to be exterminated by war, genocide, starvation, military and police repression, slavery, and suicide. Those whose labor-power is now deemed worthless have the choice of selling their organs, working the plantations or mines, or going into prostitution. Capital offers false hope but as it fails to deliver on its promise, the search for alternatives to its social universe continues. More false hope comes in the form of full-blown theocracies, or governments slouching towards theocratic ideals, and when these are seen for the perversities that they are, there is hope that a socialist alternative will prevail.

The Marxist, neo-Marxist and Radical Left critiques found in the pages of *Education, Equality and Human Rights* in my mind more adequately address the differentiated totalities of contemporary society and their historical imbrication in the world system of global capitalism than progressive trends most often found in the educational literature in the United States. The text as a whole raises issues and unleashes the kind of uncompromising critique that more domesticated currents of critical education studies in the United States do not. And it brings some desperately needed theoretical depth to the tradition of critical education in general. Such theoretical infrastructure is absolutely necessary for the construction of concrete pedagogical spaces in schools and in other sites where people can be critically nourished in their struggle for educational change and social and political transformation.

Cole and his contributors collectively assert – each with their own unique focus and distinct disciplinary trajectory – that the term 'social justice' all too frequently operates as a cover for legitimizing capitalism or for tacitly admitting to or resigning oneself to its brute intractability. Consequently, it is essential to develop – as this marvelous book has done – a counterpoint to the way in which social justice is used in progressive education by inviting students to examine critically the epistemological and axiological dimensions of social democracy so that they might begin to reclaim public life from its embeddedness in the corporate academic-complex. It is precisely this challenge that has been taken up and exercised with such success by the authors of this important collection.

A true renewal of thinking about educational and social reform must pass through a regeneration of Marxist theory within an ecosocialist framework if the great and fertile meaning of human rights and equality is to reverberate in the hopes of aggrieved populations throughout the world. One way to fuel the political agency of those who seek a non-capitalist future is to bring Marx out of the academic storage bins and into teacher education programs and explore the rich history of revolutionary struggle which for me would include movements within the revolutionary or utopian romantic traditions (here I am referring to revolutionary romanticism as a critique of bourgeois modernity distinguished from its other incarnations such as restitutionist, conservative or fascistic romanticism – see Lowy and Sayre, 2001). If critical educational studies is to avoid being corralled into accepting the dominant ideology, or annexed to pro-capitalist forces among the left, or transformed into a recruiting ground for liberal reform efforts, or even worse, turned into an outpost for reactionary populism, it will largely be due to the efforts of people such as Mike Cole and his cadre of authors. This is a book that will reinvigorate the debate over educational change. Not only will *Education, Equality and Human Rights* become required reading for North American educators, social workers, students and professionals, but it will help tilt the scales of the social in the direction of real justice.

Peter McLaren
University of California, Los Angeles

Reference

Lowy, M. and Sayre, R. (2001) *Romanticism Against the Tide of Modernity*. Translated by Catherine Porter. Durham and London: Duke University Press.

Introduction

Human rights, equality and education

Mike Cole

Human rights legislation

As currently formulated, the concept of 'human rights' is a comparatively recent phenomenon. The President of the United Nations General Assembly, Dr E.H. Evatt, observed at the proclamation of the Universal Declaration of Human Rights in December 1948 that this was 'the first occasion on which the organised world community had recognised the existence of human rights and fundamental freedoms transcending the laws of sovereign states' (Laqueur and Rubin, 1979, cited in Osler and Starkey, 1996, p. 2).

Article 1 of the United Nations Universal Declaration of Human Rights states: 'All human beings are born free and equal in dignity and rights. They are endowed with reason and conscience and should act towards one another in a spirit of brotherhood' (cited in ibid., p. 173).[1] One might respond charitably to the exclusion of women in the affirmation of brotherhood, when one reads Article 2, which affirms: 'Everyone is entitled to all the rights and freedoms set forth in this Declaration, without distinction of any kind, such as race, colour, sex, language, religion, political or other opinion, national or social origin, property, birth or other status' (ibid). However, although Article 2 stresses 'without distinction of any kind' I would want to cite 'disability', 'sexuality' and 'age' specifically, in addition to the other examples given.

As far as education is concerned, Article 26 declares:

> Everyone has the right to education. [It] shall be free, at least in the elementary and fundamental stages. Elementary education shall be compulsory . . . [and] shall be directed to the full development of the human personality and to the strengthening of respect for human rights and fundamental freedoms. It shall promote understanding, tolerance and friendship among all nations, racial or religious groups and shall further the activities of the United Nations for the maintenance of peace.
>
> (ibid., p. 174)

Forty years later, in November 1989, the United Nations adopted the UN Convention on the Rights of the Child. Defining a 'child' as anyone under 18, 'unless by law majority is attained at an earlier age' (ibid., p. 175), the Convention reiterated the principles enshrined in the United Nations Charter and stated that

> the education of the child shall be directed towards . . . respect for the child's parents, his or her own cultural identity, language and values [and] the preparation of the child for responsible life in a free society, in the spirit of understanding, peace, tolerance, equality of sexes, and friendship among all peoples, ethnic, national and religious groups and persons of indigenous origin . . . [C]hildren of minority communities and indigenous populations [have the right] to enjoy their own culture and to practise their own religion and language.
>
> (ibid., pp. 178–9)

In addition, 'children with disabilities' have the right to 'special care, education and training designed to help them to achieve the greatest possible self-reliance and to lead a full and active life in society' (ibid., p. 177). I would want to add to this Convention the right, when this becomes apparent, of children to their own sexuality.

On 12 May, 2004, the British Government published a White Paper which paved the way for legislation to set up a single Commission for Equality and Human Rights (CEHR), envisaged to come into being in 2007. This will be created by the Equality Bill which was announced, along with other bills connected with equality, in the Queen's speech in November, 2004. The CEHR will take over the work of the Commission for Racial Equality, the Equal Opportunities Commission and the Disability Rights Commission. Its brief is to *fight discrimination* on grounds of 'race', gender and disability; but also on grounds of religion or belief, sexual orientation and age.[2]

In addition, the Equality Bill will require the public sector to *promote* gender equality. The sector is already required to promote 'race' equality under the Race Relations (Amendment) Act (2000). A separate bill, the Disability Discrimination Bill will do the same for disability. There are no provisions for this requirement to be extended to religion or belief, sexual orientation or age. Regulations outlawing discrimination *at work* on grounds of religion or belief or sexual orientation came into force in 2003, and a ban on ageist discrimination at work will come into force in 2006.

Another bill will outlaw incitement to religious hatred. On the surface, this seems very positive, but there are concerns about how it will be interpreted, and any implications it may have for academic freedom (Natfhe Equality News http://www.natfhe.org.uk/help/EqNews.html: accessed 28 January 2005).

As far as the private sector is concerned, a 'lighter touch' will be applied. This means apparently that private companies will be encouraged to follow new codes of practice which might stress the importance of specified holidays for religious staff, of changing the nature of family away days to be more inclusive of lesbian or gay staff, and of recognising the crucial role that older staff can play (Travis, 2004).

On the wholly negative side is the widely publicised raft of measures concerned with security and the so-called 'war on terror' which will impact disproportionately on Muslims (Natfhe Equality News http://www.natfhe.org.uk/help/EqNews.html: accessed 28 January 2005).

The CEHR and New Labour

In a very telling article on New Labour and the new Commission, *Guardian* columnist, Jackie Ashley (2004) distances the concept of 'equality' from its socialist roots: 'the dinosaur years of taxing the rich till their pips squeaked' (ibid.). 'Now', she states, 'equality is less about tax and more about giving women, minority ethnic groups, disabled people and gay people rights and muscle in the labour market' (ibid.). To underline the point, she continues: '[i]t is still about money and power . . . but it is less about class' (ibid.). 'Britain, like other European countries, will thrive or wither depending on how well it exploits the whole labour force' (ibid.). We must bring 'ethnic minorities', 'older working people', 'disabled people' ('[p]oliticians are beginning to realise that disablement rights mean more than being kind to people in wheelchairs') fully into the economy since '"[e]quality" will be vital to sustaining not just the NHS but also private profits, all our pensions and the tax base' (ibid.).

'Equality in its new meaning', she goes on 'is not going to be much easier for New Labour to sell than "old equality" was for old Labour 25 years ago. This is why the new commission, when it finally launches, must make much of the hard-edged case for equality as a founding principle for our economic success in the decades ahead, as well as the social justice case' (ibid.). '[W]e need a workforce that uses all its talent', she concludes.

Ashley's contention that New Labour's primary motivation for the creation of the new Commission is to foster an inclusive 'workforce that uses all its talent' in sustaining the economy and making profits seems well placed from this 'modernising' party that has fully distanced itself from its socialist roots, and totally embraced neo-liberal global capitalism (e.g. Cole, 2005). Having said that, for socialists, the reforms embraced by the new Commission are, of course, to be welcomed. While socialist commitment is to a transformed world (see below) any progressive reforms should be supported in principle.

The concern is that the new Commission will be as weak or weaker than the old Commissions. It is important that the Commission 'has teeth'; that is able to act decisively and effectively. Clearly there is a need for new harmonised but diverse equality legislation covering all equality issues, and for such legislation to extend beyond the confines of the world of work (although if the preceding analysis is correct, it is clear why this is the Government's priority). A good start might be to extend the excellent provisions of the Race Relations (Amendment) Act to all issues of equality. This seems to be already on the cards for gender and disability. With respect to education, this would make it incumbent on educational institutions to be pro-active and to create equality policies for all the equality issues. It would also require educational institutions to monitor all racist, sexist, homophobic, disablist and classist incidents. As with the specifications of the Race Relations (Amendment) Act, such incidents should be deemed as such (until proven otherwise) if any member of the educational community perceives them as such.

The government seems to have responded to some of the pressure which followed the May 2004 White Paper by agreeing to greater enforcement powers than originally intended, and making the CEHR's first task a consultation on a single Equality Act. In these consultations, further pressure will hopefully result in six separate strands for each of the issues, and guaranteed greatly increased funding (Natfhe Equality News: http://www.natfhe.org.uk/help/EqNews.html: accessed 28 January 2005).

It is envisaged that the CEHR will come into being in 2007, although the Commission for Racial Equality (CRE), which was previously opposed to the new Commission, seems to have dropped its opposition in return for a concession that the CRE will not have to join the merged body until 2008/9 (ibid.)

The aims of the book

The purpose of this book is twofold; first to create a better understanding of equality issues; second, to relate these issues to education. Hence the chapters of this book introduce the issues of gender, 'race' and racism, sexuality, disability and social class in their own right, before specifically relating each to education.

With respect to these five equality issues, five important points need to be made.[3] First, they are all social constructs, which reflect particular social systems; they are not inevitable features of any society, but rather crucial terrains of struggle between conflicting social forces in any given society. In other words, I do not believe that societies *need* to be class-based, to have 'racialized' hierarchies, to have one sex dominating another. I refuse to accept that people are *naturally* homophobic or prone to marginalizing the needs of disabled people. On the contrary, I believe that, in general we are socialized into accepting the norms, values and customs of the social systems in which we grow up, and schools have traditionally played a major part in that process. Where these social systems exhibit inequalities of any form, those at the receiving end of exploitation, oppression or discrimination have, along with their supporters, historically resisted and fought back in various ways, as the chapters of this book bear witness. Schools do not have to be places where pupils/ students are encouraged to think in one-dimensional ways. Indeed, were this the case, there would be no point in this book. They can and should be arenas for the encouragement of critical thought, where young people are provided with a number of ways of interpreting the world, not just the dominant ones.

Second, each of the issues under consideration in this book has a material and institutional parameter (differences in wealth and power, laws which disfavour certain groups) and a personal parameter (modes of thinking and acting both by the exploiters and discriminators, and those on the receiving end of exploitation and discrimination).

Third, these inequalities are interrelated and need to be considered in a holistic way. Every human being has multiple identities. To take a case in point, there are, of course, lesbian, gay, bisexual and transgendered people in all social classes, among the Asian, black and other minority ethnic communities and among the white communities. There are lesbian, gay, bisexual and transgendered people with disabilities and with special needs.

Fourth, while recognizing the interrelation of various inequalities, at the same time, their separateness must also be acknowledged. As will become clear in the chapters of this book, people are not only exploited and oppressed in similar ways, they are exploited and oppressed in different and specific ways.

Since each chapter is introductory in its own right, I do not propose to discuss each equality issue here. However, there is one final point to make in this Introduction. It is necessary to make a distinction between equality and equal opportunities. Equal opportunities policies, in schools and elsewhere, seek to enhance social mobility within structures which are essentially unequal. In other words, they seek a meritocracy where people rise (or fall) on merit, but to grossly unequal levels or strata in society – unequal in terms of income, wealth, lifestyle, life chances and power. Egalitarian policies, policies to promote equality, on the other hand, seek to go further. First, egalitarians attempt to develop a systematic critique of structural inequalities, both in society at large and at the level of the individual school. Second, egalitarians are committed to a transformed economy, and a more socially just society, where wealth and ownership is shared far more equally, and where citizens (whether young citizens or teachers in schools, economic citizens in the workplace or political citizens in the polity) exercise democratic controls over their lives and over the structures of the societies of which they are part and to which they contribute. While equal opportunity policies in schools and elsewhere are clearly essential, it is the view of the contributors to this volume that they need to be advocated within a framework of a longer-term commitment to equality. It is in this spirit that the book is written.

Acknowledgement

I would like to thank Hugh Starkey for his advice on the human rights legislation in this chapter.

Notes

1   This citation from the *Universal Declaration of Human Rights* and the following citations from the *Universal Declaration of Human Rights* and the *Summary of the UN Convention on the Rights of the Child* are taken from Osler and Starkey (1996), Appendices 1 and 2 respectively. I have indicated the page number of Osler and Starkey's book on which each citation occurs.
2   Social class is not mentioned. For socialists, social class equality is an oxymoron, since capitalism is fundamentally dependent on the exploitation of one class by another. The end of this exploitation would herald the end of capitalism and its replacement by socialism (see Chapter 9 of this volume for a discussion). However, it is my view that discrimination with respect to social class origin (classism) should be part of the legislation. Thus, it is pleasing to note that, signalling the low achievement of white working class boys, Trade and Industry Secretary, Patricia Hewitt has stated that as

well as 'disadvantaged Muslim communities' the CEHR will have within its remit such boys growing up

> in families and communities where the old manufacturing jobs have disappeared, many of the parents aren't in work and where if you do apply for a job, many employers will take one look at the post-code and not even offer you an interview.
> (Travis, 2004)

Whether this is a genuine concern for all deprived people, or more a reflection of the backlash against multiculturalism (Vaz, 2004) is another question.

3   The rest of this Introduction draws on Cole and Hill (1999).

References

Ashley, J. (2004) Politically Correct (http://www.guardian.co.uk/comment/story/ 0,,1250977,00.html: accessed on 7 August, 2004)

Cole, M. (2005) 'New Labour, Globalization and Social Justice: The Role of Education', in G. Fischman, P. McLaren, H. Sünker and C. Laukshear (eds) *Critical Theories, Radical Pedagogies and Global Conflicts*, Lanham, Md: Rowman & Littlefield

Cole, M. and Hill, D. (1999) Introduction in P. Hill, and M. Cole (eds), *Promoting Equality in Secondary Schools*, London: Cassell

Osler, A. and Starkey, H. (1996) *Teacher Education and Human Rights*, London: David Fulton

Natfhe Equality News: http://www.natfhe.org.uk/help/EqNews.html

Travis, A. (2004) Minister Defends New Equality Body (http://www.guardian.co.uk/ guardianpolitics/story/0,,1215402,00.html: accessed 6 August, 2004)

Vaz, K. (2004) Divided We Stand, United We Fall, *The Guardian*, 21 May

1 Women thirty-five years on
Still unequal after all this time

Jane Kelly

Introduction: women's liberation or post-feminism?

Although some women claim that we are in a post-feminist era, we have only to look at the demands of the first Women's Liberation Conference, held at Ruskin College, Oxford, in 1970, to recognize that we are still far from having achieved equality. The 1970 conference demanded equal pay, twenty-four-hour childcare,[1] free contraception and abortion on demand. Later, other demands were added – the right to determine one's own sexuality; the rights of black women, including the right to determine their own demands autonomously; reproductive rights; and the right to education.

If we look at just the first three, none of these has been achieved. Despite the Equal Pay Act of 1973, and the highest number ever of women working – over 70 per cent – women still only earn 82 per cent of the male wage; and these figures are based on full-time work. Of course the high proportion of women working part-time, do not earn anything like that percentage.[2] The highest percentage of part-time women workers, 48 per cent, is to be found amongst those with dependent children. Despite the fact that nearly 40 per cent of employees have dependent children and 55 per cent of women with children under five years are at work, the high cost of nursery provision means that part-time work is often the only option for women.

The New Labour government has put in place a policy of a nursery place for every three and four year old by 2004 and there has been a threefold increase in spending from £66 million in 2001 to £200 million in 2003–4, creating one million new childcare places by March 2004. However, since large proportions of mothers are returning to work soon after the birth of their child, the cost of childcare for the under threes remains very high and only 5 per cent of employers contribute to childcare costs, with another 5 per cent offering nursery places.[3] So the government's increase in spending on childcare is scarcely an adequate response to the needs of mothers for pre-school childcare, whether they are raising children on their own or not.

As for free abortion on demand, while abortion rights are less threatened by legal attacks than they were in the 1970s and 1980s, the service is still geographically patchy. Recent attempts to investigate a doctor for carrying out an abortion for a women carrying a foetus with a cleft lip and palate show that thirty-seven years after the 1967 Abortion Act was passed, women still do not have a right to choose whether to have a baby. The provision for in vitro fertilization (IVF) is also a geographical lottery with couples, including same-sex couples, often having to pay for private treatment because of poor NHS provision.

Postmodern feminism

The current fashion for postmodern theory is quite incapable of explaining why, thirty-five years after the founding of the modern Women's Liberation Movement and the achievement of several pieces of equal rights legislation, such as the Equal Pay Act of 1973 and the Sex Discrimination Act of 1975, the original demands have not been met. The adoption of various post-feminist frameworks by many feminist writers and theorists has not helped us to understand why this should be the case. Postmodernism's refusal to analyse society as an entity and its determination to concentrate on the local situation means it is unable to understand women's oppression. Some feminists who have adopted postmodernism even encourage the use of distinct and often contradictory theories to look at different elements (e.g., Fraser and Nicholson, 1990, p. 26) which leads to incoherence and an inability to understand the interrelation between these different elements of the oppression of and discrimination against women.

Since the 1980s, the writings of the French female psychoanalysts Luce Irigaray and Julia Kristeva, who had been students of Jacques Lacan, have been increasingly adopted by feminists, along with the writings of Michel Foucault, Jacques Derrida and Roland Barthes. The stress these writers put on the place and role of the individual in society leads to real difficulties in analysing the position of women. They argue that individual consciousness is in a state of constant change, unstable and in flux; that the female subject enters the conscious world of male-dominated language and is thus inevitably discriminated against, forced to speak an alien language; that power is not centralized, for example in the state, or some other recognizable authority, but located within the individual herself. Consequently, the acquisition of knowledge or the ability to judge truth from falsity is an impossible ideal, best forgotten.

At the same time, many one-time feminists have assumed that so much has been achieved there is little left to fight for. Successful careers have been built – as journalists, as politicians, as academics – from analyses once made of the rights and roles of women, but, whether out of pessimism that little can now be changed, or through a misunderstanding that their own lives represent all women's lives, a certain smugness has set in so that actual investigations into the real lives of ordinary working women are rare today. Instead the notion that women can make it if they try hard enough has taken hold, leaving the lives of the vast majority of working women unrepresented and invisible.

Despite the necessity of strategic thinking when dealing with something as pervasive as women's oppression, we are left with a choice between postfeminists who deny that anything needs changing or postmodernists who recognise women's oppression but whose framework is incoherent and contradictory.

The refusal of postmodernism and postfeminism to think about the whole world and its relationships is thoroughly pessimistic and totally inadequate when it comes to changing the lives of half the world's population – namely women. Rather than using these theories I want to suggest like other writers, such as Mike Cole (2003, 2004, 2005) that Marxism is much better placed to explain why women have not been able to achieve equality over the last thirty-five years.

Against those who say that Marxist and socialist theory is gender- and colour-blind, that it 'has used the generalising categories of production and class to delegitimise demands of women, black people, gays, lesbians, and others whose oppression cannot be reduced to economics' (Fraser and Nicholson, 1990, p. 11), I want to argue for a return to the ideas of socialism and Marxism, to reject the criticism that it ignores and is ignorant of the position of women (and other oppressed groups), in order to discuss the position of women today in Britain. I think it is important to relate the ideological offensive against women, carried out by the Tory governments since 1979 and continued by New Labour, to the real position of women, at home and in the paid workforce, and to sketch out some areas of fruitful campaigning activity for the development of feminism and to fight for equal rights (see, for example, Kelly, 1992, 1999).

In this chapter I am going to look first at some examples of discrimination against women in the nineteenth century, as well as various struggles resulting in legislative or women's rights, including for both middle- and working-class women. Second, I will discuss some issues relating to women, work and the labour market today. I will explain why equal rights legislation has failed to alter women's position at work, and ask whether discrimination and inequality are direct results of biology – in the famous phrase: is biology destiny? – or whether the social position of women, especially the role played by women in the family, is more influential. Finally, I want to to suggest one or two theories based on Marxism which may help us understand these problems, to put us in a better position to continue the struggle for equality.

Gendered divisions: women in the nineteenth century

While we should continue to press for the demands made in the early 1970s, we should not assume that nothing has been gained. If we look back to the position of women in nineteenth-century Europe, we can see just how many gains have been made since then. The Industrial Revolution, which moved production out of the home into the factory, had profound effects on both middle- and working-class women. It resulted in different spheres of influence and a gendered division, at least for middle-class women, between the domestic or private space of the home – the woman's world – and the public world of men.

In Victorian Britain, sexual hypocrisy meant that middle-class women were not supposed to enjoy sexual contact, while their husbands, partners in promoting the family values of thrift, sobriety and piety, used prostitutes in their thousands. The secondary position occupied by both middle- and working-class women in Britain in the nineteenth century is symbolized by the so-called 'rule of thumb'. Nowadays this means a more or less accurate measurement; then it meant that a man was legally entitled to hit his wife or partner, as long as the stick was no thicker than his thumb!

These changes were not confined to Britain. Women were in a similar position in France, for example. Berthe Morisot, an impressionist painter, was unable to help organize the impressionist exhibitions, despite the fact that she showed in all but one of them, because the organizers (Monet, Pissarro, Renoir – all men) met in cafés which were out of bounds to middle-class women. One of the reasons middle-class women were barred from so many public places in the French cities was because working-class women *were* present: as barmaids, laundresses, sales-girls and especially prostitutes, on the streets and in cafés. So this private/public division was not only gendered but divided by class (Lipton, 1987; Pollock, 1988; Garb, 1993). The barring of middle-class women from the sights and sounds that constituted modernity, which was the subject matter of impressionism, meant that female artists like Morisot, Mary Cassatt and Eva Gonzales painted different and more restricted subjects, such as domestic interiors, views from balconies: the street, the café, backstage at the theatre were barred to them. As a result, until the recent development of a feminist art history, many books on impressionism omitted the women artists from the history altogether, refusing to recognize that discrimination led them to different subjects; despite the fact that in Morisot's case her style was classically impressionist.

In Austria, too, Freud's discovery that many middle-class women suffered from what he described as 'hysterical symptoms', including temporary paralysis of limbs, has also been partially explained by reference to their seclusion within the home. Oppressive domesticity, daily unchanging routines, complete economic and social dependence on men led some women to rebel in the only ways open to them. Whether such hysterical symptoms were the result of real sexual abuse by their fathers, other male relations or close family friends or whether the experiences had been fantasized is open to question; that the women experienced extreme physical symptoms for which there were no physiological explanations cannot be denied.

While the Industrial Revolution constructed a norm of oppressive domesticity for middle-class women, it also led to the growth of a new class, the proletariat, or working-class, which included men, women, and initially children as well. The contradiction between the ideal of a genteel, domestic femininity for women and the reality of working women's lives, fulfilling the needs of the capitalist economy, produced a number of struggles for women's rights, fought for by both middle- and working-class women, most notably for female suffrage – the right to vote.

The demand for women's suffrage in Britain, fought for on and off during the whole of the second half of the nineteenth century and the first decades of the twentieth, saw the British labour movement divided. The Chartist demands in the 1840s for annual parliaments, proportional representation and universal suffrage did not include the vote for women: they were opposed to female suffrage, as were many in the Independent Labour Party (ILP) during the last decade of nineteenth century and the first of the twentieth, and the Labour Representation Committee (LRC), the early form of the modern Labour Party.

Conversely, at the turn of the century Keir Hardie, a supporter of women's right to vote and a radical member of the ILP, said that:

> he valued the zeal of middle and upper class suffragettes, but felt that 'without the active support and cooperation of working women they will have no chance whatever of being successful.' Much of his speech [in 1902 to suffragettes at Chelsea Town Hall] was devoted to countering the arguments against women's suffrage he had come across on the Labour Representation Committee. Socialists were fearful of the influence of the priest and the parson if women got the vote: Hardie said he preferred that to the influence on men voters of the publican (usually Tory) and the bookmaker. Trade unionists sometimes argued that votes for women could lead to domestic discord: what sort of domestic peace is it, Hardie asked, if it is based on the wife being treated as an 'inferior domestic animal'?
>
> (Liddington and Norris, 1978, p. 153)

The vote for women aged thirty years and over was eventually won in Britain in 1918 and in 1928 for those over twenty-one, but it should be remembered that in France women only gained suffrage in 1944.

Other feminist campaigns in Britain produced reforms such as the Married Women's Property Acts, in 1870, which gave women the right to keep their inheritance and earnings; the Custody of Infants Act of 1886, which gave widowed mothers rights over their children, previously the responsibility of a male guardian after the husband's death; and in 1888 maintenance for deserted wives as long as the husband was at fault.

There were changes in education too, especially with regards to middle-class women. In 1850 North London Collegiate School, the first academically oriented day school for the daughters of the middle-class was opened, and in 1873, along with a number of general changes in education, Girton College, Cambridge, the first college for women, was founded. The setting up of mass education in the last decades of the nineteenth century is a telling example of the institutionalization of inequality. Always related both economically and ideologically to the needs of the state, mass education was set up with class and gender divisions structured in. From the 1870s to the end of the century, working-class girls' education was dominated by training in domestic economy, in cookery and laundry – education for motherhood. In the early twentieth century, childcare was added.[4] In this same period the majority of middle-class girls were educated at home or in small private boarding schools, apart from the few more academic schools like North London Collegiate School and Cheltenham Ladies College (1854). These two had a broader educational content than schools for working-class girls, but like other middle-class girls' education, it too was primarily a training for marriage and homemaking.[5]

Until the end of the nineteenth century most changes pertained solely to middle-class women, for working-class women could afford access to neither education nor the law. However, legislation was passed which altered the lives of working-class women. In the 1870s and 1880s laws restricting the conditions of work for women were gradually introduced; for example, women (and children) were banned from working in the mines and from night work. This latter was a double-edged sword: women were only barred from night work where men were also employed, and this was usually better-paid work; they were allowed to work at night in the caring professions – nursing – and in places of entertainment, for example, bars and music halls. The exclusion from better-paid night work was achieved in the name of reform with the connivance of the male-dominated trade union movement which used the argument that a man was entitled to a 'family wage', enough to keep his wife and children so that the former should not have to take paid work.

In trying to emulate the middle-class ideal, the working-class wife and mother was made dependent on the male wage earner and the man was made responsible for his whole family. In practice, of course, women continued to take paid work, but in the less well-paid and less protected areas.

This contradictory reform was not accepted without a fight. For example, in 1874 the Women's Protective and Provident League (WPPL) was formed to oppose both restrictive legislation for women as well as their exploitation at work. Launched by Emma Paterson, who was a bookbinder from Bristol, with the help of Mrs Mark Pattison (later Lady Dilke), the WPPL sought:

> 'the protection afforded by combination', thereby avoiding exploitation by employers and the hostility of working men who, fearful 'that the employment of women . . . [would] lower their wages', were 'forbidding their members to work with women' and agitating 'to limit the hours of women's work in factories and workshops'. To Paterson, such legislation was offensive because it both reduced female earning power and put women on a par with children, for whom protection was also sought.
>
> (Bolt, 1993, p. 175)

But the legislation was passed anyhow.

This is not merely a matter of historical debate, for as recently as the 1970s, trade unionists at the Cowley car plant in Oxford fought a long battle for the right of women to work nights, alongside men and for better wages than daytime work offered. This debate is part of the equality versus difference debate: do you fight for women's rights on equal terms with men – for example, making pregnancy and childbirth a temporary disability akin to breaking your leg – or do you argue that women's lives are fundamentally different from men's so that they need different rights and legislation to men, including protection from certain types of work, and in particular circumstances, during pregnancy, for example? Alexandra Kollontai a leading member of the Bolshevik Party, took the latter view. In the period after the 1917 revolution in Russia she took up these issues and wrote a number of papers on them. As Alix Holt writes in her introduction to Kollontai's writings:

Some of the first laws prepared by the commissariat related to the protection of maternity: women were given a legal equality that took their reproductive function into consideration. Women were not to be employed in various jobs harmful to their health, they were not to work long hours or night-shifts, they were to have paid leave at childbirth.

(Holt, 1977, p. 117)

Kollontai had been discussing the needs of women in pregnancy and after childbirth well before 1917, including in a 1914 pamphlet entitled 'Working Woman and Mother'. Some of the demands she developed here included maternity insurance schemes to provide benefits for women for sixteen weeks, or longer if the doctor thought necessary, both before and after the birth of a child. These were to be given directly to the mother, whether there was a live birth or not, and were to be one and a half times the woman's normal wage, or of the average wage if the woman was not employed. She was also to be entitled to benefits, equalling one-half of the normal wage, for the whole period of breast feeding, and for at least nine months (Holt, 1977, pp. 137–8). For Kollontai, the reproductive capacity of women had to be taken into account as a special circumstance, not only for the sake of the mother, but for the child's health.

Compared to nineteenth-century legislation in Britain, framed by the demand for a 'family wage', and leading to the exclusion of women from well-paid work, the changes introduced into the new Soviet Union were based on the equality of women, and their right not to be discriminated against because of reproduction.[6]

Women and work

Economic independence, paid work outside the home, has been seen by many as a prerequisite of freedom for women. The ability to take paid work depends on the control of fertility. From the outset the modern Women's Liberation Movement recognized the centrality of choice in matters of reproduction in the fight for equality for women. The development and introduction of the contraceptive pill, while it carried some unacceptable health risks, was still the first contraceptive method that could be relied upon to be effective, and meant that women could increasingly control their fertility: sexual intercourse did not any more lead inevitably to pregnancy and childbirth. The Abortion Act of 1967 also helped women in their right to choose whether, when, where and how to have children.

The control of fertility was an important development in the process of the incorporation of women into the workforce from the 1960s onwards. Women had been drawn into the workforce during the Second World War but were moved out of heavy industry and munitions afterwards. Although immigration from the Caribbean and from the Asian subcontinent was initially used to fill the labour gap, by the early 1960s this immigration was being restricted, and women were once again drawn into the workforce in increasing numbers.[7]

Women now make up 50 per cent of the workforce in Britain, an increase of ten per cent since 1973. The largest proportion of women ever work for a great part of their lives.[8] However, in the main, women's work is different from men's; it is within a segregated labour market, in worse conditions, for less pay and is more frequently part-time. The suggestion made by some who have adopted a post-feminist agenda that women have achieved equality at work is far from the truth. Even for middle-class women in such jobs as company financial managers and treasurers, where women's average hourly earnings amount to only 60 per cent of men's, equality remains far away. It is true that in some professions women's pay is nearer men's, but in most cases women are paid well below their male counterparts. Ironically the difference is at its narrowest at the bottom of the low pay scale, for example among check-out operators and retail cashiers where women's average hourly earnings amount to more than 99 per cent of men's.[9]

In addition the majority of women at work are segregated both *horizontally*, in different jobs from men, for example in nursery and primary teaching, where the majority of workers are women; and *vertically*, in jobs that men do as well, but where women are usually lower down the scale or career ladder.

All this has an impact on the lower pay women receive. In the segregated labour market 49 per cent of women are employed in three areas of work: secretarial and personal assistants, sales and customer services and personal services such as childcare, all of which are poorly paid.[10] For example childcare workers, who are 97.5 per cent female, earn on average £8,000 in a private day nursery, rising to between £10,000 to £13,000 for a qualified worker in an educational or social services setting. The average age of these workers is thirty-two, many will be parents themselves. Such segregation leaves women in poorly paid work, in the service sector, in the caring professions, replicating expectations of women's work in the home.

One change which has taken place over the last five years or so is the significantly higher number of mothers who return to work after maternity leave, though this is often into part-time employment. In 2003 19 per cent of women with a child under five years and who were married or co-habiting, were working full-time; but 39 per cent were working part-time. For single mothers these figures were 10 per cent and 23 per cent. These figures rise as the child goes into full-time education. However, it is still the case that women rather than men, take a break for childrearing – euphemistically called a career break – which also interrupts work patterns, affecting work and career prospects.

Jobs normally carried out by men are also undervalued when women are the majority of the workers. For example, in the ex-USSR most doctors were women and were very badly paid compared to industrial workers.

Where women work in sectors alongside men, they work in the lower grades with less pay. For example, the majority of teachers are women, but the majority of head teachers are men. This is replicated in the teaching unions: the National Union of Teachers has a majority of women members but the General Secretary has always been a man.

The Dual Labour Market thesis (Barron and Norris, 1976) describes this segregated labour market, pointing to the way women workers are segregated into areas of work associated with their domestic roles and responsibilities, but it does not explain why women are in this situation, why they have accepted this secondary position, why it is seen as normal, nor what employers gain from hiring women, rather than men.

Women now represent around 50 per cent of the workforce, and the right to work and the right to choose both seem firmly embedded in contemporary thinking, yet women still only earn 75 per cent of the male wage. Why have the Equal Pay Act and the Sex Discrimination Act of 1975 not eradicated inequality?

To understand all this we need to look at the history of the last twenty-five years. The attacks by the Tory governments of the 1980s and 1990s have continued under the New Labour governments. The neo-liberal economic agenda, along North American lines, has led to cuts in the welfare state, increasing privatization of public sector provision, worsening working conditions, including working very long hours or having more than one job: all this affecting the position of women for the worse. At home, women are now responsible for more caring than in the past, including for the sick, the disabled and the elderly, picking up the pieces of the disintegrating welfare system. In their paid work outside the home, women are the majority of workers in the public sector – in the NHS, in education, in social services – where conditions have worsened considerably.

Dramatic and startling changes in employment took place in Britain in the 1980s and 1990s. There was a massive loss of traditional jobs in engineering, mining and manufacturing. These were jobs with high status, good conditions and pay, full-time and unionized, with trade unions that fought to improve conditions, such as the installation of pit-head baths for miners, and they were jobs for men. There was a parallel increase in the service sector, jobs with flexible hours, part-time and short-term contracts, poorly paid and non-unionized: these are women's jobs.[11]

These structural changes go some way to explaining why women have not achieved equal pay: there is both horizontal and vertical segregation between men and women at work. Women work in the segregated labour market and in jobs at the bottom of the ladder. Assumptions about women's wider roles of responsibility for home and children make their paid work secondary. This not only includes women with husbands or partners but single women and female single parents.

Does this mean, therefore, that the oppression of women is based on biological difference? Does the biological fact of women's procreative capacity inevitably lead to this position of inequality? Is this position unalterable? Or is it rather a result of the particular ways in which our society operates, and therefore would another type of society have different solutions? I will now turn to elements of Marxist theory to offer some possible explanations for women's inequality which suggest that this is not simply a function of biology, but is fundamentally determined by the economic and social demands of capital, which uses biology to reinforce the secondary role of women and sustains gender divisions to maintain its rule.

Divide and rule: production, reproduction and the reserve army of Labour

Capitalist society not only divides by class, but takes advantage of other divisions, including sex and 'race', to maintain its rule. Recognizing that women's oppression had been used by the ruling class to maintain power in all societies, Engels linked together the production of goods for use or sale and the reproduction of life. 'The decisive element of history is pre-eminently the production and reproduction of life and its material requirements' (Engels, 1978 [1884], p. 4). In *The Origin of the Family, Private Property and the State*, Engels shows that the way in which a society reproduces itself (makes things, provides food and shelter, and so on) will affect everything about that society.[12] Thus he argues that where the capitalist mode of production predominates, where the law of value reigns, where production for profit supersedes production for use, the same ideas also influence such intimacies as marriage and family life. Within the family, he says, women are oppressed as a secondary partner – within the family he is the bourgeois and the wife represents the proletariat used to reproduce both the present and future labour force cheaply, as well as providing a source of cheap labour outside the home.[13]

Women are expected to reproduce the future labour force, by childbearing. In addition they are expected to 'service' the other members of the family for free: shopping, preparing food, cooking, cleaning, giving emotional support; all these are the responsibility of women, to such an extent that women often find themselves without any knowledge or understanding of their own emotional and practical needs.

Marx and Engels gave insufficient weight to the way in which women's entry into the workforce is determined by her role in the family; instead they analysed the family and paid work separately.

> Marx's analysis of the general tendencies within capitalism provides the foundation for the analysis of female wage labour, but . . . his specific, and extremely fragmentary, allusions to the position of women are unsatisfactory because he, like Engels, does not adequately analyse the relationship between the family and the organisation of capitalist production.
>
> (Beechey, 1987, p. 56)

Domestic roles played by women clearly influence the way they work and the kinds of jobs they do. Putting women's reproductive and domestic roles first, women's paid work outside the home is less valued than male work. Even when the woman is in fact the sole wage earner and where women make up half the workforce, it is assumed that their work is secondary to a male wage. This devaluing of women's work is based on the idea of the 'family wage' referred to above, a wage earned by the man, enough to cover the cost of housing and feeding the wife and family so that when a woman works, this cost is assumed to have already been paid – whatever the actual situation – so that she can be paid less. Thus women's work is seen as less important than men's and is paid at a lower rate.

Alongside the analysis of the oppression of women in the family, the Marxist concept of the reserve army of labour is also relevant. In the nineteenth century, Marx identified young people and agricultural workers who had been replaced by machinery, as well as the unemployed, as 'the industrial reserve army of surplus-population' (cited in Beechey, 1987, p. 46). More recently feminists have located women, too, as a social group used in the same way (Bruegel, 1986, pp. 40–53; Beechey, 1987, pp. 45–50, 87–8). The use of women as part of the reserve army depends on existing, in this case sexual, divisions in the working class.

The reserve industrial army is necessary to capital in at least two ways:

> it provides a disposable and flexible population . . . labour power that can be absorbed in expanding branches of production when capital accumulation creates a demand for it, and repelled when the conditions of production no longer require it . . . It is also seen as a condition of competition among workers, the intensity of which depends on the pressure of the relative surplus population. This competitive pressure has two consequences. It depresses wage levels: Marx argues that the general movements of wages are regulated by the expansion and contraction of the industrial reserve army, which in turn corresponds to periodic changes in the industrial cycle. Competition also forces workers to submit to increases in the rate of exploitation through the pressure of unemployment.
>
> (Beechey, 1987, pp. 47–8)

The first point is best exemplified by the way in which women were drawn into engineering and munitions factories during World War II to replace the male population who were fighting. Nurseries were provided for children to facilitate this. With the return of soldiers into civilian life in 1945, women were encouraged to go back to their domestic roles, or into the caring and service sectors.

The second point, the ability of the reserve army to depress wages (and conditions), partly explains what took place during the 1980s and 1990s. These two decades saw a massive growth of women's jobs, alongside a loss of male ones, but it was not an equal swap. Male jobs in engineering, steel, mining, manufacturing, jobs which were unionized, with decent wages and security, were lost. Work normally associated with women and young people, in the service sector, in sales, and so on, jobs which are predominantly non-unionized, poorly paid, often part time, sometimes on short-term, even zero-hours contracts – the infamous 'Mc Job'[14] – were created. In the process women, and young people, brought into the workforce were used to undermine the conditions and wages of traditional, male work and to introduce and normalize to the whole workforce such notions as part-time working and short-term contracts. This is the so-called 'flexible workforce'.

By the middle of the 1990s the composition of the labour force had changed. According to *Labour Market Trends*, March 1997, over 70 per cent of women between the ages of sixteen and fifty-nine were economically active at the start of 1996. Forty-four per cent were working part-time, compared to 8 per cent of men.

Of the 5.8 million people working part-time, 82 per cent were women (Sly, Price and Ridson, 1997). However the 8 per cent of men working part-time doubled between 1986 and 1996, whereas the percentage of women working part-time had increased by only 1 per cent. The figures for temporary work are even more striking: the number of women in temporary jobs increased by 23 per cent, while for men the figure was 74 per cent.

It seems to be the case that the work of women, defined by their expected domestic roles, has been used to undermine both the level of wages and the conditions of work in the late twentieth century. While there have been a number of other factors in this process, including economic stagnation, de-industrialization, high levels of general unemployment and attacks on trade union rights, women's position as part of the reserve army of labour is at least one element in the process.

More recently the reserve army of labour has been augmented by a new group of workers – documented and undocumented migrant workers. Nobody knows how many undocumented migrant workers there are in Britain, but it is probably in the low hundreds of thousands They have come from all over the world, including eastern Europe, Asia, and Africa and have little or no protection under law against their employers, landlords or others who control their lives. They are added to by the more numerous migrant workers with visas or work permits. But such legality does not guarantee dignity, decent wages, working conditions and lodgings. On the contrary, as recent events in Britain have exposed, legal and illegal workers can be equally exploited. Such migrant labour is used in food harvesting, food packaging, catering, construction and cleaning. In cities, especially in London, casual work in the building trade is increasingly carried out by migrant workers from eastern Europe rather than from Ireland as was the tradition.[15]

With the new accession countries now part of the European Union (EU), two classes of migrant workers are emerging: those from the EU who may stay, and those from outside the EU, who will only be allowed to stay for a short period, and without their families. This is creating a new 'reserve army of labour'.

Amongst these workers are many women; not working in agriculture or the building trade, but in the leisure and service industry, especially in the south east and in London. Cooking, serving and cleaning in the restaurants and bars, cleaning offices in the early morning and at night, and in the sex industry, in massage parlours, sex clubs, including lap dancing clubs, and as prostitutes on the streets: women from eastern Europe, from African countries and from Asia, are doing the work which many women born here now refuse to do – at least for the minimum wages offered for these jobs, or in the conditions imposed in the sex industry.

Having used women born here to undermine wages and conditions in the 1980s and 1990s, this new reserve army, women and men forced to flee countries devastated by the neo-liberal economic policies imposed by the International Monetary Fund and by the World Bank, is being used to maintain and raise the profits of capitalism. Whilst racist attacks by politicians and the media on asylum seekers and economic migrants continue to try to divide and rule working people, anti-racists must argue for equal rights for these workers, so that their role as a reserve army is reduced as much as possible.

Conclusion

While formal equality may seem to have been achieved by equal pay laws and legislation outlawing sexual discrimination, capital works in devious ways to outwit and undermine such reforms. Formal legal equality within a capitalist society can never be real equality. Even though campaigning for such legislation is important in raising consciousness on these issues, we cannot depend on the legal process alone to achieve it. Underlying, structural reasons, the way in which capital operates, at both economic and ideological levels, make real equality more or less impossible to achieve under capitalism. However many women are in work, it is unlikely that we will be given equal pay, access to all levels and grades of work, adequately paid maternity leave (to say nothing of paternity leave), free childcare, equal rights in practice, without a complete change in the system. But fighting for changes now is not a waste of time. The achievements of the Women's Movements in the nineteenth and twentieth centuries put us in a better position than ever before to fight for equality with men. However, without realistically assessing our actual situation, that fight will take place with one hand tied behind us.

Thirty-five years after the first Women's Liberation Conference in Oxford, women remain unequal – at work, in the home, in legal and social institutions. Achievements in some areas such as divorce, reproductive rights and legislation on equal pay and against sex discrimination are open to reversals and are often unenforceable. Capitalists and their supporters gain from social division and will always impede genuine equal rights for all, for capitalism is a system premised on inequality and the right of the rich to exploit the poor.

Notes

1 This should not be misunderstood as care for each child for twenty-four hours, but the availability of childcare for women at all times, thus allowing women to choose when to work and to have some leisure time without childcare responsibilities.

2 The largest difference in the average full-time hourly rate is in London where women earn only 76.4 per cent of the male rate. Furthermore if you look at weekly earnings, on average women work 3.5 hours less than men, so the figure drops to 75.4 per cent of male earnings. All figures from National Statistics at www.statistics.gov.uk unless otherwise stated.

3 A typical cost for full-time childcare for an under-two year old is £134 a week (£7,000 a year) rising to £168 a week in London and the south-east (£8,730 a year). Figures from the Day Care Trust, www.daycaretrust.org.uk

4 This was in response to fears of a decline of the 'race' in the face of the growing Empire, and more particularly the discovery of the poor health of working-class recruits in the Boer War 1899–1902 and World War I in 1914. There was also a falling birthrate and rising infant mortality rates (see Chapter 3 of this volume).

5 While it will not come as a surprise to anyone that in the nineteenth century education was oppressively gendered, it may come as more of a shock to discover that as late as 1963 the Newsom Committee Report, *Half Our Future*, published by the Central Advisory Council for Education, 1963, argued that for girls of average or less than average ability (whatever that is): '. . . their most important vocational concern [is] marriage', and therefore domestic science, as it became known, remained high on the

curriculum agenda, with girls given the chance to run a flat for a week. Incidentally the mothers of these same girls were by this time almost certainly working outside the home! (Open University, 1984; for a detailed discussion of gender and education, see Chapter 2).

6 It is of course true that the appalling economic plight of the Soviet Union in the years following the revolution meant that, as Holt tellingly states, 'the collective was unable to do its duty towards women' (Holt, 1977, p. 120).

7 The percentages of women in work show an upward curve from around 30 per cent in 1918 to around 50 per cent today, but the sharpest increase is from the 1960s.

8 Seventy per cent of women are now part of the labour force in Britain.

9 'The gender pay gap – why it widened in 2002', Incomes Data Service, 20 January 2003. www.incomesdata.com

10 Only 13 per cent of men work in these areas.

11 Income Data Services Ltd (1993) shows women as 49 per cent of workforce, with a rise between 1973 and 1993 of 2 million women's jobs and a loss of 2.8 million male jobs. But this was not a straight swap for at least 45 per cent of women in the 1990s are working part-time. In 1993. 35 per cent of all workers were not in full-time, permanent jobs.

12 Engels, (1978) *The Origin of the Family, Private Property and the State*, Foreign Language Press, p. 85.

13 The costs of rearing children, shopping for and cooking for a family, if paid at a going rate, would be astronomical.

14 This term comes from the employment practices of fast-food outlets, which include zero-hours contracts and employees clocking on and off dependent on the level of custom. Most of the employees are young.

15 I am indebted to Bill MacKeith's article, 'Migration: An Issue 'for Britain' or for Workers' Rights?', in *Socialist Outlook* 3, Spring, 2004 for material in this section.

References

Barron, R.D. and Norris, E.R. (1976) 'Sexual Divisions and the Dual Labour Market' in D.L. Barker and S. Allen, *Dependence and Exploitation in Work and Marriage*, London: Longman

Beechey, V. (1987) *Unequal Work*, London: Verso

Bolt, C. (1993) *The Women's Movements in the United States and Britain from the 1790s to the 1920s*, London: Harvester Wheatsheaf

Bruegel, I. (1986) 'The Reserve Army of Labour, 1974–1979', in Feminist Review (ed.), *Waged Work: A Reader*, London: Virago

Central Advisory Council for Education (England) (1963) *Half Our Future: A Report of the Central Advisory Council for Education*, London: HMSO

Cole, M. (2003) 'Might it be in the Practice that it fails to Succeed? A Marxist Critique of Claims for Postmodernism and Poststructuralism as Forces for Social Change and Social Justice', *British Journal of Sociology of Education*, 24 (4), pp. 487–500

Cole, M. (2004) 'Fun, Amusing, Full of Insights, but Ultimately a Reflection of Anxious Times: A Critique of Postmodernism as a Force for Resistance, Social Change and Social Justice', in J. Satterthwaite, E. Atkinson and W. Martin (eds) *Educational Counter-Cultures: Confrontations, Images, Vision*, Stoke on Trent: Trentham Books

Cole, M. (2005) 'The "Inevitability of Globalised Capital" versus the "Ordeal of the Undecidable"'. A Marxist Critique' in M. Pruyn and L. Huerta-Charles (eds) *Peter McLaren: Paths of Dissent*, New York: Peter Lang

Engels, F. (1978 [1884]) *The Origin of the Family, Private Property and the State*, Peking: Foreign Language Press

Fraser, N. and Nicholson, L.J. (1990) 'Social Criticism without Philosophy: An Encounter between Feminism and Postmodernism', in L.J. Nicholson (ed.), *Feminism/Postmodernism*, New York and London: Routledge

Garb, T. (1993) in F. Frascina, et al., *Modernity and Modernism: French Painting in the Nineteenth Century*, New Haven and London: Yale University Press

Holt. A. (1977) *Alexandra Kollontai: Selected Writings*, London, Allison and Busby

Income Data Services Ltd (1993) *IDS, Management Pay Review, May*, London

Kelly, J. (1992) 'Postmodernism and Feminism', *International Marxist Review*, 14, Winter, Paris: Presse-Edition-Communication (PEC)

Kelly, J. (1999) 'Postmodernism and Feminism: The Road to Nowhere', in D. Hill, P. McLaren, M. Cole and G. Rikowski (eds), *Postmodernism in Educational Theory: Education and the Politics of Human Resistance*, London: Tufnell Press

Liddington, J. and Norris, J. (1978) *One Hand Tied Behind Us: The Rise of the Women's Suffrage Movement*, London: Virago

Lipton, E. (1987) *Looking into Degas: Uneasy Images of Women and Modern Life*, Berkeley, Los Angeles and London: University of California Press

Low Pay Unit (1997) *The New Review*, November/December, London

MacKeith, B. (2004) 'Migration: An Issue "for Britain" or for Workers' Rights?', *Socialist Outlook* 3, Spring, London, International Socialist Group

Open University (1984) *Conflict and Change in Education: A Sociological Introduction*, Block 6: Gender, race and education; Unit 25: 'Women and Education', Milton Keynes: Open University Press

Pollock, G. (1988) *Vision and Difference: Femininity, Feminism and the Histories of Art*, London and New York: Routledge

Sly, F., Price, A. and Risdon, A. (March 1997) *Labour Market Trends*, London: Government Statistical Office

'The gender pay gap – why it widened in 2002', *Incomes Data Service*, 20 January, 2003.
www.incomesdata.com
www.statistics.gov.uk
www.daycaretrust.org.uk

2 Gender and education

Change and continuity

Jane Martin

Mapping change in relation to gender equality, incoming president of the NASUWT, Pat Lerew, told the annual conference:

> I know we have come a long way from my grammar school days when the only career options seemed to be teaching or nursing and when, as a young married woman in the 1960s my earnings could not be included in any mortgage application. I wasn't allowed to enter into any hire-purchase agreements and my life was not worth insuring. I suppose there was the small advantage of not being responsible for my own debts. Since then equality laws have ensured that these situations no longer apply and on the face of it there is gender equality. We all know that the truth is very different.
>
> (*The Guardian*, 13 April, 2004)

Introduction

This chapter will focus on gender equity issues in education. It has only been relatively recently that gender has come under scrutiny in British sociology of education. Until the 1970s the bias was towards the analysis of class differentials of educational achievement. This led to a simplification of the issues but a growing amount of historical and sociological research has now been published, much of which points to the fact that boys and girls experience schooling differently. At the same time, it is important not to ignore the differences that exist among groups. The interacting dynamics of class, gender and 'race' relations are crucial, as are sexuality, disability and individual biographies. So, the chapter begins with a discussion of historical perspectives on gender and education, before moving on to relate the theoretical understandings of Chapter 4 to more recent concerns, considered in their policy context.

Historical perspectives on gender and education: 1800 to 1944

The education of children in the nineteenth century was organised along the lines of social class. Elementary education was associated with the working classes and secondary education, which was not simply confined to the three Rs, was associated with the middle classes. Girls rarely feature in general histories of mass schooling and the historiography of the gender dimension has been marred by an assumption that girls and boys experienced an identical education. Among historians of women's education this assumption manifested itself in a focus on separate accounts of middle class schools. For example, there are a number of histories documenting women's struggle to secure access to secondary and higher education (Bryant, 1979; Kamm, 1965; McWilliams-Tullberg, 1975); as well as more recent accounts of the lifestyle and occupational culture of women teachers in girls' secondary schools and in higher education (Edwards, 1990; Vicinus, 1985). Yet the history of women's education has not neglected working class girl's schooling. Gomersall (1988, 1994) and Horn (1988) contributed to our knowledge of the early period and a growing body of evidence points to gendered experiences. First, there were fewer school places for girls (Hurt, 1979). Second, girls were less likely to be sent to school (Martin, 1987). Third, the two sexes did not have access to a common curriculum. Girls lost out on all the academic subjects save reading and concern about value for money led the government to introduce payment by results in 1862 when needlework became compulsory for girls. Each pupil earned the same amount for successful examination performance, but girls were permitted a lower standard of achievement in arithmetic because of the time they spent sewing (Weiner, 1994; Digby and Searby, 1981).

The 1870 Education Act was a watershed in English and Welsh education history. For the first time, locally elected, single-purpose educational authorities were empowered to raise and administer a school rate to plug the gaps in the elementary sector (Simon, 1980). Gender differences were extended and increasingly formalised after the passage of the Act. Ostensibly co-educational, in urban areas the new board schools sometimes had different entrances for the sexes, as well as separate playgrounds and separate departments for older children (Turnbull, 1987). This period also saw the promotion of a sex-differentiated curriculum. In 1878, for example, theoretical domestic economy became a compulsory specific subject for girls; four years later the government gave grants for the teaching of cookery. By the 1890s, a significant expansion in the curriculum prescriptions for working class girls saw the inclu-sion of laundry work and housewifery. Despite the addition of manual teaching, Turnbull (1987, p.86) concludes that working class boys 'did not receive practical instruction equivalent to the girls' needlework, cookery, laundry work and so on'. Further, when national efficiency became a priority in the aftermath of military failures and deficiencies highlighted by the number of recruits declared unfit for call up in the Boer War (1899–1902), the Board of Education favoured *more* domestic instruction, with lessons in the practicalities of housework and mothering for working class girls (Attar, 1990; Dyhouse, 1981; Turnbull, 1987). Hurt (1979) suggests military drill as the masculine equivalent to the separate sort of education given the girls, but fails to acknowledge the proportion of time filled by domestic subjects' instruction. From 1870 onwards, the four features of curriculum thinking – selection, differentiation, functionality and social advancement – were clearly visible within the state-aided elementary sector (Weiner, 1994). Family culture was used as a rationale for the kinds of education offered working class girls and the training in domesticity linked with erratic school attendance. Girls were frequently expected to fulfil the roles of 'good wives' and 'little mothers' on wash days, or if their mother was ill or having a baby (Dyhouse, 1981; Davin, 1996). Elsewhere Davin (1979) argues the purpose of mass schooling was to impose an ideal family form of a male breadwinner and an economically dependent, full-time wife and mother. As Gomersall has summed up:

> This was an ideal that came broadly to be shared by the bourgeoisie and men and women of the working classes alike, each for their own particular economic, political, cultural and social reasons. That it was unattainable for most outside the ranks of skilled and unionised labour was seen as unprob-lematic; it integrated the goals of the powerful men of the working classes with those of the dominant social and economic groups and served as an aspirational ideal to the unskilled, unorganised work-force.
>
> (Gomersall, 1994, p.238)

Although Mary Wollstonecraft applied ideas of equality to women in a *Vindication of the Rights of Women* (1792), her vision did not find much favour in Victorian Britain. Unlike their male counterparts, middle class girls were largely educated for the marriage market and Wollstonecraft did not consider the frivolous education they received as any education. In the words of the suffragette leader, Emmeline Pankhurst (1979, pp 5–6): 'My parents, especially my father, discussed the question of my brothers' education as a matter of real importance. My education and that of my sister were scarcely discussed at all'. Likewise Emily Davies (who led the campaign for access to secondary and higher education), resented the fact that whereas her three brothers all went to well-known public schools followed by Trinity College, Cambridge; she only received a limited education. This included a brief spell at a day school supplemented by occasional paid lessons in languages and music (Caine, 1992). Divisions within the education of the middle class and the working class reveal a dichotomy between the experience of girls and boys in terms of expectations and opportunities.

Both working people and women members of the school boards had much to lose from the educational re-organisation that followed the 1902 Education Act (Hollis, 1989; Martin, 1999; Turnbull, 1983) – working people because the division between elementary and secondary schooling was more firmly defined; women because they were disqualified by sex for election to the new education authorities. The Act abolished the school boards and made subcommittees of county councils responsible for the board schools, now called public elementary schools. For the first time the local education authorities were permitted to establish rate-aided secondary schools whose form and curricula were to follow those of the elitist, public schools. Secondary school fees were set at £3 per annum and this excluded all save the high ability working class child who won a free-place on the basis of an attainment test. Purvis (1995, p.14) has suggested those who benefited were highly likely to be lower middle class males.

As I have already mentioned, the intentions in educating boys and girls were different. Increasingly a similar policy was pursued in elementary and secondary schools. For instance, both the 1905 Code of Regulations for Public Elementary Schools and the Regulations for Secondary Schools imposed practical training in the female role. Policy guidelines incorporated a set of linked assumptions advocating separate but complementary adult roles for men and women. On the one hand, the female curriculum was discussed in terms of girls' biology and what this meant for their future after school. On the other, the principle of male-as-norm meant the teaching of other subjects was informed by the assumption that boys were breadwinners and secondarily fathers (Hunt, 1991). This was approved school practice by the 1920s and a report on the differentiation of the curriculum in secondary schools concluded that there were two main aims for education: first, to prepare children to both earn their own livings and second, to be useful citizens. However ideologies of femininity dictated that girls also needed to be prepared for family life and motherhood, since their primary vocation was to be 'makers of homes' (HMSO, 1923, cited in Hunt, 1991, p. 119). This one role was seen to supersede all other social principles, both inside and outside school.

State policy endorsed the view that women were different from men; not only biologically but socially, intellectually and psychologically as well. Within the school girls were more likely to be taught by women, while the men tended to teach the boys, especially older boys (Purvis, 1995). This was crucial to the National Association of Schoolmasters (NAS), formed in 1923, who deplored the influence of female teachers on male students (Littlejohn, 1995). Only male teachers could reinforce 'normal' masculinity. As a writer in the union journal, the *New Schoolmaster* put it:

> in the matter of managing and instructing young children the sex of a person may matter but little [. . .] in the great task of educating children the sex of the teacher is of paramount importance. The character of children is the essential consideration, and the essentials of character lie in the sex of the person.
>
> (*New Schoolmaster*, November 1936, cited in Littlejohn, 1995, p. 50)

By the 1920s approximately three-quarters of elementary school teachers were women. In these circumstances the NAS continued to press their demands for men teachers for all boys over seven, and headmasters in mixed schools. Indeed they did not relinquish the first objective until 1976. Clearly this insistence on the importance of gender in teaching has implications for the construction of patriarchal relations in teachers' work. Indeed Littlejohn claims 'the most volatile and explosive issue of all was the appointment of women to the inspectorate with special responsibility for handicraft and physical education' (1995, pp 53–4). To subject men teachers to the authority of women passing judgement on the teaching of technical crafts and sports was more than they could bear. It was emasculating.

Overall education policies remained tailored to processes of class formation in the inter-war years. Beyond that, there was evidence of gender-based asymmetries in terms of access to schooling; curriculum content and years of education attained.

Historical perspectives on gender and education II: 1944 to 1975

The 1944 Education Act encouraged intense speculation about the potential impact of free secondary education for all. Many saw the reform as primarily about the realisation of class equality and the production of a new type of society. But this did not mean 'that all children now received what had before the Act been described as secondary education' (Thom, 1987, p.131). Scarcity of grammar school places necessitated selection procedures on the lines of 'age, ability and aptitude' as recommended in the Norwood Report (1943). However the official ideology for girls' education still assumed homogeneity of female interests. Thus, for example, while Norwood interspersed the word 'child' with 'boy', criteria particular to girls' schooling featured in a lengthy chapter on domestic subjects. Different social roles were taken for granted and the question of gender was perceived very differently from that of class. Little had changed, as Thom (1987) makes clear:

> Gender was raised, but it was raised as a general social question, that is, the issue of whether girls and boys should receive a separate sort of education as a whole, not whether one girl should receive a different sort of education from another. No one asked what the implications were for equality in this; rather, whether boys and girls required a fundamentally different organisation of education.
>
> (Thom, 1987, p. 125)

Throughout the 1940s and 1950s (when selection through the 11+ examination predominated); girls had to do much better than boys to obtain a place at a grammar or technical school (Deem, 1981; Thom, 1987). This was justified on the grounds that girls' academic superiority in the early stages made it necessary 'to tilt the balance in the favour of those late-developing boys' (Grant, 1994, p. 37). The accepted theory was that boys would catch up by the age of 14. Gender stereotypes about male superiority were reinforced earlier by medical practitioners who warned female students of the risks evoked by too much intellectual work (Dyhouse, 1981). As late as the 1930s, it was professed that a girl who worked hard might get brain fever (Rendel, 1997, p. 56). So, when it came to male-female 11+ result patterns, common sense and social observation suggested the difference 'is not real because it does not last, it is not a phenomenon produced by the test, it is a phenomenon produced by "nature"'(Thom, 1987, p. 141). The fact that girls frequently scored better marks than boys prompted some local authorities to set up different norms; others added new tests to level up the sexes (Thom, 1987). Technical adjustment was necessary to balance the numbers of successful girls and boys; there was also a historic shortage of girls' grammar school places. It has to be accepted 'that there is no such thing as a fair test' (Gipps and Murphy, 1994, p. 273) but this went unremarked in 1940s and 1950s Britain.

More recent analyses redress the balance. Examining the education policy context after the Labour Party came to power in July 1945; Dean (1991) discusses the gendered nature of education policies and the impact of those policies on practice. In particular, he develops the argument that the victorious politicians saw the domestic role of women as crucial for the construction and rehabilitation of social harmony and cohesiveness. For the young female population leaving school at age 15, the Ministry of Education continued to point to that special curriculum for girls, organised around familial concerns. Further, the influential school inspector John Newsom attacked the academic grammar schools for ignoring domestic skills and placing too much emphasis on public examinations and obtaining professional careers. Yet even here the cult of motherhood and domesticity was still prevalent. Two-thirds of those who went to university were men; more women trained as teachers. In 1958 there were 100 teacher training colleges for women, as opposed to 18 for men and 18 mixed-sex colleges (Heward, 1993, pp. 23–4). Class and gendered concepts of adult destiny were similarly evident in the curriculum recommendations of the 1959 Crowther Report on the education of 15–18 year olds. In the secondary modern schools (virtually synony-mous with working class schooling), this report suggested that: 'The prospect of courtship and marriage should rightly influence the education of the adolescent girl [. . .] her direct interests in dress and personal experience and the problems of human relationships, should be given a central part in her education' (Crowther Report, p. 124, quoted in Riley, 1994, p. 37). However there is evidence of female disaffection with schooling in this period. Early leaving generated attention in the Gurney-Dixon Report of 1954 and Crowther commented on the fact that grammar school girls were more likely to leave school at the statutory age (Deem, 1981). Imputing motivation is difficult, but it is conceivable that early leaving was prompted by fear of failure. More recent research into female truancy found this was the main reason given for 'bunking' lessons (Le Riche, 1988). As Spender and Sarah (1980) argue very forcefully, in education women have learnt *how* to lose even though they may have had the ability to succeed academically. The educational biography of the American Pulitzer prize-winning novelist, Carol Shields (1935–2003), is revealing. A college graduate and trained teacher, as a young woman her expectations were simple: 'a baby, a TV, a fridge-freezer and a car' (*The Guardian*, 23 May 1998).

By the 1960s a radical restructuring of English state education opened up new possibilities for change. This programme of educational reform was informed by human capital theory with its main tenet that the role of education was crucial to the development of economic growth (Schultz, 1970; see Simon, 1991, pp. 222, 229 and 291 for a discussion). Reassessments of the concept of equal access saw the gradual shift to a non-selective system of secondary schooling in England and Wales, a change that accelerated the number of children educated in mixed schools in the state sector. This meant a changing balance of power among women and men staff in senior and managerial positions as schools became mixed, larger and more complex; however the accepted norm was that mixed-sex schooling was preferable to single-sex schooling on academic, as well as social grounds (Deem, 1984). Simply put, it was hoped that the presence of female pupils would have a 'civilising' influence on their male peers. As Arnot (1984, p. 50) has noted, 'never it would seem has the argument been reversed'. Overall the removal of barriers to female success in the 11+ examination inevitably benefited some, predominantly middle class girls; discussion of who benefits academically from mixed or single-sex schooling runs on and will be returned to later.

In theory, Deem (1981) maintains the expansion of the curriculum in state-maintained secondary schools should have been 'helpful' to girls. In practice, Benn and Simon (1972) found that very few schools offered a common curriculum to all their pupils in the early days of the comprehensive reform. Divergence in the content of education was clearly seen in the provision of gender-specific courses in subjects like domestic science, typing and childcare, which were not open to boys; and woodwork, metalwork and technical drawing (TD), which were not open to girls. Links between the distribution of educational knowledge and patterns of women's work remained in evidence despite the rise of a new feminist movement (see Chapter 1) and the greater participation of women in the labour force.

Breaking boundaries I: equal opportunities?

When the Sex Discrimination Act of 1975 was passed by the Labour government under Harold Wilson, it made direct and indirect discrimination on the grounds of gender illegal in a number of spheres of public life, including education (Carter, 1988). Previous attempts[1] to get sex included within the scope of the Race Relations Act had failed but on this occasion the support of the minister, Roy Jenkins, helped overcome the opposition of some Home Office officials (Rendel, 1997, pp. 3, 12). Although the then Department of Education and Science was unenthusiastic, the Act outlawed discrimination in the provision of curricular and non-curricular facilities, and extra-curricular activities. Additionally, it covered standards of behaviour, rules regarding pupils' dress and appearance, school discipline and careers guidance, but did not apply to private schools. It is in this context that we have to see the influence of what Stone (1994) calls 'education feminism' that is, the women's movement within the educational system. For feminist educationists and historians, this was a spur to groundbreaking work as they exposed the educational system to a critique which revealed the enduring importance of a patriarchal order and gendered differences in outcomes. In so doing, they 'uncovered ideas and practices inimical to the full development of potential, not only girls but often of boys, too, and those disadvantaged by social or ethnic origin' (Watts, 2002, p. 146).

There was criticism of gender differentiation across a diversity of areas as the research in and on the 1970s and 1980s showed the ways in which patriarchal relations are deployed and used in schools (Deem, 1978). Collaborative rather than competitive kinds of teaching were encouraged in the belief that it would be more productive of good teaching and learning for boy and girl students. Attention also focused on male dominance within the work of schools, government and teacher unions. Generally men ran the schools, dominating the administrative and policy-making side of education. Women mostly operated within female spaces. Hence female heads of department in secondary schools were likely to be found in low status subject areas like home economics and girls' physical education. At the same time, it should be noted that primary education, like women, is itself constructed as 'Other' and subjugated in several ways (Paechter, 1998). For example, less state funding is provided for the education of younger children in England and Wales and virtually all primary education is provided by women who often find themselves made responsible for the failure of boys. However, it seems that even here sexual divisions were constantly reinforced. Feminist analysis showed that primary school teachers readily clustered behaviour into two categories, one for boys and another for girls, drawing on oppositional constructions of masculinity and femininity (Clarricoates, 1980). On the one hand, boys were livelier, adventurous, boisterous, self-confident, independent, energetic, couldn't-care-less, loyal and aggressive. On the other, girls were obedient, tidy, neat, conscientious, orderly, fussy, catty, bitchy and gossipy. Stanworth (1986) drew a similar picture in her account of the ways in which gender divisions were sustained in a co-educational college of further education. Higher teacher expectations towards boys had implications for the self-image of one young woman:

> I think he thinks I'm pretty mediocre. I think I'm pretty mediocre. He never points me out of the group or talks to me, or looks at me in particular when he's talking about things. I'm just a sort of wallpaper person.
>
> (Stanworth, 1986, p. 37)

Of course, such a description may reflect the use of discipline and control in teaching styles. This raises the point that the control of working class boys, understood in terms of the problems of violence and truancy, also received a good deal of attention in research and public discussion.

Early texts dealing with the production of masculinity through resistance to schooling show how anti-school working-class 'lads' block teaching (Willis, 1983). Similarly, in *Schooling the Smash Street Kids*, Corrigan (1979) used the analogy of a 'guerrilla struggle' to represent the ability of white, working class, heterosexual, boys in the north east of England to monopolise space in the classroom, despite the 'occupying army' of teachers. Examples of disruptive behaviour included 'running about in classrooms', 'running under chairs' and 'tossing chairs about' (Corrigan, 1979, p. 58). By contrast, the resistance of anti-school girls was individual and personalised or 'invisible' – they 'skived off' school (Llewellyn, 1980). Although some rebellious girls used a feminine preoccupation with appearance in order to position themselves in opposition to school (Payne, 1980; Riddell, 1989).

In relation to fields of study selection, the 1975 report on curricular differentiation highlighted the areas in which sexism flourished (DES, 1975). There were high levels of sex stereotyping in option choices and teachers found themselves being criticised for influencing pupil preferences. Beyond that, evidence of illegal segregation of craft subjects was found in 19 per cent of the schools studied by Her Majesty's Inspectorate (HMI) from 1975 to 1978 (cited in Pascall, 1997, p. 119). Research on schoolgirls' option choices shows significant patterns of gender segregation informed by expectations of future employment. As a result it was argued that if any group benefited from moves to promote equal access to curricular options, it was likely to be the boys:

> Male students who took 'girl's subjects' were assumed to be learning a skill for future use in the labour market. They were taken more seriously than their female peers in the same classes, to whom such skills were supposed to come naturally for use in their future roles as wives and mothers [. . .] Female students who took 'boys' subjects' were either presumed to be interested solely in flirting with the boys or discounted as unique exceptions.
>
> (Griffin, 1985, pp. 78–9)

Riley (1994) also found the working class girls attending a coeducational south London comprehensive in the early 1980s experienced a very sex-differentiated curriculum. Institutionalised sexism meant girls were channelled out of technical drawing in order to preserve the subject as a male-only space. Despite the achievement of equal rights legislation, most girls were still sitting examinations in a narrow cluster of subjects seen as supporting natural female interests, needs and choices with respect to personal/domestic life. The effects were carried forward into further study and employment at precisely the point when, for the first time since World War II, there was a growing problem of youth unemployment. Working class boys and men were particularly affected by the decline of vocational apprenticeships and industrial jobs with release for college training. On the other hand, cutbacks in teacher training and fierce competition for university places in arts courses reduced opportunities for some young women.

In educational establishments, staff who were involved in the women's movement tried to act as agents of change, by raising the consciousness of many teachers and encouraging small-scale school-based initiatives on equal opportunities. Despite the lack of top-down reform of schooling to help girls, feminist teachers were concerned with staffing, classroom interaction, sexual harassment, and the division of girls/boys in both administration and curriculum, besides extra curricular activities (see Stantonbury Campus Sexism in Education Group, 1984). One of the best known projects, the Girls into Science and Technology initiative, was set up in Manchester (Kelly, 1985). Here researchers worked alongside and with teachers in 10 schools to encourage girls to take traditionally 'male' subjects, even after they became optional (then at age 14). To this end, the project team brought adult women scientists to act as role models, tried to raise awareness about the gender dynamics of classrooms, and experimented with single-sex classes.

Although the ambivalence of girls' responses to science changed little, early analyses of the education provisions of the Sex Discrimination Act indicate mild success (Deem, 1981). Using the indicators identified by Stromquist (1990, p. 137) to assess women's progress, more access must be noted, as must girls' successes: the ratio of male entry to female entry in the GCE O-level and CSE examinations had changed and fewer of the female candidates failed. Nonetheless, fewer girls than boys achieved the three good A-levels which would have given them access to higher education and there were prevailing inequities in curriculum and attitudes (Arnot *et al.*, 1999). Thus Arnot (1983, p. 71) argues the development of co-educational state comprehensive secondary schools 'did not represent [. . .] a challenge to the reproduction of dominant gender relations but rather a modification of the *form* of its transmission.' The ubiquity of those relations is borne out by a homily recorded in a comprehensive secondary school in 1978:

> In assembly the lower school is addressed by the Senior Mistress, Mrs Marks. Pupils are told they will soon be given a form to take home – school wants the phone number of where mother works. Mrs Marks says that if they are ill or have an accident, school tries to get mother. The school try not to bother father, because he is the head of the family, his wage keeps the family while mother's is only for luxuries [. . .] If there is no-one at home – mum, granny or auntie – they will be put to bed at school.
>
> (Delamont, 1983, p. 93)

By the 1980s, it was observed that the New Right agenda, with its commitment to 'family values', might conflict with moves that could improve career prospects for girls (David, 1983).

Breaking boundaries II: social justice?

Arguments about social justice were shunned when the then Secretary of State for Education and Science, Kenneth Baker, proposed a radical restructuring of the school system. Introducing the Education Reform Bill at the 1987 Conservative Party Conference he declared 'the pursuit of egalitarianism is over' (quoted in Arnot, 1989/90, p. 21). The national goal was quality. According to Baker, the National Curriculum would deliver it 'for all our children, over all our country' (quoted in *From Butler to Baker: the 3Rs*, 1993). Effective opposition was contained by the language of access and entitlement (Simon, 1991), but the idea of a common 'entitlement' curriculum was not new. HMI had been arguing for it since at least 1977 (Benn and Chitty, 1997, p. 277). Feminist educators also supported the notion of a common curriculum experience, albeit one that encompassed the hidden curriculum of schooling and *not* one posited on a male educational paradigm (Benn *et al.*, 1982). However this position is very different from the liberal reformist perspective that is limited by a failure to recognise that educational gender differentiation does not occur in a social and political vacuum. Knowledge is not a neutral commodity, but the emphasis on equal opportunities' serves to reinforce the illusion of neutrality (Arnot, 1989/90). The National Curriculum gave equal entitlement to all pupils (within the state sector) but gender hierarchies were reinforced by the privileging of maths, science and technology. The status accorded male-centred forms of knowledge did little to challenge the values and practices of patriarchy/androcentricity:

> In short, while girls must be educated in the skills and attitudes to achieve an academic equality with boys – and to challenge inequalities within the labour market – the education of boys in the skills and attitudes to address their equal responsibilities within the family are of equal if not greater importance. And this is where the formal equality accorded by the National Curriculum is most lacking, in the 'masculinisation' of the schooling of girls with no corresponding 'feminisation' of the schooling of boys.
>
> (Gomersall, 1994, p. 246)

What this position represents is a concern to restructure boys' education in such a way as to break the circulation of stereotypical sex-role expectations. The views expressed emphasise that the majority of schooling operates for a particular form of hegemonic masculinity.

Arnot's (1994) review of gender research in British sociology of education highlights two theoretical traditions – the cultural and the political economy perspective. Whereas cultural analyses concentrate on different socialisation processes, political-economy theories use the method of historical materialism. In this latter tradition, reproduction theory is particularly influential, suggesting that schools reproduce the values and ideologies of the dominant social group-ings, as well as the status rankings of the existing class structure.[2] Building on this work, Arnot adjusts the theory to enable her to combine a class and gender analysis. Here she develops the concept of gender codes, which is now fairly well established, to refer to 'the principles which govern the production, repro-duction and transmission of gender relations and gender hierarchies' (Arnot, 2002, p. 176). Hegemony is put to the fore to show the possibility of accommodation and resistance, to allow us to explore the strategies and methods by which a particular way of seeing gender/power relations becomes projected as the 'natural' order.[3] Sociological analysis can provide insight into how powerful groups within society maintain control, while showing how teachers, students and other human agents, can and do, play a crucial role in moderating or changing existing social norms. It is accepted that individuals within the school may generate counter-hegemonic forces and thereby offer routes to change in the name of, for example, women's rights.

Research undertaken for the Equal Opportunities Commission has revealed how English and Welsh education reforms of the late 1980s impacted on gender equality by institutionalising a National Curriculum which gave equal entitlement to all pupils (within the state sector) to develop the same learning skills and experience the same subjects. Studying the figures on assessment performance for 1985–94, Arnot *et al.* (1996) used a statistical construct of a 'gender gap' to consider comparative achievement figures. The time period covered the introduction of a new common examination, the General Certificate of Secondary Education, plus coursework assessment, seen to have improved the performance of girls noticeably, as they have the performance of boys, though less dramatically. In the compulsory sector, the pattern of male advantage was sustained in the increasing dominance of boys in chemistry, computer studies and economics. On the other hand, a more balanced entry pattern was found in English, mathematics and history. Overall more girls than boys were entered for GCSE examinations and girls were more successful in terms of the proportion of A–C grades gained, though the elite minority of girls in private single-sex schools seemed to be at a substantial advantage (Arnot *et al.*, 1996).

In the post-compulsory sector, the data showed sex segregation in subject choice was still marked. Far more young men completed A-levels (used for university entrance) in mathematics, physics and technology, and at 18 the gender balance in the pattern of examination performances had shifted (Arnot *et al.*, 1996, p. 64). Similarly in vocational examinations and the various training schemes, the less prestigious types like business and commerce, hairdressing and beauty and service courses were mostly taken by women. Gender patterns in post school education show how being male or female impacts on career ambition. They also suggest that:

> a girl's experience of gender cannot be abstracted so neatly from any other aspects of her life. Girls from different social backgrounds will not experience patriarchal culture in identical ways, and the adult lives they anticipate will promise different kinds of opportunity, responsibility and experience. Their priorities as girls will reflect these disparities.
>
> (Miles and Middleton, 1995, p. 133)

This is corroborated by Murphy and Elwood (1998) who observe that children's learning out of school has important consequences for what they choose to do within school. It has an effect on performance, views of relevance, expectations, styles of expression and achievement.

In her research, Lees' (1993) found that whereas academic girls expect careers, non-academic girls anticipate the need to combine unskilled and part-time employment with the responsibilities of housework and child care. Pro-school and academically or work-oriented girls were typically white females from middle class homes with strong parental support. Mirza (1992) comments that the Irish girls in her study saw their futures as home-makers, child-carers and part-time workers; whereas the black girls she interviewed anticipated a career. Clearly the way in which women perform relative to men varies according to class and ethnicity, as does the value of having or not having educational qualifications. Significantly, the mature women students interviewed by Pascall and Cox (1993) saw education as an escape route from a lifetime of domesticity and low-paid work. However, the gradual abolition of mandatory grants, the introduction of loans and the prospect of incurring high levels of debt have had a major impact on this group of students.

The range of social and economic reforms instigated by the Conservative governments of the 1980s and the New Labour policies of the 1990s have continued to support and foster a market philosophy. Pupils and students have been cast as educational clients, and parents have been recast as the consumers of education systems. Examination and assessment performance league tables, a more stringent school inspection process (set up in 1992) all serve as mechanisms to 'measure' standards, with an unprecedented emphasis on the phenomenon of the failing school. These new regimes have had a dramatic impact and Ball and Gewirtz (1997) note the accretive value of 'successful' girls in their study of contemporary school provision. Not only do they become 'a valuable and sought after resource' but 'their presence in school normally conveys positive impressions to parents about ethos and discipline' (Ball and Gewirtz, 1997, p. 214). It is important to note, however, that these assumptions operate differentially among girls: the 'good' girl is constructed across class lines. In a qualitative investigation drawing on data spanning nearly 20 years, Walkerdine *et al.* (2001) found that none of the working class girls who succeeded in education trod a straightforward academic path, whereas only one middle class girl did not go on to university entrance. The educational trajectories of two girls, Patsy (working class) and Julie (middle class), who went to the same nursery, infant and junior schools, and whose parents did all the 'right things', may help to explain why. At 10, both girls were doing equally badly at junior school but whereas Patsy's performance was read as lack of ability by the teacher, Julie's performance was viewed as a problem of motivation. At 16, both girls got poor GCSE results and Patsy left school while Julie went on to university: 'at 21 Julie was back on track and was likely to become a graduate professional, while Patsy, painfully aware of her lack of qualifications, was equally likely to remain in relatively poorly paid, low-status work' (Walkerdine *et al.*, 2001, pp. 125–6).

In their history of postwar education and social change, Arnot *et al.* (1999) argue that feminist campaigners were able to manipulate the concerns of the Conservative governments of the 1980s and 1990s by integrating equal opportunities work into debates about educational standards and performance and good schools. Sixteen-year old girls were already improving their results in the 1970s but 20 years on, the alarm at girls' successes in statutory assessments would bring different aspects of the patterns that form the kaleidoscope of gender, education and equality to the fore. Feminists might have been forgiven for thinking the dream of gender equality was nearer. And yet, it was the underachievement of boys which made hearts race, *not* the extraordinary success of schools and teachers in improving girls' academic performance (Watts, 2002).

In the 1990s, the rise in female performance roused media reports obsessed with threats to male breadwinning, the collapse of family life and the crisis of fatherhood, and a spill over into an increase in problematic and anti-social behaviours, crime and deviance. On the face of it, gendered reactions to the annual publication of the GCSE results developed a generalised narrative of female academic success and male failure. This received official legitimation in 1996, when Chris Woodhead, then Chief Inspector of Schools for England, wrote a column in *The Times* entitled 'Boys who learn to be losers: on the white male culture of failure'. In it he said that the apparent failure of white working class boys was 'one of the most disturbing problems we face within the whole education system' (quoted in the *TES*, 26 April 1996). Two years later, when the publication of new official statistics showed girls outperforming boys in terms of the proportion of pupils obtaining five A–C grades at GCSE in all but one local authority (Kensington and Chelsea), concern for boys' underachievement led then Schools Standards Minister Stephen Byers to intervene. In a speech at the eleventh International Conference for School Effectiveness and Improvement, he argued that the 'laddish, anti-learning culture' was impeding boys' achieve-ment (*The Guardian*, 6 January 1998). Henceforth each local authority was required to address the issue of male disadvantage in drawing up its Education Development Plan.

Others added their own recipes for change. In May 1997 the Professor of Education at Exeter University, Ted Wragg (1938–2005), entered the public debate when he put forward a 10-point plan to help the boys. But the plan did not extend to girls, nor did it consider the interests of girls. Thus the old-fashioned problem of boys behaving badly was resolved by a recommendation that teachers appeal to boys' interests – humour, adventure and sport (*TES*, 23 May 1997). Elsewhere some of the arguments underpinning the drive to recruit more male primary school teachers bear a striking similarity to the NAS backlash in the 1920s and 1930s (see *Daily Mail*, 5 January 1998). In addition, Arnot (1996, p. 13) cites evidence from a 1995 sample that suggests the majority of new teachers are 'more supportive of class and ethnic equality than of gender equality'. Such attitudes are likely to be reinforced by rhetoric about a generation of male losers and teaching strategies for the future that may lead to a further masculinisation of classroom environments (Raphael Reed, 1998). Anti-sexist work to raise achievement for all pupils might go further. Boys/men negotiate and take up a variety of masculinities and some of these confer power and prestige, while others are stigmatised and subordinate. We can relate this to the question of special educational needs. Young boys positioned as slow learners, poor at sport and lacking physical strength and skill, may resort to overtly challenging behaviour that may, in turn, make them liable to being classified as having special needs (Benjamin, 2003). Indeed, working class boys are found in greater numbers in 'less acceptable' categories of emotional and behavioural difficulties and moderate learning difficulties and middle class boys dominate the non-stigmatised category of specific learning difficulties.

But boys are not the only ones to suffer from a lack of insight into the effects of gender. Indeed not all boys *are* losing. To paraphrase David and Weiner (1997) we need to keep balance on the 'gender agenda'. Several factors have been glossed over amid the hysteria about the current positions of pupils in schools. First of all, boys and girls are both much more successful at school than they were 50 years ago, making the phenomenon one of relative rates of improvement for both sexes. Second, it is obvious that poverty (as measured by eligibility for free meals), plus factors of 'race' and ethnicity, remain crucial for both sexes (Burgess *et al.*, 2003). In the third place, when the attainment figures are checked carefully we see a tendency to confuse percentages and percentage points, and a tendency not to use proportionate figures (Gorard *et al.*, 1999). Consideration of the Welsh data and comparable English data for 1992–7 shows girls doing better at Key Stages 1 to 4 in English and Welsh, at Key Stage 4 in languages, some design subjects and humanities, no achievement gaps in mathematics and science, and gaps at other levels either static or declining. On the basis of these research findings Gorard *et al.* (1999) speculate that the educational phenomenon of the 'growing gender gap' does not actually exist. Fourth, comparative literacy rates have sparked panic about boys' achievement, even though girls have traditionally excelled at language-based subjects and despite empirical evidence to suggest boys' greater show of interest in film, computer and CD-ROMs may be a better preparation for changing world literacy than may often be the case for girls (Marsh, 2003). Fifth, data from the Leverhulme Numeracy Research Programme, a study of teaching and learning in English primary schools between 1997 and 2002, shows girls do not match boys' performance in mathematics (Lucey *et al.*, 2003). At GCSE level, the tendency to play safe with examination entries of girls in mathematics means more girls than boys achieve grade C from the Intermediate tier, but mathematics departments in schools only encourage continuation with a B or C grade gained from the Higher tier. In August 2003 more boys got A* grades in GCSE mathematics, biology, chemistry and physics, and more boys took the elite single science subjects than the balanced science associated with state schools (http://educationguardian.co.uk accessed 29 October 2003). Finally, it is deeply ironic that evidence once used to help explain the underachievement of girls is being used across time to signify different conclusions. Twenty years ago, perceptions of the differential abilities of boys and girls triggered a very different reaction to concerns about schoolgirl attainment in maths and science. Consequently, as Mahony (1998, p. 39) notes, 'it took a good deal of persuasion by (mainly) feminists before policy makers would look beyond the innate capacities of girls themselves for explanations'. In contrast, the perception of boys as innately clever continues. Conversely, so does a tendency to imply that girls' academic attainment is the result of compliant hard work: even though the reduction of the coursework element at GCSE did not redress the balance in favour of boys (Arnot *et al.*, 1999). Female school performance has improved but there is plenty of evidence to support the argument that this is *despite* the continuing male dominance in the classroom, the playground, curriculum content and greater demands on teacher time and energy (Francis, 2000).

Conclusion

A historical perspective shows that girls have continued to do better in education whenever they have been offered more opportunities (Miller, 1996). Instead of celebration, however, we have seen an extraordinary media debate over female academic success which has been interpreted as a problem for boys, in particular working class boys (Epstein *et al.*, 1998). Much has changed since the 'fourth-year leavers' Jane Miller taught in the early 1970s 'were given to marvelling at our willingness to work so hard for so little, when they could have fixed us all up with something far more lucrative in Shepherd's Bush market (Miller, 1996, p. 6). Thirty years on, we expect boys to be unemployed when they leave school without 'high levels of literacy, a particular accent, articulacy or stylish attractiveness' (Walkerdine *et al.*, 2001, p. 112). At the same time, girls appear to have greater career ambition, to be mindful of the gender-discriminatory nature of the adult workplace and inequality of housework and childcare, all of which may have provided new motivation (Francis, 2000). But where will girls' successes get them? Despite any early learning disadvantage top jobs continue to go to men. Female graduates can expect to earn 15 per cent less than their male equivalents by the age of 24 and it is mostly men on very high salaries who comprise the new elite in the financial and multinational sectors. Meanwhile professions like law and medicine are losing much of their traditional power and status just at the time when large numbers of women are coming into them (Walkerdine *et al.*, 2001).

To come full circle and return to the quote with which we started, inequalities of gender still have consequences in relation to educational systems, practices and institutions, even if the principle of gender differentiation is neither as explicit nor as legitimate in the twenty-first century as it was in the twentieth. In a context of restructured schools and broader social change, the form of its transmission is more likely to be found in the micro-world of classroom interaction and the more subtle differentiated curriculum tracks (Arnot, 2002). So, while the issue of boys' in crisis has 'effectively silenced work on girls, women and femininities' (Archer and Leathwood, 2003, p. 227) the old inequalities, though changed, have not ceased. Hegemonic masculinities and social class continue to dominate the state education system.

Notes

1   This was by the backbench MPs and campaigners Joan Vickers (1907–94, Conservative) and Lena Jeger (Labour).
2   Louis Althusser (1918–90) illustrated this point through an analysis of the role played by the repressive state apparatus and the ideological state apparatus. In this framework of ideas, schools form part of the ideological apparatus of the state, functioning in part to mould individuals into subjects that fit the requirements of capitalism. Besides particular knowledge and skills imparted through the content of education, students learn submission, deference and respect for the established organisation of work and their place in it. The structuralist Marxism of Althusser takes social structure as its central focus. Here the emphasis is on institutional domination through the institutions created by dominant groups to ensure the continuance of their domination.

3   The term hegemony was used by the Italian Marxist Antonio Gramsci (1891–1937) founder and briefly leader of the Italian Communist Party. Gramsci was imprisoned by Mussolini and his writings in captivity were later published as *The Prison Notebooks*. Gramsci defines hegemony as the organising principle or world view diffused through agencies of ideological control and socialisation into every area of social life. In this context the key conceptual tool is what Gramsci calls cultural hegemony. Central to this idea is the notion that the dominant class lays down the terms and parameters of discussion in society; it tries to define and contain all taste, morality, and customs, religious and political principles. However, hegemonic control has to be won and maintained. Subordinate classes can always produce a counter hegemony in an attempt to modify, negotiate, resist or even overthrow the dominant culture. In humanist Marxism as articulated by Gramsci, humankind and the question of agency becomes the central focus.

References

Archer, L. and Leathwood, C. (2003) 'New times – Old inequalities: diverse working-class femininities', *Gender and Education*, Vol. 15, No. 3, pp. 227–35.

Arnot, M. (1983) 'A cloud over co-education: an analysis of the forms of transmission of class and gender relations', in S. Walker and L. Barton (eds) *Gender, Class and Education*, Lewes: Falmer, pp. 69–91.

Arnot, M. (1984) 'How shall we educate our sons?', Deem, R. (ed.) *Co-education Reconsidered*, Milton Keynes, Open University Press, pp. 37–56.

Arnot, M. (1989/90) 'Consultation or legitimation? Race and gender politics and the making of the national curriculum', *Critical Social Policy*, 29, pp. 20–38.

Arnot, M. (1994) 'Male hegemony, social class and women's education', in L. Stone (ed.) *The Education Feminism Reader*, London: Routledge, pp. 84–104.

Arnot, M. (1996) 'The return of the egalitarian agenda? The paradoxical effects of recent educational reforms', *NUT Education Review*, 10 (1), pp. 9–14.

Arnot, M. (2002) 'Sociological understandings of contemporary gender transformation in schooling in the UK' in *Reproducing Gender*, London: Routledge, pp. 175–99.

Arnot, M., David, M. and Weiner, G. (1996) *Educational Reforms and Gender Equality*, Manchester: Equal Opportunities Commission.

Arnot, M., David, M. and Weiner, G. (1999) *Closing the Gender Gap: Postwar Education and Social Change*, Cambridge: Polity Press.

Attar, D. (1990) *Wasting Girls' Time. The History and Politics of Home Economics*, London: Virago.

Ball, S.J. and Gewirtz, S. (1997) 'Girls in the education market: choice, competition and complexity', *Gender and Education*, 9 (2), pp. 207–22.

Benjamin, S. (2003) 'Gender and special educational needs' in C. Skelton and B. Francis (eds) *Boys and Girls in the Primary Classroom*, Maidenhead: Open University Press, pp. 98–112.

Benn, C. and Simon, B. (1972) *Half Way There. Report on the British Comprehensive-School Reform*, Harmondsworth: Penguin.

Benn, C., Parris, J., Riley, K.A. and Weiner, G. (1982) 'Education and women: the new agenda', *Socialism and Education* 9 (2), pp. 10–13.

Benn, C. and Chitty, C. (1997) *Thirty Years On. Is Comprehensive Education Alive and Well or Struggling to Survive?*, 2nd edn, London: Penguin.

Board of Education (1943) *Curriculum and Examinations in Secondary Schools* (Norwood Report), London: HMSO.

Bryant, M. (1979) *The Unexpected Revolution*, Studies in Education, University of London.

Burgess, S., McConnell, B., Propper, C. and Wilson, D. (2003) 'Girls rock, boys roll: an analysis of the age 14–16 gender gap in English schools', *CMPO Discussion Paper* No. 03/084.

Caine, B. (1992) *Victorian Feminists*, Oxford: Oxford University Press.

Carter, A. (1988) *The Politics of Women's Rights*, London: Longman.

Clarricoates, C. (1980) 'The importance of being Ernest, Emma, Tom, Jane. The perception and categorization of gender conformity and gender deviation in primary schools', in R. Deem (ed.) *Schooling for Women's Work*, London: Routledge and Kegan Paul.

Corrigan, P. (1979) *Schooling the Smash Street Kids*, London: Macmillan.

David, M. (Winter 1983) 'Thatcherism *is* anti-feminism', *Trouble and Strife*, 1, pp. 44–8.

David, M. and Weiner, G. (1997) 'Keeping balance on the gender agenda', *TES*, 23 May 1997.

Davin, A. (1979) 'Mind that you do as you are told', *Feminist Review*, 3, pp. 80–98.

Davin, A. (1996) *Growing Up Poor. Home, School and Street in London 1870–1914*, London: Rivers Oram Press.

Dean, D.W. (1991) 'Education for moral improvement, domesticity and social cohesion: the Labour government, 1945–1951', *Oxford Review of Education*, 17 (3), pp. 269–86.

Deem, R. (1978) *Women and Schooling*, London: Routledge, and Kegan Paul.

Deem, R. (1981) 'State policy and ideology in the education of women, 1944–1980', *British Journal of Sociology of Education*, 2 (2), pp. 131–43.

Deem, R. (ed.) (1984) *Co-education Reconsidered*, Milton Keynes: Open University Press.

Delamont, S. (1983) 'The conservative school? Sex roles at home, at work and at school', in S. Walker and L. Barton (eds) *Gender, Class and Education*, Lewes: Falmer, pp. 93–105.

Department of Education and Science (1975) Curricular Differences for Boys and Girls, Education Survey, No 21, London: HMSO.

Digby, A. and Searby, P. (1981) *Children, School and Society in Nineteenth Century England*, London and Basingstoke: Macmillan.

Dyhouse, Carol (1981) *Girls Growing Up in Late Victorian and Edwardian England*, London: Routledge and Kegan Paul.

Edwards, E. 'Educational institutions or extended families? The reconstruction of gender in women's colleges in the late nineteenth and early twentieth centuries', *Gender and Education*, 2 (1), pp. 17–35.

Epstein, D., Elwood, J., Hey, V. and Maw, J. (eds) (1998) *Failing Boys? Issues in Gender and Achievement*, Buckingham: Open University Press.

Francis, B. (2000) *Boys, Girls and Achievement*, London: RoutledgeFalmer.

Gipps, C. and Murphy, P. (1994) *A Fair Test? Assessment, Achievement and Equity*, Milton Keynes: Open University Press.

Gomersall, M. (1988) 'Ideals and realities: the education of working-class girls', 1800–1870, *History of Education*, 17 (1), pp. 37–53.

Gomersall, M. (1994) 'Education for domesticity? A nineteenth century perspective on girls' schooling and domesticity', *Gender and Education*, 6 (3), pp. 235–47.

Gorard, S., Rees, G. and Salisbury, J. (1999) 'Reappraising the apparent under-achievement of boys at school', *Gender and Education*, 11 (4) 441–54.

Grant, L. (1994) 'First among equals', *Guardian Weekend*, 22 October, pp. 37–46.

Griffin, C. (1985) *Typical Girls? Young Women From School to the Job Market*, London: Routledge, and Kegan Paul.

Heward, C. (1993) 'Men and women and the rise of professional society: the intriguing history of teacher education', *History of Education*, 22 (1), pp. 11–32.

Hollis, P. (1989) *Ladies Elect. Women in English Local Government, 1865–1914*, Oxford: Clarendon Press.

Horn, P. (1988) 'The Education and Employment of Working Class Girls, 1870–1914', *History of Education*, 17 (1), pp. 71–82.

Hunt, F. (1991) *Gender and Policy in English Education 1902–1944*, London: Harvester Wheatsheaf.

Hurt, J. (1979) *Elementary Schooling and the Working Classes 1860–1918*, London: Routledge and Kegan Paul.

Kamm, J. (1965) *Hope Deferred. Girls Education in English History*, London: Methuen.

Kelly, A. (1985) 'Changing schools and changing society: some reflections on the Girls into Science and Technology project' in M. Arnot (ed.) *Race and Gender: Equal Opportunities Policies in Education*, Oxford: Pergamon.

Le Riche, E. (1988) *Why Do Teenage Girls Truant?*, London: Roehampton Institute of Higher Education, Department of Sociology and Social Administration.

Lees, S. (1993) *Sugar and Spice: Sexuality and Adolescent Girls*, London: Routledge.

Littlejohn, M. (1995) 'Makers of Men', in L. Dawtrey, J. Holland and M. Hammer with S. Sheldon (eds) *Equality and Inequality in Education Policy*, Clevedon: Multilingual Matters in association with The Open University, pp. 46–55.

Llewellyn, M. (1980) 'Studying girls at school: the implications of confusion' in R. Deem (ed.) *Schooling for Women's Work*, London: Routledge and Kegan Paul, pp. 42–51.

Lucey, H., Brown, M., Denvir, H. Askew, M. and Rhodes, V. (2003) 'Girls and boys in the primary maths classroom' in C. Skelton and B. Francis (eds) *Boys and Girls in the Primary Classroom*, Maidenhead: Open University Press, pp. 43–58.

Mahony, P. (1988) 'Girls will be girls and boys will be first', in D. Epstein, J. Elwood, V. Hey and J. Maw (eds) *Failing Boys? Issues in Gender and Achievement*, Buckingham: Open University Press, pp. 37–55.

Martin, J. (1987) 'The origins and development of gendered schooling', unpublished MA dissertation, University of Warwick.

Martin, J. (1999) *Women and the Politics of Schooling in Victorian and Edwardian England*, Leicester: Leicester University Press.

Marsh, J. (2003) 'Superhero stories' in C. Skelton and B. Francis (eds) *Boys and Girls in the Primary Classroom*, Maidenhead, Open University Press, pp. 59–79.

McWilliams-Tullberg, R. (1975) *Women at Cambridge*, London: Victor Gollancz.

Miles, S. and Middleton, C. (1995) 'Girls' education in the balance: the ERA and inequality', in L. Dawtrey, J. Holland and M. Hammer with S. Sheldon (eds) *Equality and Inequality in Education Policy*, Clevedon: Multilingual Matters in association with The Open University, pp. 123–39.

Miller, J. (1996) *School for Women*. London: Virago.

Mirza, H.S. (1992) *Young, Female and Black*, London: Routledge.

Murphy, P. and Elwood, J. (1998) 'Gendered experiences, choices, and achievement – exploring the links', *The International Journal of Inclusive Education*, 2 (2), pp. 95–118.

Pankhurst, E. (1979) *My Own Story*, London: Virago.

Paechter, C. (1998) *Educating the Other: Gender, Power and Schooling*, London: The Falmer Press.

Pascall, G. (1997) *Social Policy, A New Feminist Analysis* London: Routledge.

Pascall, G. and Cox, R. (1993) 'Education and domesticity', *Gender and Education* 5 (1), pp. 17–35.

Payne, I. (1980) 'Sexist ideology and education' in D. Spender and E. Sarah (eds) *Learning to Lose*, London: The Women's Press.

Purvis, J. (1985) 'Domestic subjects since 1870' in I. Goodson (ed.) *Social Histories of The Secondary Curriculum*, Lewes: Falmer Press, 145–76.

Purvis, J. (1995) 'Women and education 1800–1914', in L. Dawtrey, J. Holland and M. Hammer with S. Sheldon (eds) *Equality and Inequality in Education Policy*, Clevedon: Multilingual Matters in association with the Open University, pp. 3–17.

Raphael Reed, L. (1998) '"Zero tolerance": gender performance and school failure' in D. Epstein with J. Elwood, V. Hey and J. Maw (eds) *Failing Boys? Issues in Gender and Achievement*, Buckingham: Open University Press, pp. 56–76.

Rendel, M. (1997) *Whose Human Rights?*, London: Trentham.

Riddell, S. (1989) 'Pupils, resistance and gender codes: a study of classroom encounters', *Gender and Education* 1 (2), pp. 183–98.

Riley, K.A. (1994) *Quality and Equality. Promoting Opportunities in Schools*, London: Cassell.

Schultz, T.W. (1970) 'The reckoning of education as human capital' in W.L. Hansen, (ed.) *Education, Income and Human Capital*, New York: National Bureau of Economic Research.

Simon, B. (1980) *Education and the Labour Movement 1870–1920*, London: Lawrence and Wishart.

Simon, B. (1991) *Education and the Social Order*, London: Lawrence and Wishart.

Spender, D. and Sarah, E. (eds) (1980) *Learning to Love*, London: Women's Press.

Stantonbury Campus Sexism in Education Group, Bridgewater Hall School (1984) 'The realities of mixed schooling' in R. Deem (ed.) *Co-Education Reconsidered*, Milton Keynes: Open University Press, pp. 57–73.

Stanworth, M. (1986) *Gender and Schooling. A Study of Sexual Divisions in the Classroom*, London: Hutchinson.

Stone, L. (ed.) (1994) *The Education Feminism Reader*, London: Routledge.

Stromquist, N.P. (1990) 'Gender inequality in education: accounting for women's subordination', *British Journal of Sociology of Education*, 11 (2), pp. 137–53.

Thom, D. (1987) 'Better a teacher than a hairdresser? "A mad passion for equality" or, keeping Molly and Betty down', in F. Hunt (ed.) *Lessons for Life. The Schooling of Girls and Women 1850–1950*, Oxford: Basil Blackwell, pp. 124–46.

Turnbull, A. (1983) '"So extremely like Parliament": the work of the women members of the London School Board, 1870–1904', in London Feminist History Group (eds) *The Sexual Dynamics of History*, London: Pluto Press.

Turnbull, A. (1987) 'Learning her womanly work: the elementary school curriculum, 1870–1914', in F. Hunt (ed.) *Lessons for Life. The Schooling of Girls and Women 1850–1950*, Oxford: Basil Blackwell.

Vicinus, M. (1985) *Independent Women*, London: Virago.

Walkerdine, V., Lucey, H. and Melody, J. (2001) *Growing Up Girl*, Basingstoke: Palgrave.

Watts, R. (2002) 'Pupils and students' in R. Aldrich (ed.) *A Century of Education*, London: Routledge/Falmer.

Weiner, G. (1994) *Feminisms in Education*, Buckingham: Open University Press.

Willis, P. (1983) *Learning to Labour. How Working Class Kids Get Working Class Jobs*, Aldershot: Gower.

Wollstonecraft, M. (1792) *A Vindication of the Rights of Woman*, Harmondsworth: Penguin (1975).

3   Racism and resistance

From Empire to New Labour

Mike Cole and Satnam Virdee

Introduction

Rather than starting with a search for empirical evidence of discrimination or the expression of racism, or analysing 'the problems' or 'differentness' of minority ethnic groups, our analysis of racism centres on the material processes themselves, the complex relationship between the state and capital and between capital and labour and the way in which racism is ideologically constructed.

We begin by considering the origin and validity of the concept 'race'.[1] Next, we examine the concepts of racism, racialisation and institutional racism. We then go on to look at the origins of the welfare state, with particular reference to racism. These origins, we suggest, lay in a political and ideological matrix of imperialism, nationalism and anti-Semitism. We then trace the continuity of racism up to the present day, concluding with a discussion of Islamophobia and Xeno-racism and of forms of resistance to them.

'Race'

The formalization of the concept 'race' in the English language can be traced back to 1508 (*Oxford English Dictionary*), when it began to take on a specific economic connotation with the burgeoning development of the slave trade (Williams, 1964). For most of that century, however, it was used to refer to a class or category of persons or things; there was no implication that these classes or categories were biologically distinct. During the seventeenth century, an historical dimension was added, and there developed a view that the English were descendants of a German 'race' and that the Norman invasion of the eleventh century had led to the domination of the Saxons by an 'alien race'. This interpretation of history gave rise to a conception of 'race' in the sense of lineage back to the Saxons. Distinction, however, was based on separate history, rather than biological differences. During the late eighteenth and early nineteenth centuries, the term finally became associated with physical traits, both within the boundaries of Europe and beyond (Miles, 1982, pp. 10–11). According to Banton, by 1850, it is probable that 'a significant section of the English upper class subscribed to a rudimentary racial philosophy of history' (Banton, 1977, p. 25).

Racism

Before tracing the continuity of racism from these times up to the present, we would like to offer a definition of racism. Overt intentional racism, based on biology or genetics, whereby people are declared inferior on racial grounds, is now generally unacceptable in the public domain (it is freely available, of course, on Nazi and other racist websites). Contemporary racism, nonetheless, might best be thought of as a matrix of biological and cultural racism. Following Cole, 2004a, pp. 37–8, we would argue that in that matrix racism can be based on genetics (as in notions of white people having higher IQs than black people: see Herrnstein and Murray, 1994) or on culture (as in contemporary manifestations of Islamophobia). Quite often, however, it is not easily identifiable as either, or is a combination of both. A good example of the latter is when Margaret Thatcher, at the time of the Falklands/Malvinas war, referred to the people of that island as 'an island race' whose 'way of life is British' (Short and Carrington, 1996, p. 66). Here we have a conflation of notions of 'an island race' (like the British 'race' who, Mrs Thatcher believes, built an empire and ruled a quarter of the world through its sterling qualities; Thatcher, 1982, cited in Miles, 1993, p. 75) and, in addition, a 'race' which is culturally like 'us': 'their way of life is British'.

There are forms of racism, which are quite unintentional. The use by some people, *out of ignorance*, of the term 'Pakistani' to refer to everyone whose mode of dress or accent, for example, signifies that they might be of Asian origin is one example. The use of the nomenclature 'paki', on the other hand, we would suggest, is generally used in an intentionally racist way.

Racism can also be overt, as in racist name-calling in schools, or it can be covert, as in racist mutterings in school corridors. In other situations, seemingly positive attributes ascribed to an ethnic group will probably ultimately have racist implications. For example, the sub-text of describing a particular group as having a strong culture might be that 'they are swamping our culture'. In addition, attributing something seemingly positive – 'they are good at sport' – might have implications that 'they are not good' at other things. In still other situations, racism may well become apparent given certain stimuli (racist sentiments from a number of peers who might be collectively present at a given moment, for example). Stereotypes of ethnic groups are invariably problematic and, at least potentially, racist.

We would argue, therefore, that, in order to encompass the multifaceted nature of contemporary racism, it is important to adopt a broad concept of racism, rather than a narrow one, based, as it was in the days of the British Empire, for example, on notions of overt biological inferiority. Elsewhere, one of us (Cole, 2004a, pp. 37–8) has advocated a definition of racism which includes intentional as well as unintentional racism; biological as well as cultural; racism that is 'seemingly positive' as well as obvious negative racism; dominative racism (direct and oppressive) as opposed to aversive racism (exclusion and cold-shouldering) (cf. Kovel, 1988) and overt as well as covert racism. All of these forms of racism can be individual or personal as well as institutional, and there can, of course, be permutations among them.

We will shortly attempt to justify this wider definition in a context of racialization and institutional racism in Britain from the origins of the Welfare State up to the rise and fall of the Radical Right, and the ascendancy of New Labour (see also Chapter 4 for the educational connections), but first we would like to consider the interconnection between racialization and institutional racism.

Racialization and institutional racism

The concept of 'racialization' is useful to understand this process. Robert Miles has defined racialization as an ideological[2] process that accompanies the exploitation of labour power (the capacity to labour), where people are categorized into the scientifically defunct notion of distinct 'races'. As Miles puts it, the processes are not *explained* by the fact of capitalist development (a functionalist position). However 'the process of racialization cannot be adequately understood without a conception of, and explanation for, the complex interplay of different modes of production and, in particular, of the social relations necessarily established in the course of material production' (1987, p. 7). It is this interconnection which makes the concept of racialization inherently Marxist.

We will argue, following Cole, 2004a, that the Marxist concept of racialization transcends the rather nebulous and ahistorical definition of institutional racism provided by Macpherson (1999) and makes it possible to relate racism to these historical, economic and political factors, essential in understanding and combating racism.

For Marxists, any discourse is a product of the society in which it is formulated. In other words, 'our thoughts are the reflection of political, social and economic conflicts and racist discourses are no exception' (Camara, 2002, p. 88). Dominant discourses (e.g. those of the government, of big business, of large sections of the media, of the hierarchy of some trade unions) tend to directly reflect the interests of the ruling class, rather than 'the general public'. The way in which racialization connects with popular consciousness, however, is via 'common sense'. 'Common sense' is generally used to denote a down-to-earth 'good sense' and is thought to represent the distilled truths of centuries of practical experience, so that to say that an idea or practice is 'only common sense' is to claim precedence over the arguments of Left intellectuals and, in effect, to foreclose discussion (Lawrence, 1982, p. 48). In fact, common sense:

> is not a single unique conception, identical in time and space. It is the 'folklore' of philosophy, and, like folklore, it takes countless different forms. Its most fundamental characteristic is that it is . . . fragmentary, incoherent and inconsequential.
>
> (Gramsci, 1978, p. 419)

The rhetoric of the purveyors of dominant discourses aims to shape 'common sense discourse' into formats which serve their interests.

Following on from this, institutional racism may be defined as

Collective acts and/or procedures in an institution or institutions (nation-wide, continent-wide or globally) that intentionally or unintentionally have the effect of racialising, via 'common sense', certain populations or groups of people. This racialisation process cannot be understood without reference to economic and political factors related to developments and changes in national and global capitalism.

(Cole, 2004a, p. 39)

The relationship between institutional racialization, common sense and the fore-closure of Left perspectives is vividly at work in the media at the time of writing (January, 2005). Opposition Leader Michael Howard, announcing new Tory policy on further immigration restriction for asylum seekers, declared that immigration controls were not racist, but 'plain common sense'. Asylum seekers are the group most commonly racialized in media discourse in Britain at the moment (see below; see also Cole, 2004b). The following day, in its Leader, Britain's most popular tabloid, *The Sun* (25 January 2005, p. 8) repeated the message *twice* underlined in bold: 'That is not racist. It is common sense'. Howard's reference to 'common sense' was again repeated in an article by its political editor, Trevor Kavanagh, with huge headlines declaring: 'This isn't racism. It's COMMON SENSE' (ibid., pp. 8–9). In the same edition, columnist Richard Littlejohn used the phrases 'the Fascist left' and 'the Labour/ Liberal/BBC/Guardianistas axis' and informed readers that 'the Left always, always tell lies' (ibid., p. 11), while the Leader in *The Daily Mail* (25 January, 2005) ranted on about 'Left-wing politicians, liberal newspapers and reps of the race relations industry'.

'Calm and rational stand for common sense' appeared in Jane Moore's column in *The Sun* the following day (26 January, 2005, p. 11). The same paper (ibid., pp. 12–13) revealed that 97 per cent of its readers backed Howard. Juxtaposed to this revelation (ibid., p. 13), as if to underline that *The Sun's* purpose was to racialize specific groups, the paper featured an article about Yardie 'crack dealers flooding into Britain'.

As will become clear in the following analysis, institutional racism and insti-tutional racialization have been biological and cultural; overt and covert; 'seem-ingly positive' as well as negative; dominative as well as aversive.

The pre-World War Two period[3]

Racialization is historically and geographically specific. Thus, in the British colonial era, implicit in the rhetoric of imperialism was a racialized concept of 'nation'. British capitalism had be to regenerated in the context of competition from other countries, and amid fears that sparsely settled British colonies might be overrun by other European 'races'.

By the end of the nineteenth century, the ideology of the 'inferiority' of Britain's colonial subjects and the consequent 'superiority' of the British 'race' were available to all. There were a number of reasons for this. First, important social and economic changes had occurred, especially the transformation of Britain into a predominantly urban, industrial nation (Lorimer, 1978, p. 107). Basic state education, available after the 1870 Act and underpinned by imperial themes (see Chapter 4 of this volume; see also Mangan, 1986), and technical developments (Williams, 1961, pp. 168–72; see also Richards, 1989) facilitated the introduction of a cheap popular imperialist fiction (Miles, 1982, pp. 110 and 119). In addition, missionary work was seen as 'civilizing the natives'. In fact, a plethora of imperial themes permeated popular culture in the late Victorian era (Cole, 1992, pp. 36–42). As well as in the education system, from the late 1800s to 1914, patriotism, Empire and racism were highly marketable products in music hall (Summerfield, 1986), in juvenile fiction (Bratton, 1986) and in popular art (Springhall, 1986). Springhall writes of the importance of 'hero-worship and sensational glory, adventure and the sporting spirit: current history/falsified in coarse flaring colours, for the direct stimulation of the combative instincts'. 'It was no accident', he goes on:

> that the 'little wars' of Empire, which took place in almost every year of Queen Victoria's reign after 1870, provided the most readily available source for magazine and newspaper editors of romantic adventure and heroism set in an exotic and alien environment.
>
> (Springhall, 1986, p. 49)

Such images, Springhall (1986, p. 50) continues, were also apparent in commercial advertising, school textbook illustrations, postcards, cigarette cards, cheap reproductions and other ephemera which appropriated and mediated the work of popular British artists of the time. Racism had thus become institutionalized in popular culture in the British Imperial era in many ways.

Those at the receiving end of this 'heroism' had to be constructed as biologically inferior.[4] While the biological 'inferiority' of Britain's imperial subjects was perceived secondhand, the indigenous racism of the period was anti-Irish and anti-Semitic (Kirk, 1985; Miles, 1982). From the 1880s, there was a sizable immigration of destitute Jewish people from the Russian pogroms, and this fuelled the preoccupation of politicians and commentators about the health of the nation, the accompanying fear of the degeneration of the 'race', and the subsequent threat to imperial and economic hegemony (Holmes, 1979; Thane, 1982). 'National efficiency' served as a convenient label under which a complex set of beliefs, assumptions and demands could be grouped – it completed the racist chain of Empire, nation and 'race'.

In 1905, the Liberal government passed the Aliens Act which halted further Jewish immigration. The Act did not exclude 'Jews' by name – just as post-World War Two legislation does not refer specifically to 'Asian', 'black' or other minority ethnic groups.

Anti-Semitism was not merely the province of the ruling élite. Ten years earlier (1895), the Trades Union Congress (TUC) had convened a special conference at which it compiled a list of questions to be asked of all members of Parliament. These questions were described as a 'labour programme' and included a number of progressive demands: for the nationalization of land, minerals and the means of production; old age pensions; adequate health and safety facilities; the abolition of the House of Lords; workers' industrial injury compensation; the eight-hour day and the reform of the Poor Law system. They also demanded the restriction of Jewish immigration (Cohen, 1985, pp. 75–6). Robert Blatchford, a founding member and representative of the Manchester and Salford Independent Labour Party (ILP) and one of the leading socialist journalists of his generation, queried the 'racial results likely to follow on the infusion of so much alien blood into the British stock' (Howell, 1983, p. 292). As Cohen argues, 'it was a common theme amongst many socialists that England was eugenically doomed if it carried on sending its own citizens to the colonies while receiving Jews from Europe' (Cohen, 1985, p. 80).

Thus, an 'imperial race' was needed to defend the nation and the colonies (Miles 1993, p. 69), while Jews needed to be barred to ensure the survival of the British 'race'. Intentional and overt institutional racism was rampant in all the major institutions of society: in the government, the TUC and, of course, at the heart of capitalism itself. It had become 'common sense' to view the world in this way. Britain had become a dominative and overtly institutionally racist society.

Such racist thinking went largely unchallenged apart from during those periods of intense class conflict like that witnessed during the New Unionism in the late 1880s and early 1890s, when Jewish and English workers united in pursuit of common economic goals (Buckman, 1980; Williams, 1980).

It is important to note that anti-Semitism was not solely based on the stereotype of the poor Jew – a member of the lower social orders – threatening to pollute the racial purity of the British 'race', but on the ideology of the 'Jewish-capitalist conspiracy' and perceived attempts at world domination. In 1904, the ILP issued a pamphlet entitled *The Problem of Alien Immigration*, the first page of which mounted an attack on 'the rich Jew who has done his best to besmirch the fair name of England and to corrupt the sweetness of our national life and character' (Cohen, 1985, p. 76).[5]

Following World War One, it was emigration rather than immigration which dominated the agenda (Branson, 1975; Mowat, 1968; Stevenson, 1984). However, this did not prevent the state from renewing anti-alien legislation throughout the 1920s. By the 1930s, the focus had shifted to a concern about falling birth rates, in the light of worries about both 'race' preservation and the efforts of dictators in Italy and Germany to increase birth rates in those countries (Mowat, 1968, pp. 517–18).

It is within the context of these historical antecedents that the Beveridge Report of 1942, one of the key documents informing the founding of the welfare state, was written. Here, the links between welfare and 'race', and indeed gender and nation, were made explicit. For example, the argument deployed in favour of introducing child allowances was that: 'with its present rate of reproduction the British race cannot continue, means of reversing the recent course of the birth rate must he found' (paragraph 413). Women were assigned the role of baby-machines in the service of capitalism and British hegemony and were told: 'In the next thirty years housewives as Mothers have vital work to do in ensuring the adequate continuance of the British Race and British Ideals in the world' (paragraph 117).

The clearest example of Beveridge's own racism can be seen in his essay *Children's Allowances and the Race*. In it he stated:

> Pride of race is a reality for the British as for other peoples . . . as in Britain today we look back with pride and gratitude to our ancestors, look back as a nation or as individuals two hundred years and more to the generations illuminated by Marlborough or Cromwell or Drake, are we not bound also to look forward, to plan society now so that there may be no lack of men or women of the quality of those earlier days, of the best of our breed, two hundred and three hundred years hence?
>
> (cited in Cohen, 1985, pp. 88–9)[6]

The post-World War Two period[7]

In this section we limit our discussion of migrant labour to the postwar experience of Asians and Caribbeans and their English-born children. This is not to deny that 'white' groups have been subject to a process of racialization: they clearly have (see the preceding discussion of Jewish experiences in the nineteenth century; see also Grosvenor's reference (1998, p. 118) to the Cypriot experience in twentieth-century England; see as well Kirk, 1885 and Miles, 1982 for a discussion of anti-Irish racism). Additionally, we restrict our analysis to England. The small literature that exists on racism in Scotland (see, for example, Miles, 1982, pp. 121–50; Miles and Dunlop, 1986) suggests that it has taken a rather different form and trajectory to that in England and cannot be adequately assessed within the limited confines of this chapter.

The demands of an expanding postwar economy meant that Britain, like most other European countries, was faced with a major shortage of labour (Castles and Kosack, 1985). The demand for labour was met by a variety of sources, including 500,000 refugees, displaced persons and ex-prisoners of war from Europe between 1946 and 1951, and a further 350,000 European nationals between 1945 and 1957 (Sivanandan, 1976, p. 348). However, the overwhelming majority of migrants who came to Britain were from the Republic of Ireland, the Indian subcontinent and the Caribbean (Miles, 1989).

On the whole, the labour migration from the Indian subcontinent and the Caribbean proceeded by informal means with little effort made to relate employment to vacancies. Instead, it was left to free market forces to determine the size of immigration (Sivanandan, 1976, p. 348). However, those industries where the demand for labour was greatest actively recruited Asian, black and other minority ethnic workers[8] in their home countries (Fryer, 1984; Ramdin, 1987). Employers such as the British Transport Commission, the London Transport Executive, the British Hotels and Restaurants Association and the Regional Hospitals Board all established arrangements with Caribbean governments to ensure a regular supply of labour (Ramdin, 1987, p. 197). By 1958, and a decade of labour migration, there were 125,000 Caribbean and 55,000 Indian and Pakistani workers in England (Fryer, 1984, p. 373).

Despite the heterogeneous class structure of the migrating populations (see Heath and Ridge, 1983), they came to occupy, overwhelmingly, the semi-skilled and unskilled positions in the English labour market (Daniel, 1968; Smith, 1977). Furthermore, they found themselves disproportionately concentrated in certain types of manual work characterized by a shortage of labour, shift working, unsocial hours, low pay and an unpleasant working environment (Smith, 1977).

Importantly, research suggests that elements of organized labour colluded with employers to exclude Asian and Caribbean workers from key forms of employment, especially skilled work (Fryer 1984; Wrench, 1987). With little evidence of a class consciousness constructed around an identity of working-class solidarity but rather a sectionalist class consciousness characterized by the primary concern of protecting the terms and conditions of their immediate work colleagues (Kelly, 1988; Hyman, 1972; Beynon, 1984) elements of skilled organized labour, fearful of the perceived threat posed by migrant labour, colluded with employers to ensure that the trade union strategy of restrictive practices took on an added racist dimension by excluding migrant labour from skilled jobs (Virdee, 1999b).

It was not only in the economic sphere that Asian, black and other minority ethnic workers found themselves discriminated against during this period. It is important to emphasize that the state played a critical and formative role in restricting the immigration of non-whites. In the late 1950s, there was growing concern within Parliament, the media and the major political parties of the 'dangers of unrestricted immigration'. This contributed to an important shift in public policy towards migrant labour from one of support for unrestricted immigration to one that stressed that the immigration of 'non-whites' had to be curbed if the social fabric and cohesion of the country was not to be irreparably undermined. As a result, in 1962, an Immigration Act was introduced which had as its primary objective the curbing of 'non-white' labour from the Indian subcontinent and the Caribbean only, with immigration from the Republic of Ireland remaining unaffected (see Miles and Phizacklea, 1984).

The consequences of this process of racialization were clear. According to Miles (1982, p. 165), these different racialized groups came to

> occupy a structurally distinct position in the economic, political and ideological relations of British capitalism, but within the boundary of the working class. They therefore constitute a fraction of the working class, one that can be identified as a racialised fraction.[9]

'Black' self-organization: a strategy of collective antiracist action

Apart from a few exceptions (see, for example, Virdee and Grint, 1994; Virdee, 1999b), an often neglected aspect of the racialization process has been any critical investigation of the forms of resistance to it (see Solomos, 1993). If we undertake an assessment of the 1950s and 1960s, it is clear that apart from isolated cases such as the campaign mounted by black community organizations and individual whites against the operation of a 'colour bar' introduced by white bus workers in Bristol in 1955 (see Dresser, 1986 for a detailed discussion) there is little evidence of collective resistance to such racist exclusionary practices from any workers until the mid-1960s. As Sivanandan (1982, p. 5) argues, 'resistance to racial abuse and discrimination on the shopfloor was more spontaneous than organised'.

However, by the mid-1960s, the discriminatory practices enforced by employers and trade unions alike came under growing pressure from a series of strikes by racialized workers in the textile and foundry industries (Moore, 1975; Duffield, 1988; Wrench, 1987). Importantly, nearly all of these disputes were character-ized by a substantial level of support from the different racialized communities and an almost complete lack of support from the white working class (Sivanandan, 1982; Wrench, 1987).

Drawing inspiration from the civil rights struggles in the USA and the visits to Britain of the two main leaders of the American antiracist movement – Martin Luther King in December 1964 and Malcolm X in January 1965 (Sivanandan, 1982) – this period witnessed the racialized community establishing numer-ous organizations committed to challenging racism through self-organization constructed around the identity 'black'. Importantly, and unlike the USA, 'black' became an identity that was inclusive of all the main 'non-white' social groups that were subject to racialization during this period. Shukra (1996, pp. 30–1) describes how activists within these communities set about attempting to establish an Asian–Caribbean alliance against racism:

> The 'black' radical activist was usually an unpaid campaigner who operated intensively with a small group of like-minded people, went from meeting to meeting, distributed pamphlets, spoke at rallies, carried banners and organised demonstrations to convince what was termed 'West Indian', 'Indian' and 'Pakistani' people that their experience of inferior treatment at the hands of employers, schools, local authorities, government officials, politicians and the police was unacceptable. Crucially, they also argued that this situation could be changed through militant political activity, primarily against employers and the state . . . the black activists used the term 'black' to build a movement to mobilise and cohere self-reliant communities of resistance to racism.

Among some of the more prominent organizations that Asians and Caribbeans joined to combat racism and exclusionary practices were the Racial Action Adjustment Society (RAAS), a 'black' radical organization whose slogan was 'Black men, unite . . . we have nothing to lose but our fears' (cited in Sivanandan, 1982, p. 16) and the Black People's Alliance (BPA) see below; see also Josephides (1990). The outcome was that an identity previously employed to disparage particular racialized social groups was appropriated by the racialized communities themselves and infused with new meaning and an ideology of resistance – a process which Gilroy (1987) in Britain and Omi and Winant (1986) in the USA have come to define as 'race' and 'racial' formation, respectively.

The impact of such 'racial' formation coupled with growing academic evidence which demonstrated that 'racial' discrimination in the labour market ranged from the 'massive to the substantial' (Daniel, 1968) forced the state into introducing reforms to curb the worst excesses of racist exclusionary practices. One of the most important measures was the introduction of a Race Relations Act in 1968 which outlawed discrimination in the areas of employment, housing and the provision of goods, facilities, services and planning. Additionally, the Race Relations Board, established in 1965 by the first Race Relations Act, was given stronger enforcement powers, and a new body – the Community Relations Council (CRC) – was created to promote 'harmonious community relations' (Wrench, 1996, p. 24).

Consequently, by 1968, accompanying the legislation designed to curb 'non-white' immigration was the recognition by the state of the need for anti-discrimination legislation for those racialized migrants and their children already resident in Britain. These two aspects of state policy were neatly encapsulated by Roy Hattersley (a former Home Office minister) in his formulation: 'Integration without control is possible, but control without integration is indefensible' (cited in Solomos, 1993, p. 84).

However, for some elements of the British élite and white working class, the introduction of reforms, even while conceding the need for racist immigration controls, was tantamount to undermining the social basis of a much revered imagined community (Anderson, 1983) – the British (i.e. 'white') 'race' and its 'traditional' way of life. This current of opinion was most significantly reflected in the speeches of Enoch Powell, who, ironically, in a previous guise as Minister of Health had been responsible for the recruitment of Caribbean nurses during the postwar era of capitalist expansion (Fryer, 1984). In April 1968, Powell set out his opposition to attempts by the state to curb racist discriminatory practices when he claimed that racialized migrant labour and their children should not be 'elevated into a privileged or special class . . . The discrimination and the deprivation, the sense of alarm and of resentment, lies not with the immigrant population but with those among whom they have come and are still coming' (cited in Miles and Phizacklea, 1984, p. 3). The ideological hold of such racist thought over parts of the white working class was forcefully demonstrated by the marches in support of Powell by the Smithfield meat porters and the dockers of east London (Sivanandan, 1982; Miles and Phizacklea, 1984) who chanted 'Back Britain, not Black Britain' (*The Trial of Enoch Powell*, Channel 4, 20 April 1998).

Racialized workers responded to this racist threat by establishing the Black People's Alliance (BPA), an organization which marked the high-point of the antiracist 'racial' formation project in Britain, including both Asian and Caribbean activists, with Jagmohan Joshi, the leader of the Indian Workers Association (IWA-GB), becoming its general secretary (Josephides, 1990). Despite such collective resistance, persistent pressure from the racist right served to forge the necessary political climate for the Labour government to introduce the Common-wealth Immigrants Act in 1968. This piece of legislation removed the right of entry into Britain from all British passport holders who did not have a parent or grand-parent born in Britain (Miles and Phizacklea, 1984, p. 60). Such racist immigration controls were further strengthened with the election of a Conservative adminis-tration in 1970, which, within a year, had introduced an Immigration Act that effectively marked the end of Asian and black immigration for settlement (Gordon and Klug, 1985, p. 7).

By the early 1970s, research conclusively demonstrated that after having been resident in Britain for over a quarter of a century and despite almost a decade of collective resistance by the racialized communities themselves, racialized workers from the Indian subcontinent and the Caribbean continued to be substantially disadvantaged in the British labour market, as well as in other areas of resource allocation (Smith, 1977). A national survey carried out during this period showed the continuing importance of biological racism in defining the life chances of these social groups who were all lumped together as 'coloured people' (ibid., p. 111).

However, at the same time, wider events, in particular the growing class conflict between organized labour and the state and employers (Hyman, 1972; Crouch, 1977) were increasingly undermining the highly sectionalist working class con-sciousness that had hindered the formation of a current of white antiracism during the 1950s and 1960s.

Growing class conflict in the 1970s and the formation of a current of white antiracism

The attempts to curb unofficial trade union activity by the state during the late 1960s and early 1970s served to politicize key elements of organized labour and contributed significantly to the formation of an oppositional class identity (Hyman, 1972; Kelly, 1988). In particular, there began to take place a significant shift beyond the narrow, sectionalist class consciousness of the 1950s and 1960s to a more politicized form of class consciousness which recognized the value of working class solidarity and collective action to defend working class interests.

This important development coupled with almost a decade of industrial struggles against racism and exclusionary practices by racialized workers and the growing fear of far-right influence in trade unions (see Miles and Phizacklea, 1978) created the necessary conditions for antiracist ideas and the need for solidarity between 'black' and 'white' labour to gain a wider audience within many trade unions. By the mid-1970s, the TUC (see Miles and Phizacklea, 1978) and major trade unions, including the TGWU, GMBWU, NALGO, CPSA and the SCPS, recognized that working class solidarity, necessary to combat growing employer and state encroachment of trade union rights, could only be achieved by explicitly challenging racism both within the workplace and outside. It was during this period that most large trade unions introduced anti-discriminatory measures (see, for example, the annual reports of NALGO 1977; 1979; 1981) which marked the beginnings of a decisive shift in policy within British trade unions from the 'problem of integration' to the 'problem of racism' (Miles and Phizacklea, 1978).

Importantly, it was amid this growing industrial unrest and the shift to the left among key sections of organized labour (Hyman, 1972; Crouch, 1977; Marsh, 1992; Kelly, 1988), that the incoming Labour government introduced several important pieces of legislation, the Sex Discrimination Act in 1975 and the Race Relations Act in 1976 (Marsh, 1992). While the latter piece of legislation was subsequently shown to have been largely ineffective in challenging the prevalence of racism and exclusionary practices because of the sheer magnitude of the problem (see McCrudden *et al.*, 1991), its introduction nevertheless represented a highly symbolic indication of the commitment to combat racism and exclusionary practices by the state under pressure from the organized labour movement and the racialized communities.

However, the most visible manifestation of the solidarity between Asian and white labour came during the course of the Grunwick dispute when thousands of white (and non-white) workers, including miners, dockers (some of whom had demonstrated in favour of immigration controls in 1968), transport workers and post office workers, undertook secondary picketing to support South Asian women on strike (Rogaly, 1977; Ramdin, 1987). While the dispute ended in defeat for the strikers in 1978, it nevertheless demonstrated that amid the growing radicalization of parts of the organized labour movement, many white workers overcame the ideology of racism and acted along the fault line of class in solidarity with racialized workers.

There is some evidence to suggest that this current of white antiracism at work was also influential in building resistance to racism outside of the workplace. In particular, primary research evidence suggests that parts of the organized labour movement played a decisive role in the formation of such antiracist and anti-fascist organizations as the Anti-Nazi League (ANL) (see, for example, the annual reports of Civil and Public Servants Association (CPSA), 1980, p. 13; 1981, p. 11; Society of Civil and Public Servants (SCPS), 1983, p. 26; 1984, p. 54; and National and Local Government Officers (NALGO), 1981, p. 15). In addition to the longer-established 'black' antiracist groups, by 1973–4, many 'whites' had also begun to establish antiracist committees supported by local trades councils. The racist pronouncements of some rock stars led to the formation of a national organization called Rock Against Racism in August 1976 (Gilroy, 1987, pp. 120–1). The years 1976 and 1977 were important because they saw growing confrontation between racists and antiracists which culminated in antiracists preventing the far-right National Front from marching through Lewisham in south London – an area of relatively high 'black' concentration. In 1977 the National Front polled 119,000 votes in the Greater London local council elections and threatened to become the third party in British politics. The Anti-Nazi League (ANL) was established in 1977 to counter the threat from the National Front (Gilroy, 1987), and, in alliance with more locally based antiracist organizations such as the Campaign Against Racism and Fascism (CARF) (CARF, 1992, p. 2), they successfully exposed the National Front as 'Nazis', contributing greatly to driving a wedge between them and a potentially sympathetic 'white' British public, and ultimately leading to their electoral demise (Messina, 1989).

Of course, such evidence by no means suggests that the white working class moved *en bloc* towards an antiracist position; otherwise, there would have been little need for the establishment of a national antiracist organization in the first instance. Rather, this chapter has highlighted an important yet greatly neglected aspect of antiracist politics during this period – the formation of a current of white antiracism. The consequences of such political developments were that by the late 1970s Britain had a significant antiracist movement built around the dual ideological currents of 'racial' formation and working class solidarity.

Antiracism in an era of neo-liberalism: the 1980s and early 1990s

The economic and political forces that had helped to shape the formation of an activist 'inter-racial' unity within parts of the organized labour movement was not to last long, however. The failure of the 1974–9 Labour government and 'left' trade union leaders to arrest the rising levels of unemployment and the decline in real wages of many sectors of organized labour contributed greatly to a sense of disillusionment with such politics which ultimately manifested itself in the return of the Conservative Party to office in May 1979 with a substantial working class vote (Marsh, 1992).

However, the introduction of neo-liberal economic policies designed with the primary purpose of curbing public spending through the stringent use of monetarist procedures served merely to accelerate the de-industrialization of Britain that had been under way since the mid-1970s (Eldridge *et al.*, 1991). The recession was particularly marked in parts of the north and north-west of England, Scotland and many of the inner-city areas of the major conurbations (including Greater London) where both white and racialized workers were laid off in large numbers (Brown, 1982). Due to a complex interaction of the occupational and regional distribution of different racialized social groups, some were worse affected than others by the decline in manufacturing employment. Specifically, workers of Pakistani origin who found themselves disproportionately concentrated within the collapsing textile industry and, residentially concentrated in the north and north-west, were more adversely affected than workers of Indian and African-Asian origin (or, for that matter, whites) who were relatively more evenly distributed across several major manufacturing industries and were also more residentially dispersed (see Modood, 1997).

It was this economic decay coupled with the exacerbation of more specific problems, such as the growing deterioration in the relationship between the police and inner-city youth, that contributed greatly to the urban unrest in many of the English conurbations during the early 1980s (Benyon, 1984; Solomos, 1988). Although the research evidence strongly suggests that the participants of the urban unrest comprised white youths as well as Asian and black youths (see Benyon 1984; Gilroy, 1987; Solomos, 1988), two mutually antagonistic sets of social forces ensured that racism, or, more precisely, the social construction of 'race', came to dominate public policy debate about the main causes of the unrest.

On the one hand, the antiracist movement insisted that the root causes of the unrest lay in the systematic destruction of the lives of racialized communities through the operation of racism and exclusionary practices and state (mainly police) harassment which had served to create a 'racially defined' sub-proletariat (see Sivanandan, 1993). On the other hand, the tabloid press forcefully denied that the unrest was the result of racism, and instead attempted to criminalize the unrest by claiming it was the product of a black criminal underbelly within society (see Solomos, 1988, Gilroy, 1987). In both sets of analyses, far less attention was paid to explaining the plight of white working class youth who had also been active participants of the unrest (Benyon, 1984).

It was amid this highly charged political atmosphere that the Scarman Inquiry into the urban unrest was published in November 1981 (Scarman, 1981). The report advanced a series of recommendations: including calling for a more effective co-ordinated approach to tackling the problem of the inner cities; adopting a policy of affirmative action to combat 'racial' discrimination among racialized social groups; reforming the police force and introducing new methods of policing (Taylor, 1984, p. 29). However, apart from giving qualified support to the findings contained in the Scarman Report (see Raison, 1984, pp. 244–57), the right-wing Conservative administration proved to be highly averse to introducing even minor reforms necessary to tackle racism and exclusionary practices because of its disagreement with the material explanations of the unrest advanced by the Scarman Inquiry (Ball and Solomos, 1990).

At this juncture, the trade unions could have colluded with employers to exclude racialized workers from the remaining areas of employment growth and stability (such as the service sector) within the British social formation. However, they did not: the political relations in 1980s England were rather different to those during the 1950s and 1960s when the prevalence of a highly sectionalist class consciousness had greatly hindered the formation of an indigenous current of white antiracism.

While the mass 'inter-racial' rank-and-file solidarity evident at Grunwick had subsided, the trade union activists who had come to prominence during the 1970s on a platform that articulated the defence of general working class interests remained in positions of responsibility. As a result by the early 1980s, activists in the trade union movement were, in political terms at least, far to the left of their membership over a range of important issues (Marsh, 1992), including the need to combat racism.

An antiracist coalition comprising 'black' activists, trade union activists and the left of the Labour Party ensured that the recommendations of the Scarman Report, and in particular the need to tackle 'racial' disadvantage, was forced on to the social policy formation agendas of the local state. Under such pressure, the recommendations acted as a catalyst, particularly in those local authority areas that were politically controlled by left-wing Labour parties in the Greater London area where nearly half of the racialized population resided (Owen, 1993), to undertake antiracist action (Ball and Solomos, 1990).

One practical example of the kind of antiracist initiative launched during this period was collection by employers of systematic data on the ethnic origin of their applicants and employees so that the extent of disadvantage could be effectively assessed and thereby more systematically remedied through the adoption of affirmative action programmes.

Specifically, non-manual forms of employment, albeit at the lower grades, were opened up to large numbers of racialized workers for the first time. This process acted as a catalyst and other large employers were forced to consider the employment and promotion of racialized workers. These developments have led to an important reconfiguration in the position of racialized social groups in economic relations: they no longer occupy a position in the semi-skilled and unskilled sites of the manual working class but instead display strikingly similar class cleavages to those of the white population.

Racism, antiracism and New Labour

While the introduction of the Race Relations (Amendment) Act (2000) (http://www.hmso.gov.uk/acts/acts2000/20000034.htm) is to be thoroughly welcomed (Cole, 2004a; Cole and Stuart, 2005), the onset of a Labour government has done little, despite the rhetoric of 'an inclusive society', to challenge the fundamental racism inherent in British society. Gillborn (2001) argues that the politics of 'race' and nation which were discussed earlier in this chapter, and which were made explicit during the government of Margaret Thatcher, have been kept alive in the new rhetorics of the Labour government. Indeed, on 14 January, 2003, British Home Secretary, David Blunkett, suggested that 'institutional racism' was a slogan that let individual managers 'off the hook' in tackling racism (Travis, 2003).[10] He said that it was important that the government's 'diversity agenda' tackled the fight against prejudice but also took on the long-standing need to change attitudes:

> That is why I was so worried about people talking about institutional racism because it isn't institutions. It is patterns of work and processes that have grown up. It's people that make the difference.
>
> (ibid.)

Questioned about his comments afterwards, he added that 'I think the slogan created a year or two ago about institutional racism missed the point. It's not the structures created in the past but the processes to change structures in the future and it is individuals at all levels who do that' (ibid.).

Blunkett's comments are, of course, related to the Stephen Lawrence Inquiry (Macpherson, 1999).[11] It is well known that, while the inquiry admits the existence of racism among some *individual* police officers (an acknowledgement which we would suggest is understated) it accentuates *institutional racism* as the key problem. Blunkett's intervention represents an attempt to turn back the tide; to trivialize institutional racism by describing it as a 'slogan'; indeed to deny its existence and to revert back, in Blunkett's own words, to 'individual prejudice' as being the major problem. If it is the case that managers in the police and elsewhere are using the acceptance of the existence of 'institutional racism' as an excuse for inaction, then this should, of course, be challenged. What is problematic in Blunkett's remarks is the shift in focus from 'institutional racism' to a conception of racism as an autonomous *personal* problem – a move from 'institutional racism as collective failure' to the 'rotten apple theory' of racism. There are two main problems with this. First of all, the psychological concept of prejudice divorces discriminatory practices from wider structural factors: institutional racism usually refers to racism *permeating* major institutions, e.g. the police force, the education system, the political system, and so on, at the local level, the national level and/or beyond. Second, in stressing *individual* blame, the need for structural change – local, national, international – is negated. Acknowledging structural and institutional injustices opens up the possibilities for institutional and structural change, whereas the accentuation of personal prejudice does not.

Blunkett's deficit and Thatcherite view of minority peoples is underscored in another intervention, in which, on BBC Radio 4's Today programme, speaking of educating the children of asylum seekers separately while their applications are processed, he stated: 'Whilst they're going through the process, the children will be educated on the site, which will be open. People will be able to come and go, but importantly not swamping the local school'.[12]

One of us (Mike Cole) argued the case, in October 2003, on BBC Radio 4's *The Learning Curve* (audio link available at http://www.bbc.co.uk/radio4/factual/learningcurve.shtml), that it is inappropriate for a British National Party (BNP) activist and local election candidate to retain his position as a primary school governor because the BNP has policies that directly lead to discrimination on grounds of ethnicity and religion. The government was invited to send a spokesperson to the studio. Instead, it read a statement from Junior Schools Minister, Stephen Twigg, which merely stated that, 'the most successful schools are those that have an antiracist ethos and celebrate diversity and that systems should be in place to ensure that no governor acts in a way that is against the school's ethos'. This gives no encouragement to those of us who believe that the *very presence* of a BNP member in a school is against the ethos of antiracism and cultural diversity.

Indeed in many ways, the New Labour government seems to be attempting to steal the thunder from the BNP, particularly with respect to Islamophobia and asylum-seekers. We will deal with each in turn.

Islamophobia[13]

Just as in the days of the British Empire there is an ideological requirement for racialization. As Zephaniah states:

> when I come through the airport nowadays, in Britain and the US especially, they always question me on the Muslim part of my name. They are always on the verge of taking me away because they think converts are the dangerous ones.
>
> (2004, p. 19)

Islamophobia is a key component of racialization connected to the new imperialism, in its ongoing quest for global profits. According to the Commission on British Muslims and Islamophobia (CBMI), Britain is 'institutionally Islamophobic', with hostility towards Islam permeating every part of British society (Doward and Hinsliff, 2004). The report produces a raft of evidence suggesting that since 9/11, there has been a sharp rise in attacks on followers of Islam. Ahmed Versi, editor of the Muslim News, who gave evidence, said:

> We have reported cases of mosques being firebombed, paint being thrown at mosques, mosques being covered in graffiti, threats made, women being spat upon, eggs being thrown. It is the visible symbols of Islam that are being attacked.
>
> (cited in ibid.)

More than 35,000 Muslims were stopped and searched in 2003, with fewer than 50 charged (ibid.).

Islamaophobia, like other forms of racism, can be cultural or it can be biological, or it can be a mixture of both. Echoing the quote from the school textbooks, cited in Chapter 4, p. 74 of this volume, where Asia was denigrated as 'a continent of dying nations rapidly falling back in civilisation', and where reference was made to 'the barbaric peoples of Asia', the former Archbishop of Canterbury recently defended a controversial speech in which he criticised Islam as a faith 'associated with violence throughout the world'. At the Gregorian University in Rome he said that Islam was resistant to modernity and Islamic societies had contributed little to world culture for hundreds of years (http://www.timesonline.co.uk/article/0,,1-1052154,00.html).

A more biological Islamophobic racism is revealed by Jamal al-Harith, a British captive freed from Guantanamo Bay. He informed *The Daily Mirror* that his guards told him: 'You have no rights here'. al-Harith went on,

> [a]fter a while, we stopped asking for human rights – we wanted animal rights. In Camp X-Ray my cage was right next to a kennel housing an Alsatian dog. He had a wooden house with air conditioning and green grass to exercise on. I said to the guards, 'I want his rights' and they replied, 'That dog is member of the US army'.
>
> (http://www.mirror.co.uk/news/allnews/content_objectid=14042696 _method=full_siteid=50143_headline=-MY-HELL-IN-CAMP-X-RAY-name_page.html)

Home Office figures showed a 300 per cent rise in the number of Asians subjected to stop and search techniques under anti-terror laws.

More people of all backgrounds were stopped and searched under the Terrorism Act 2000 in 2003, but the percentage increases among Asians were higher than most. Nearly 3,000 Asians were stopped in 2002–3, up from 744 the year before.

In the same period, stop and searches on white people rose 118 per cent, up to 14,429 from 6,629, according to the Home Office report, Statistics on Race and the Criminal Justice System. Stop and searches on black people rose from 529 to 1,745 over the year, an increase of 230 per cent (http://www.guardian.co.uk/race/story/0,11374,1252699,00.html).

Xenoracism[14]

Sivanandan has identified a new form of racism:

> It is a racism that is not just directed at those with darker skins, from the former colonial territories, but at the newer categories of the displaced, the dispossessed and the uprooted, who are beating at western Europe's doors, the Europe that helped to displace them in the first place. It is a racism, that is, that cannot be colour-coded, directed as it is at poor whites as well, and is therefore passed off as xenophobia, a 'natural' fear of strangers. But in the way it denigrates and reifies people before segregating and/or expelling them, it is a xenophobia that bears all the marks of the old racism. It is racism in substance, but 'xeno' in form. It is a racism that is meted out to impoverished strangers even if they are white. It is xeno-racism.
>
> (A. Sivanandan, cited in Liz Fekete, *The Emergence of Xeno-racism*, Institute of Race Relations, 2001)
> (http://www.irr.org.uk/2001/september/ak000001.html)

The ongoing *process* that accompanies this new form of racism is a new form of racialization, which one of us (Cole, 2004b) has referred to as xeno-racialization. So how can we explain the current process of xeno-racialization? Globalization in the twenty-first century requires labour market flexibility. However, resurgent economic crises have intensified the contradictions faced by states. As Gareth Dale (1999, p. 308) puts it with great clarity:

> On the one hand, intensified competition spurs employers' requirements for enhanced labour market flexibility – for which immigrant labour is ideal. On the other, in such periods questions of social control tend to become more pressing. Governments strive to uphold the ideology of 'social contract' even as its content is eroded through unemployment and austerity. The logic, commonly, is for less political capital to be derived from the compact's content, while greater emphasis is placed upon its exclusivity, on demarcation from those who enter from or lie outside – immigrants and foreigners.
>
> (ibid.)

The Observer gives a cameo of the ongoing process of xeno-racialization, a process, which, in Plymouth, seems to be leading to (voluntary) incarceration. Attacks on asylum seekers have become routine there since the beginning of 2003, when an Iraqi was beaten up outside a supermarket in the city centre (http://observer.guardian.co.uk/politics/story/0,6903,987273,00.html).[15] 'Many times they swear at me in the street', a 20-year-old, who arrived in Britain three years ago, told the newspaper. 'It is upsetting when you smile and say "Hi" and someone says "Fuck you"'. The city is largely white and still dominated by the military and naval presence in the dockyards. Asylum seekers make up a tiny proportion of Plymouth's 250,000 population, with a total of just 1,000 refugees in the city, including those who have successfully claimed asylum there (ibid.).

Official police figures show that Plymouth averages between 22 and 30 racist incidents a month, many of which involve asylum seekers. Refugee groups believe as many as six times more incidents go unreported. Of the dozen or so asylum seekers who chose to talk to *The Observer* in Plymouth, most had been attacked and all had been verbally abused (ibid.).

The report also refers to the Raglan Road estate in Devonport, former naval quarters which have been converted into asylum seeker accommodation. The site is run by Adelphi Hotels under contract from the Home Office. Security is tight, with a single access road patrolled 24 hours by guards employed by the hotel group. Such is the Home Office sensitivity about the site that staff are under strict instructions not to talk to the press. All inquiries to Adelphi are referred to the Home Office and *The Observer* was asked not to enter the site without first obtaining clearance from the Home Office' (ibid.).

The estate is just outside the centre of the city in one of the poorest parts of Devon. The grey concrete flats are standard-issue army blocks from the 1970s. Inside they are shabby and underfurnished, but clean and secure. Most of the men here who talked to *The Observer* felt safe here but it was a different matter when they left the estate. 'It's like a community here, a village that no one can enter. I stay at home. I don't go to the city centre. I don't really ever leave', one 'inmate' told the paper (ibid.).

Not all newspapers provide sympathetic coverage to such issues. Indeed, as Geddes (2003, p. 40) notes (certain) newspapers play an intermediate role in an orchestrated government campaign to downgrade the public perception of asylum seekers. He gives an example of the local newspaper in the coastal town of Dover, which ran a front page editorial in December, 1998, claiming that

> Illegal immigrants, asylum seekers, bootleggers and scum of the earth drug smugglers have targeted our beloved coastline. We are left with the back draft of a nation's human sewage and no cash to wash it down the drain.
>
> (ibid., p. 43)

Xeno-racialization directed at Britain as a whole is clearly visible in a week's reading of *The Sun*. On 1 March, day one, we were told in the Leader that 'endless appeals by failed asylum seekers have been a source of irritation for years' (p. 8). On day two, we heard that '[l]ottery chiefs have been blasted over grants given to help asylum rejects fight deportation' (*The Sun*, 2 March 2004, p. 2). In the same edition of the paper, a reader wrote in to inform other readers that '[t]his Government will always be soft on asylum seekers, because they are scared of upsetting Left-wingers and union groups'. Everyone he knows, he went on, 'is sick of the asylum madness' (ibid., p. 37).

On day three, another reader asked how 'an asylum seeker, expelled from this country, [was] able to return and set up a vice empire worth millions?' (*The Sun*, 3 March 2004, p. 34). Day four had the paper's political correspondent, Nic Cecil, proudly proclaiming that 'David Blunkett told Britain's top judge last night to stop carping at his bid to end abuse of Britain's asylum system' (*The Sun*, 4 March 2004, p. 2). Cecil was concerned about legal attempts to 'attack . . . plans to allow asylum rejects only **ONE** appeal' (original emphasis) (ibid.). On the readers' page, a reader stated that Blunkett's plan to restrict asylum seekers to just one appeal 'is the most feasible idea the Government has come up with and could end lucrative payments for greedy lawyers who choose to defend asylum cheats' (ibid., p. 46).

On day five, *The Sun* Leader hurled abuse at Lord Woolf, 'one of the most foolish and wrong-headed men in the land' who 'has made a career out of posturing to liberal hand-wringers responsible for so much of the decline in British life' and 'who campaigned more than any other judge to saddle Britain with all the suffocating red tape of the European Convention on Human Rights' (*The Sun*, 5 March 2004, p. 6). It doesn't take much imagination to guess his current 'crime'. '[H]e has been strutting his stuff at Cambridge University, threatening that judges will revolt' if Mr Blunkett does not drop his 'sensible and fair proposals to speed up the asylum appeals process' (ibid.). Elsewhere, in the same edition, *Sun* reporters managed to find one member of the public whose instinct was 'somewhere between the Government and Lord Woolf', but another eight who were anti-Woolf: '[too] many Eastern Europeans'; 'Lord Woolf is an idiot'; 'Asylum seekers should be thrown out of Britain if they fail just one appeal' and so on (ibid. pp. 36–7).

So how did *The Sun* round off this particular week's coverage of migration issues? Saturday's *The Sun* informed its readers that 'Tory MP Ann Winterton has blasted Britain's political correct culture'. This refers to a letter Winterton has written to all Tory MPs bemoaning the end of 'free speech' (*The Sun*, 6 March 2004, p. 2). This was in response to negative reactions to a racist 'joke' she made about the death by drowning in Britain in February 2004 of twenty suspected 'illegal immigrants' (some of whom were known to the police as asylum seekers) working in conditions of extreme exploitation.[16]

Conclusions

In this chapter we began by considering the concepts of 'race', racism, racialization and institutional racism. We then briefly considered the racist origins of the welfare state and traced the racist practices of the state, capital and sections of organized labour in the post-World War Two period. It was not until the mid-1960s that collective action against such racist practices emerged. Owing to the continued prevalence of a sectionalist class consciousness among elements of 'white' labour and the dominance of racist sentiment, it was racialized workers organizing independently who first began to challenge such practices. However, attempts to curb unofficial trade union activity in the late 1960s and early 1970s served to politicize key elements of organized labour and resulted in the formation of an oppositional working class identity. This major development, coupled with almost a decade of industrial struggles against racism by racialized workers and growing fear of far-right influence in trade unions, created the necessary preconditions for the ideas of antiracism and solidarity between racialized and 'white' labour to gain a wider audience in the trade unions. By the mid-1970s, the TUC and some of the larger affiliated trade unions explicitly recognized that working class solidarity could only be achieved through combating racism.

However, it required the urban unrest and the political pressure that followed from organized labour and the racialized communities themselves finally to force the state to introduce reforms to curb the worst excesses of racist discriminatory practices.

We concluded by examining racism in the 1980s, 1990s, and beyond; up to and including the onset of the New Labour government.

We regret to conclude that British society remains institutionally racist. Islamophobia and xeno-racism have reached epidemic proportions. In addition, major institutions in the society remain rampantly racist, albeit racist in forms less biological and more cultural; less dominative and more aversive.

For example an official enquiry into the National Health Service (Carvel, 2004: http://society.guardian.co.uk/mentalhealth/story/0,8150,1142309,00.html: accessed July 21 2004) found the NHS to be riddled with institutional racism, persistently failing to give patients from Asian, black and other minority ethnic communities the services they need and deserve. The report blamed the Department of Health for failing to tackle what it called 'this festering abscess which is at present a blot upon the good name of the NHS'.

In addition, an interim report by the Commission for Racial Equality (CRE, 2004) uncovered a 'disturbing racial pattern' in recruitment to the police force, with 42 per cent of Chinese, 33 per cent of Asian and 34 per cent of black applicants rejected, as compared to 23 per cent of white people. The report also revealed the existence of 'stealth racism', with many officers treating 'race' and diversity awareness as 'a big joke'.

The struggle for antiracism and an equitable society is an ongoing one. It is hoped that this chapter will encourage readers to take part in and continue that struggle. The struggle takes place on many terrains. The major trade unions are, to varying degrees, now committed to antiracism, and many are affiliated to antiracist action groups. In addition, there has been a recent increase in the number of TU leaders who identify more openly with socialist antiracist policies.

As far as political parties are concerned, the Respect Coalition, which is 'upfront' in its opposition to all forms of racism, including Islamophobia, xeno-racism and imperialist wars, gained what veteran BBC pundit, Anthony Howard described as 'staggering' 12.66 per cent and 6.27 per cent shares of the vote, respectively, in by-elections in July, 2004 (*Respect*, 2004, unpaginated).

Another major arena of institutional racism, and, in our view, a crucial terrain of antiracist struggle is the education system. Racism and Education is addressed by Mike Cole and Maud Blair in the next chapter.

Notes

1 We put 'race' in inverted commas because we question its validity as a scientitic concept. Robert Miles has argued cogently against the notion that there exist distinct 'races' (1982, pp. 9–16). After a review of the literature, he gives three reasons for this. First, the extent of genetic variation within any population is usually greater than the average difference between populations. Second, while the frequency of occurrence of possible forms taken by genes does vary from one so-called 'race' to another, any particular genetic combination can be found in almost any 'race'. Third, owing to interbreeding and large-scale migrations, the distinctions between 'races', identified as dominant gene frequencies, are often blurred (ibid., p. 16).

2 As Hill (2001, p. 8) has pointed out, the influence of ideology can be overwhelming. He cites Terry Eagleton (1991, p. xiii) who has written, '[w]hat persuades men and women to mistake each other from time to time for gods or vermin is ideology'. The efficacy of this observation resonates throughout this chapter.

3 This section draws on Cole, 1997, pp. 451–2 and Cole, 1992.

4 For the role of education in the construction of colonial citizens as biologically inferior, see Chapter 4.

5 Not all leaders of the Labour movement at the time were pro-imperialist and anti-Semitic. William Morris, Sylvia Pankhurst, Annie Besant, Fenner Brockway and George Lansbury are notable exceptions.

6 Our historical contextualizing of the foundation of the welfare state should not be seen as a critique of the notion of a welfare state *per se*. As socialists, we would see it as something we must defend. It is the most equitable institution possible under capitalism. We would particularly wish to rise to its defence, in the present historical conjuncture, when its very existence is under threat (Cole 1998b; Hatcher 1998).

7 The following analysis draws heavily on Virdee, 1999a.

8 There has been an ongoing debate on nomenclature in Britain (e.g. Cole, 1993; Johnson *et al.*, 2000; Aspinall, 2002). We would maintain that the formulation, 'Asian, black and other minority ethnic', despite its imperfections, remains the best way to collectively describe the minority ethnic constituency in Britain. Following Cole 1993, pp. 672–3 (see also Cole and Stuart, 2005), we prefer the nomenclature, 'Asian, black and other minority ethnic' to the more common nomenclature, 'black and ethnic minority' for four reasons. First, the term 'black' once popular as an all-encompassing nomenclature had ceased to have that purchase from the late 1980s onwards: hence the need for the wider formulation. Second, with respect to this nomenclature, the omission of the word 'other' between 'and' and 'ethnic minority' implies that only 'ethnic minorities' (people of Cypriot and Irish origin, for example) are minority constituencies whereas black people are not. This is, of course, not accurate. Third, the use of the term, 'ethnic minority' has, in practice, meant that members of the dominant majority group are not referred to in terms of their ethnicity, with the implication that they do not have ethnicity (the sequencing of 'minority' before 'ethnic' does not carry this implication, since, the creation of a new formulation, together with the prioritizing of the former over the latter, facilitates the conceptualization of a *majority* ethnic group too). Fourth, 'black and ethnic minority' has the effect of excluding people of Asian and other origins who do not consider themselves 'black'. The fact that people of Asian origin form the majority of 'non-white' minority ethnic women and men is masked. Having said that, two points follow: first, we are very much open to alternative suggestions; second, it can be necessary to sub-divide within 'Asian, black and other minority ethnic' people, in order, for example, to examine differential rates of achievement (see Chapter 4, for a discussion). We are aware, of course, that nomenclatures change. For example, as we shall see, the all-inclusive term, 'black' was common for a number of years in Britain. We are not attempting to make a definitive statement. If readers can improve on it, this is of course to be welcomed. Ideally, we

believe in ethnic self-definition, recognizing that there can be differences in preferred nomenclature among ethnic groups. For the benefit of readers from outside the UK, 'Asian', in the British context, refers to people from, or with origins in, the Indian sub-continent.

9 From the 1980s these racialized (non-white) groups also occupied different positions according to whether they were male or female. They were a racialized fraction, differentiated by gender (Cole, 1989).

10 The following analysis is based on Cole, 2004a, pp. 35–6, 47.

11 This report looked at racism in the Metropolitan Police and other British institutions. It followed a lengthy public campaign initiated by the parents of black teenager Stephen Lawrence, murdered by racist thugs in 1993. A bungled police investigation means that there have been no convictions.

12 This is, of course, reminiscent of Thatcher, who, in 1978, remarked after a riot in Wolverhampton: 'People are really rather afraid that this country might be swamped by people of a different culture' (Guardian Unlimited: http://politics.guardian.co.uk/homeaffairs/story/0,11026,689919,00.html).

13 This section of the chapter draws heavily on Cole, 2004c, p. 533.

14 This section of the chapter draws heavily on Cole, 2004b, pp. 160–2.

15 Plymouth is a garrison town which sent 15,000 service personnel out of a total of 40,000 to Iraq. Such attacks are thus also a feature of the new Imperialism (Cole, 2004c).

16 The week beginning 1 March was not atypical. An inspection of *The Sun's* archives on 6 March 2004 revealed over the last year an astonishing 629 references to 'asylum seekers' and 288 references to 'refugees' (http://www.thesun.newsint-archive.co.uk).

References

Anderson, B. (1983) *Imagined Communities*, London: Verso

Aspinall, P. (2002) 'Collective Terminology to Describe the Minority Ethnic Population: the Persistence of Confusion and Ambiguity in Usage', Sociology 36(4), pp. 803–816

Ball, W. and Solomos, J. (eds) (1990) *Race and Local Politics*, Basingstoke: Macmillan.

Banton, M. (1977) *The Idea of Race*, London: Tavistock

Benyon, J. (ed.) (1984) *Scarman and after*, Oxford: Pergamon Press Limited

Beveridge, W. (1942) *Social Insurance and Allied Services (The Beveridge Report)*, London: HMSO.

Beynon, H. (1984) *Working for Ford*, London: Penguin

Branson, N. (1975) *Britain in the 1920s*, London: Weidenfeld & Nicolson

Bratton, J.S. (1986) 'Of England, Home and Duty: The Image of England in Victorian and Edwardian Juvenile Fiction', in Mackenzie, J.M. (ed.), *Propaganda and Empire: The Manipulation of British Public Opinion 1880–1960*, Manchester: Manchester University Press

Brown, C. (1982) *Black and White Britain*, London: Heinemann Educational Books

Buckman, J. (1980) 'Alien Working Class Responses', in Lunn, K. (ed.), *Hosts, Immigrants and Minorities*, Folkestone: Dawson

Camara, B. (2002) 'Ideologies of Race and Racism', in Zarembka, P. (ed.) *Confronting 9–11, Ideologies of Race, and Eminent Economists*. Oxford: Elsevier Science

Campaign Against Racism and Fascism (CARF) (1992) 'Where CARF Stands', *Campaign Against Racism and Fascism (CARF)*, 6, January/February, p. 2

Carvel, J. (2004) '"Abcess" of NHS racism exposed', (http://society.guardian.co.uk/mentalhealth/story/0,8150,1142309.00html accessed 21 July 2004)

Castles, S. and Kosack, G. (1985) *Immigrant Workers and Class Structure in Western Europe*, Oxford: Oxford University Press

Civil and Public Servants Association (1980) *1979 Annual Report*, London: CPSA
Civil and Public Servants Association (1981) *1980 Annual Report*, London: CPSA
Cohen, S. (1985) 'Anti-Semitism, Immigration Controls and the Welfare State', *Critical Social Policy*, 13, Summer
Cole, M. (1989) '"Race" and Class or "Race", Class, Gender and Community?: A Critical Appraisal of the Racialised Fraction of the Working-class Thesis', *British Journal of Sociology*, 40 (1), pp. 118–29
Cole, M. (1992) *Racism, History and Educational Policy: From the Origins of the Welfare State to the Rise of the Radical Right*, unpublished PhD thesis, Department of Sociology, University of Essex
Cole, M. (1993) '"Black and Ethnic Minority" or "Asian, Black and Other Minority Ethnic": A Further Note on Nomenclature', *Sociology*, 27, pp. 671–3
Cole, M. (1997) '"Race" and Racism', in Payne, M. (ed.), *A Dictionary of Cultural and Critical Theory*, Oxford: Blackwell Publishers
Cole, M. (1998a) 'Racism, Reconstructed Multiculturalism and Antiracist Education', *Cambridge Journal of Education*, 28 (1), pp. 37–48
Cole, M. (1998b) 'Globalization, Modernization and Competitiveness: A Critique of the New Labour Project in Education', *International Studies in Sociology of Education*, 8 (3), pp. 315–32
Cole, M. (2004a) '"Brutal and stinking" and "difficult to handle": the historical and contemporary manifestations of racialisation, institutional racism, and schooling in Britain', *Race, Ethnicity and Education*, 7 (1), pp. 35–56
Cole, M. (2004b) 'F*** you – human sewage: contemporary global capitalism and the xeno-racialization of asylum seekers', *Contemporary Politics* 10 (2), pp. 159–65
Cole, M. (2004c) '"Rule Britannia" and the new American Empire: a Marxist Analysis of the Teaching of Imperialism, Actual and Potential, in the British School Curriculum', *Policy Futures in Education*, 2 (3 and 4), pp. 523–38
Cole, M. and Stuart, J.S. (2005) '"Do you ride on elephants" and "never tell them you're German": the experiences of British Asian and black, and overseas student teachers in south-east England', *British Journal of Educational Research*, 31 (3), 349–66
CRE (2004) Cited in *The Argus*, Tuesday 15 June, p. 4
Crouch, C. (1977) *Class Conflict and the Industrial Relations Crises*, London: Heinemann
Dale, G. (1999) 'Capitalism and Migrant Labour', in Dale, G. and Cole, M. (eds), *The European Union and Migrant Labour*. Oxford: Berg
Daniel, W.W. (1968) *Racial Discrimination in England*, London: Penguin
Doward, J. and Hinsliff, G. (2004) 'British hostility to Muslims "could trigger riots"' (http://www.guardian.co.uk/race/story/0,11374,1227977.00.html)
Dresser, M. (1986) *Black and White on the Buses: The 1963 Colour Bar Dispute in Bristol*, Bristol: Bristol Broadsides
Duffield, M. (1988) *Black Radicalism and the Politics of De-industrialisation: The Hidden History of Indian Foundry Workers*, Aldershot: Avebury
Eagleton, T. (1991) *Ideology*, London: Verso
Eldridge, J., Cressey, P. and MacInnes, J. (1991) *Industrial Sociology and Economic Crisis*, Hemel Hempstead: Harvester Wheatsheaf
Esmail, A. and Everington, S. (1993), 'Racial Discrimination against Doctors from Ethnic Minorities', *British Medical Journal*, 306, March, pp. 691–2
Fryer, P. (1984) *Staying Power: The History of Black People in Britain*, London: Pluto Press
Geddes, A. (2003) *The Politics of Migration and Immigration in Europe*, London: Sage

Gillborn, D (2001) 'Racism, Policy and the (Mis)education of Black Children', in Majors, R. (ed.), *Educating Our Black Children: New Directions and Radical Approaches*, London: Routledge-Falmer

Gilroy, P. (1987) *There Ain't No Black in the Union Jack*, London: Hutchinson

Gordon, P. and Klug, F. (1985) *British Immigration Control*, London: Runnymede Trust

Gramsci, A. (1978) *Selections from Prison Notebooks*, London: Lawrence and Wishart

Grosvenor, I. (1998) *Assimilating Identities*, London: Lawrence & Wishart

Hatcher, R. (1998) 'Labour, Official School Improvement and Equality', *Journal of Education Policies*, 13, pp. 485–99

Heath, A. and Ridge, J. (1983) 'Social Mobility of Ethnic Minorities', *Journal of Biosocial Science*, Supplement 8, pp. 169–84

Herrnstein, R. J. and Murray, C. (1994) *The Bell Curve*, New York: The Free Press

Hill, D. (2001) 'Equality, Ideology and Education Policy', in Hill, D. and Cole, M. (eds) *Schooling and Equality: Fact, Concept and Policy*, London: Kogan Page

Holmes, C. (1979) *Anti-Semitism in British Society 1876–1939*, London: Edward Arnold

Howell, D. (1983) *British Workers and the Independent Labour Party, 1888–1906*, Manchester: Manchester University Press

Hyman, R. (1972) *Marxism and the Sociology of Trade Unionism*, London: Pluto Press

Johnson, M.R.D., Owen, D. and Blackburn, C. (2000) *Black and Minority Ethnic Groups in England: The Second Health and Lifestyles Survey*, London: Health Education Authority

Josephides, S. (1990) 'Principles, Strategies and Anti-racist Campaigns: The Case of the Indian Workers' Association', in Goulbourne, H. (ed.), *Black Politics in Britain*, London: Avebury, pp. 115–29

Kelly, J. (1988) *Trade Unions and Socialist Politics*, London: Verso

Kirk, N. (1885) *The Growth of Working Class Reformism in Mid-Victorian England*, London: Croom Helm

Kovel, J. (1988) *White Racism: A Psychohistory*, London: Free Association Books

Lawrence, E. (1982) 'Just Plain Common Sense: the "Roots" of Racism', in Centre For Contemporary Cultural Studies (ed.), *The Empire Strikes Back: Race And Racism In 70s Britain*, London: Hutchinson

Lorimer, D.A. (1978) *Colour, Class and the Victorians: English Attitudes to the Negro in the Mid-nineteenth Century*, Leicester: Leicester University Press

McCrudden, C., Smith, D.J. and Brown, C. (1991) *Racial Justice at Work*, London: Policy Studies Institute

Macpherson, W. (1999) 'The Stephen Lawrence Enquiry, Report Of An Enquiry By Sir William Macpherson', London: The Stationery Office

Mangan, J.A. (1986) '"The Grit of our Forefathers": Invented Traditions, Propaganda and Imperialism', in Mackenzie, J.M. (ed.), op. cit.

Marsh, D. (1992) *The New Politics of British Trade Unionism: Union Power and the Thatcher Legacy*, London: The Macmillan Press Limited

Messina, A. (1989) *Race and Party Competition in Britain*, Oxford: Clarendon Press

Miles, R. (1982) *Racism and Migrant Labour*, London: Routledge and Kegan Paul

Miles, R. (1987) *Capitalism and Unfree Labour: Anomaly or Necessity?* London: Tavistock

Miles, R. (1989) *Racism*, London: Routledge

Miles, R. (1993) *Racism after 'Race Relations'*, London: Routledge

Miles, R. and Dunlop, A. (1986) 'The Racialisation of Politics in Britain: Why Scotland Is Different', *Patterns of Prejudice*, 20 (1), pp. 23–32

Miles, R. and Phizacklea, A. (1978) 'The TUC and Black Workers: 1974–1976', *British Journal of Industrial Relations*, 16 (2), pp. 244–58

Miles, R. and Phizacklea, A. (1984) *White Man's Country*, London: Pluto Press

Modood, T. (1997) 'Employment', in Modood, T., Berthoud, R., Lakey, J., Nazroo, J., Smith, P., Virdee, S. and Beishon, S., *Ethnic Minorities in Britain*, London: Policy Studies Institute

Moore, R. (1975) *Racism and Black Resistance in Britain*, London: Pluto Press

Mowat, C.L. (1968) *Britain between the Wars*, London: Methuen

National and Local Government Officers (1977) *1976 Annual Report*, London: NALGO

National and Local Government Officers (1979) *1978 Annual Report*, London: NALGO

National and Local Government Officers (1981) *1980 Annual Report*, London: NALGO

Omi, M. and Winant, H. (1986) *Racial Formation in the United States of America*, New York: Routledge

Owen, D. (1993) *Ethnic Minorities in Great Britain: Settlement Patterns*, Census Paper 1, Coventry: Commission for Racial Equality, University of Warwick

Raison, T. (1984) 'The View from the Government', in Benyon, J. (ed.), *The View from the Government*, pp. 244–58

Ramdin, R. (1987) *The Making of the Black Working Class in Britain*, London: Gower

Respect, 'Brighton and Hove Members' and Supporters' Newsletter' (2004) 8, 18 July

Richards, J. (1989) *Imperialism and Juvenile Literature*, Manchester: Manchester University Press

Rogaly, J. (1977) *Grunwick*, London: Penguin

Scarman, Lord (1981) *The Brixton Disorders 10–12 April 1981*, London: HMSO

Short, G. and Carrington, B. (1996) 'Anti-Racist Education, Multiculturalism and the New Racism', *Educational Review* 48 (1), pp. 65–77

Shukra, K. (1996) 'A Scramble for the British Pie', *Patterns of Prejudice*, 30 (1), January, pp. 28–36

Sivanandan, A. (1976) 'Race, Class and the State: The Black Experience in Britain', *Race and Class*, 17 (4), p. 348

Sivanandan, A. (1982) *A Different Hunger: Writings on Black Resistance*, London: Pluto Press

Sivanandan, A. (1993) *Writings on Black Resistance*, London: Verso

Smith, D.J. (1977) *Racial Disadvantage in Britain*, London: Penguin

Society of Civil and Public Servants (1983) *1982 Annual Report*, London: SCPS

Society of Civil and Public Servants (1984) *1983 Annual Report*, London: SCPS

Solomos, J. (1988) *Black Youth, Racism and the State*, Cambridge: Cambridge University Press

Solomos, J. (1993) *Race and Racism in Britain*, London: Macmillan

Springhall, J.O. (1986) '"Up Guards and at Them!": British Imperialism and Popular Art, 1880–1914', in Mackenzie, J.M. (ed.), op. cit.

Stevenson, J. (1984) *British Society 1914–1945*, London: Lane

Summerfield, P. (1986) 'Patriotism and Empire: Music Hall Entertainment 1870–1914', in Mackenzie, J.M. (ed.) op. cit.

Taylor, S. (1984) 'The Scarman Report and an explanation of the riots', in Benyon, J. (ed.), op. cit.

Thane, P. (1982) *Foundations of the Welfare State*, London: Longman

Travis, (2003) 'Blunkett: Racism Tag is Aiding Racists', *The Guardian*, 15 January

Virdee, S. (1999a) 'England: Racism, Anti-racism and the Changing Position of Racialised

Groups in Economic Relations', in Dale, G. and Cole, M. (eds), *The European Union and Migrant Labour*, Oxford: Berg

Virdee, S. (1999b) 'Racism and Resistance in British Trade Unions: 1948–79', in Alexander, P. and Halpern, R. (eds), *Labour and Difference in the USA, Africa and Britain*, London: Macmillan

Virdee, S. and Grint, K. (1994) 'Black self-organisation in Trade Unions', *Sociological Review*, 42 (2) pp. 202–26

Williams, B. (1980) 'The beginnings of Jewish Trade Unionism in Manchester 1889–1891', in Lunn, K. (ed.), *Hosts, Immigrants and Minorities*, Folkestone: Dawson

Williams, E. (1964) *Capitalism and Slavery*, London: André Deutsch

Williams, R. (1961/1965) *The Long Revolution*, London: Chatto & Windus, Harmondsworth: Penguin

Wrench, J. (1987) 'Unequal Comrades: Trade Unions, Equal Opportunity and Racism', in Jenkins, R. and Solomos, J. (eds), *Racism and Equal Opportunity Policies in the 1980s*, Cambridge: Cambridge University Press

Wrench, J. (1996) *Preventing Racism at the Workplace*, Dublin: European Foundation for the Improvement of Living and Working Conditions

Zephaniah, B. (2004) 'Rage of Empire', *Socialist Review*, No. 281, January, pp. 18–20

4 Racism and education

From Empire to New Labour

Mike Cole and Maud Blair

Introduction

In this chapter, we begin by examining Britain's historical legacy of 'race',[1] class, gender and Empire, and look at the way this was represented in the school curriculum of the early twentieth century. We argue that the attitudes and images projected by school texts at this time and reinforced in government statements and policies served in part to racialize[2] the children of colonial and post-colonial immigrants as 'a problem', after mass immigration in the post World War 2 period. We then look at the educational experiences of Asian and black pupils/students,[3] before looking at some ways which were adopted to address 'the problems', which we argue lay in the education system itself and *not* in the pupils/students. We conclude with some suggestions as to how we might proceed in the new millennium.

Multicultural Britain

At the outset, we would stress that the social, cultural and religious diversity of British society is not a new phenomenon. Britain is a multicultural society and always has been. This is witnessed by the separate existences of England, Scotland and Wales. It is also evidenced by settlement from Ireland and elsewhere in Europe, both in the past and more recently.

Britain's links with Africa and Asia are particularly long-standing. For example, there were Africans in Britain – slaves and 'soldiers in the Roman imperial army that occupied the southern part of our island for three and a half centuries' (Fryer, 1984, p.1) before the Anglo-Saxons ('the English') arrived.[4] There has been a long history of contact between Britain and India, with Indian links with Europe going back 10,000 years (Visram, 1986). Africans and Asians have been born in Britain from about the year 1505 (Fryer, 1984; see also Walvin, 1973), and their presence has been notable from that time on.

Empire, 'race', class and mass schooling

Our concern in this chapter, however, is with the era of imperialism and its immediate and longer-term aftermath. In Chapter 3, Cole and Virdee argued that the origins of the Welfare State cannot be understood without reference to imperialism, nationalism and the racialization of the peoples of the (ex) colonies.

The role assigned to mass schooling in maintaining the Empire was well expressed by Lord Rosebery, leader of the Liberal Imperialists:

> An Empire such as ours requires as its first condition an imperial race, a race vigorous and industrious and intrepid, in the rookeries and slums which still survive, an imperial race cannot be reared.
>
> (Simon, 1974, p. 169)

Here we see the links between the British 'race' and social class. Schooling was seen as a way of creating workers who could compete efficiently with other capitalist nations (epitomized in the slogan, 'national efficiency'). In the 1860s, British capitalists were particularly worried about competition with Germany and the poor British showing at the Paris Exhibition in 1867 was seen as exemplifying British backwardness in technological education (Shannon, 1976, p. 86). The dual themes of nationalism and imperialism can be gleaned in the major landmark in mass schooling in the Victorian age:

> Upon this speedy provision of education depends . . . our national power. Civilized communities throughout the world are massing themselves together . . . and if we are to hold our position among men of our own race or among the nations of the world we must make up the smallness of our numbers by increasing the intellectual force of the individual.
>
> (Forster, 1870, cited in Maclure, 1979, p. 105)

This is how W.E. Forster, Vice-President in charge of the Education Department in Prime Minister Gladstone's first administration, introduced the Elementary Education Bill in the House of Commons in February 1870. Although the 1870 Education Act, passed three years after the humiliation in Paris, made education neither compulsory nor free, it laid the foundations for a system which was soon to begin to abolish fees and make attendance compulsory.

The quest for 'national efficiency' continued in the Samuelson Report of 1882–4, whose terms of reference were:

> to inquire into the instruction of the industrial classes of certain foreign countries in technical and other subjects for the purpose of comparison with that of the corresponding classes in this country; and into the influence of such instruction on manufacturing and other industries at home and abroad.
>
> (cited in Maclure, 1979, p. 122)

'National efficiency' served as a convenient label under which a complex set of beliefs, assumptions and demands could be grouped – it completed the imperial chain of social class, nation and 'race'. The survival and hegemony of the imperial 'race' were of course mutually reinforcing, as evidenced in the lead up to the 1902

(Balfour) Education Act, which established an integrated system of elementary, secondary and technical education under the general direction of the Education Department (Shannon, 1976, p. 303). There was a fear that the 'race' might be dying. For example, the Reverend Mr Usher (quoting Darwin's forecast that, if artificial limitation of families came into general use, Britain would degenerate into one of 'those arreous societies in the Pacific') in his book *New Malthusianism* was sure about this: 'yes we cannot deny it, we are a decaying race' (cited in Armytage, 1981, p. 183). Gladstone held similar views.

It was not just the ruling class that held such views. The Webbs, Sydney and Beatrice, were most interested in education. Somewhat confusedly, the former once remarked that the role of London University in the new (twentieth) century should be to combine 'a sane and patriotic imperialism with the largest minded internationalism' (cited in ibid., p. 190). Elsewhere, Sydney was less ambiguous. He once declared that he felt that at every moment he was 'acting as a Member of a Committee . . . in some affairs a committee of my own family members, in others a committee *as wide as the Ayrian race*' (Webb, 1896, p. 6) (my emphasis). Like most Fabians, Webb was an avid supporter of imperialism (Hobsbawm 1964), and, with Liberal front-bencher Richard Haldane, set up Imperial College in 1903. At one stage, Sydney, like Lord Rosebery, called for the formation of a new party to plan the aims and methods of Imperial Policy (Simon, 1974, p. 174), a party of 'National Efficiency' – a party that would advocate sanitary reform, at least 'the minimum necessary for breeding an even moderately Imperial race' (Semmel, 1960, p. 73). Since it was 'in the classrooms . . . that the future battles for the Empire for commercial prosperity are being lost', the working class wanted to know, argued Webb, 'what steps' the followers of Rosebery would 'take to insure the rearing of an Imperial race' (ibid.). The general mood of the times was that the 'inferior races' of the colonies were a direct threat to the 'superior white races' (Armytage, cited in Maclure, 1979, p. 171).

The background of the 1918 Education Act was, of course, World War 1. The higher level of German education was seen as a threat, and the Act's most important clauses concerned continuation schools, and followed the German example (Simon 1974, p. 343). What this meant was that, with certain exceptions, every young person not undergoing full-time instruction, was to be liberated from industrial toil for the equivalent of three half-days a week during forty weeks of the year – two half-days to be spent in school, and one half-day holiday (H.A.L. Fisher, MP, President of the Board of Education and architect of the 1918 Act, introducing the Bill, cited in Maclure, 1979, p. 174). However, the Act was also directly related to social control. As Fisher put it, 'Education dispels the hideous clouds of class suspicion and softens the asperities of faction' (cited in Simon, 1974, p. 344). It is encouraging to observe, he went on, that 'the sense of the value in education as an end in itself, as one of the constituent elements in human happiness, is now widely spread among the manual workers of the country' (ibid.). Note that he stresses, 'end in itself'. Fisher is most definitely not advocating a meritocracy or social class mobility. He registered his disgust at any such notions when introducing the Bill:

I notice . . . that a new way of thinking about education has sprung up among many of the more reflecting members of our industrial army. They do not want education only in order that they may become better technical workmen [*sic*] and earn higher wages. *They do not want it in order that they may rise out of their own class, always a vulgar ambition,* they want it because they know that in the treasures of the mind they can find an aid to good citizenship, a source of pure enjoyment and a refuge from the necessary hardships of a life spent in the midst of clanging machinery in our hideous cities of toil.

(cited in Maclure, 1979, pp. 173–4 (our emphasis)

The 1918 Act, then, was intended to increase 'national efficiency' – the imperial chain of social class, nation and 'race' – by promoting education. It was also intended as a means of social control, which of course also related to improved efficiency. As it turned out, by 1921, the continuation school sections of the Act had been abandoned for financial reasons (Simon, 1974, p. 30).

The imperial curriculum[5]

The curriculum of the early twentieth century was overtly racist. The primacy of the Bible and religion was replaced by the growing influence of imperialism which was very central in shaping the changing school syllabus, especially from the 1900s onwards. Thus many English readers, for example, contained passages glorifying the monarchy and celebrating Britain's commercial wealth and progress, and English teachers were increasingly encouraged to give instruction in the duties of citizenship.

The addition of subjects like history, domestic science and games to the elementary school curriculum was conceived and justified by reference to their contribution to national strength, efficiency and, of course, the Empire. Thus, history texts, for example, told their readers that the British Empire was 'gained by the valour of our soldiers, or by the patient toil and steady enterprise of colonists from the mother country', and that Britain's imperial subjects in the colonies, 'of almost every race, colour and religion' were 'all living peacefully and prospering under the British flag, and content with the knowledge that the strong arm and brave spirit that gained freedom for them will always be ready to defend the precious gift' (Pitman's *King Edward History Readers – for Juniors* (1901) cited in Chancellor, 1970, pp. 127–8). The propagation of the British 'race' depended on the continued subordination of women in the home. Thus while boys were encouraged to think that 'the only safe thing for all of us who love our country is to learn soldiering at once and be prepared to fight at any moment' (Fletcher and Kipling's *A School History of England – for Juniors* (1911) cited in ibid., p. 130) and were told not to 'forget the man in the labourer . . . he is the autocrat of the home, the father of the family, and as a voter, one of the rulers of the Empire' (Bray's *Boy Labour and Apprenticeship* (1911) – cited in Hendrick, 1980, p. 166), working class girls were being taught how to manage their homes efficiently. As Humphries (1981, p. 40) explains, the introduction of domestic science subjects was directly related to the fear of 'race' degeneracy. As he puts it, following Dyhouse and Davin:

> Subjects such as home economics, laundrywork, cookery and needlework aimed to instruct working-class girls in the correct performance of their future duties of motherhood, housework and domestic service, thereby promoting the reinvigoration of the nation and Empire through a sexist division of labour.

Geography texts were the prime conveyors of racialization. Each text laid out the conventional progression from hunting to pastoral to agricultural and finally to industrial societies (MacKenzie, 1984, p. 184). Thus, in Nelson's *The World and its Peoples* (c. 1907), the African was described as 'an overgrown child, vain, self-indulgent, and fond of idleness', while the 'wretched bushmen [were] the lowest and most debased human beings on the face of the globe' (ibid.). Asia was similarly demeaned by Nelson as a continent of dying nations rapidly falling back in civilisation (ibid.) and Australian Aboriginals were 'among the most miserable of men [*sic*]' whose 'great poverty led them to practise vices like cannibalism and the murder of the sick and helpless' (A.J. Herbertson, *Man and his Work* (1902), cited in MacKenzie, 1984, p. 185). The 'English', by way of contrast, were portrayed as morally irreproachable. As one history text put it, '[t]hey all show the bold, frank, sturdy character which so strongly marks out the Anglo-Saxon race' (T. J. Livesey, *Granville History Reader* (1902), cited in Chancellor, 1970, p. 118). In another (Cassell's *Class History of England*, cited in Chancellor, 1970, p. 122), references were made to 'the barbaric peoples of Asia' and the most frequent impression conveyed about Indians and Afghans was that they were cruel and totally unfit to rule themselves. Imperialist texts could still be found in school libraries well into the 1980s.[6]

Humphries argues that the inclusion of games and sports in the school curriculum was to encourage a corporate spirit and develop the physical strength and moral fibre of [male] working class youth – a direct transplant of elements of the public school ethos to state elementary schools, to foster the development of imperial warriors. The founding of cadet corps and rifle-shooting clubs for older children gave the fostering of imperialism a specifically militaristic form (ibid., p. 41).

Particularly influential in schools were the Empire Day Movement, the Lads' Drills Association and the Duty of Discipline Movement, all especially associated with the Earl of Meath, who particularly relished the idea of 'hardness' and believed that the 'British race . . . have ruled in the past because they were a virile race' (Lord Meath, 1910, cited in Mangan, 1986, p. 129). Meath was greatly concerned with the moral deterioration of the 'Anglo-Saxon' woman who should be prepared to face the obligations of the marriage tie (subordination to husband and state) and the sufferings and dangers of childbirth 'with as much coolness and courage as was expected of the man on the field of battle' (Lord Meath, 1910, cited in ibid.). He was also concerned with the 'Anglo-Saxon' man's increasing tendency to watch sport, rather than take part in it (ibid.). His solution was thus to train youth, via his various organizations, to build an imperial 'race', 'worthy of responsibility, alive to duty, filled with sympathy towards mankind and not afraid of self-sacrifice in the promotion of lofty ideals' (Lord Meath, 1910, cited in ibid., p. 130). Empire Day was said to have been celebrated in 1905, in 6,000 schools throughout the Empire and, by 1922, in 80,000 (ibid., p. 132)

Thus racialization ensured that the institutionalized racism (and indeed sexism) promulgated by the ruling class filtered down to the school and became part of popular culture.

Racializing the children through schooling

In Chapter 3 of this volume, Cole and Virdee analysed how the demands of an expanding post-war economy meant that Britain was faced with a major shortage of labour, and how part of this vacuum was met by mass immigration from Britain's colonies and former colonies. In this section of the chapter, we consider the effects of the arrival in the British education system of the daughters and sons of these racialized migrant workers, and look at how they, in turn, became racialized through schooling, and thereby constructed as a problem.

In the 1960s, Sir Edward Boyle, the Minister for Education, heard complaints from white parents, in Southall in London, that there were too many immigrant children in the schools. These parents demanded separate classes for fear that their children would be retarded by the newcomers from the Indian sub-continent – an aversive reaction. The policy that ensued was to disperse children from minority ethnic groups to different schools in order to ensure that there were no more than 30 per cent in any one school (Hiro, 1971). The idea was both to prevent 'a lowering of standards in the schools' and to ensure rapid assimilation of the children into the 'British culture'.[7]

In the following years it became clear from investigations carried out in London schools that another image – that of black people as threatening and needing to be firmly controlled – was also being transferred from the colonies to the 'mother country'. Bernard Coard exposed the iniquitous system of placing children into disciplinary units or 'sin-bins'. Black children, he discovered, were disproportionately represented amongst those in the units (Coard, 1971). What these actions against black children underscored was the deep-rooted nature of the racialized assumptions and stereotypes held of black people and which formed part of the 'common-sense' and 'taken-for-granted' ways in which white British made sense of 'non-white' British (Lawrence, 1982). Examples of the kinds of assumptions which underpinned suspensions of black children in British schools can be found in community and local authority journals and newsletters. A copy of *Issues* (Inner London Education Authority, 1981, p.11) states,

> A study of disruptive units in a West Midlands local authority included a range of explanations from teachers for the disproportionate numbers of ethnic minority children in the units. One teacher referred to the children of West Indian origin as being physically larger than their white counterparts, and therefore 'more difficult to handle'; another that, 'West Indian children are

lively and their liveliness gets them into trouble because teachers fear liveliness and schools like silence'.

While the belief that black children were disruptive was having an effect during the 1970s, this image was particularly strong during the 1980s when, through a series of urban disturbances, the first substantial number of black young people born in Britain began to assert their rights and rejected the assimilationist tendencies imposed on them. The manner in which these disturbances were projected via media and official sources such as the Scarman Report (Home Office, 1981) seemed to fix in the minds of white society the image of young black people (especially males) as representing trouble (see, for example, Cole, 1986, pp. 139–41). The view which carried into the classroom was that black children were not only disruptive (Wright, 1992a; Connolly, 1995), but also violent (Gillborn, 1990; Sewell 1997) – a clear extension of the racialization of their forbears.[8]

Asian school pupils/students, by contrast, were presented in seemingly benign terms as passive and studious and not presenting a disciplinary problem for teachers – a seemingly positive attribute. This notion of the 'passive Asian' student was juxtaposed against the 'aggressive' student of Caribbean origin and became, as Sally Tomlinson (1984) declared, 'a stick to beat the West Indian pupil with'.

This image of passivity applied in particular to Asian girls, but while, on the one hand, it presented them as 'ideal' pupils/students, on the other hand, this same 'passivity' was said to reflect their supposed cultural subordination (Brah and Minhas, 1985) and so was itself a 'stick to beat the Asian man with', as well as 'proof' of the 'cultural inferiority' of these groups. Here we see a form of institutional racism which exhibits seemingly positive attributes in addition to cultural manifestations. Moreover, despite this image of the 'ideal Asian pupil', this has not prevented widespread low expectations of the abilities of these pupils/students, or the inherent contradiction of the class-based view that Asian pupils/students are studious yet have no ambitions other than to be restaurateurs.

Underachievement

There were different kinds of representation for school pupils/students from different minority ethnic groups. Those of Asian background (namely Indian, Pakistani and Bangladeshi) were generally defined by the languages they spoke, and therefore were seen as an academic (and social) threat to white children (see Hiro, 1971), or as religious 'aliens' whose 'specific needs' posed a threat to the autonomy of schools (Blair, 1994) – a form of cultural racism.

By the early 1970s it had become clear that Asian and black children were not gaining the opportunities and advantages from the British education system that their parents had hoped for (Bryan *et al.*, 1985). Black pupils/students in particular were over-represented in suspensions and expulsions from school, and in units for pupils/students with emotional and behavioural difficulties, and were clearly not performing to the same level as their white peers in public examinations. Theories about the assumed disruptive, aggressive and violent natures of black children informed a number of strategies intended to contain such behaviour.

Writers have pointed, for example, to the disproportionate levels of reprimands and criticisms of, and disciplinary measures taken against, black pupils/students by teachers (see Tizzard *et al.* 1988; Mortimore *et al.*, 1988; Gillborn, 1990; Wright 1992a, 1992b; Connolly, 1995). Besides removing (male) black pupils/students from conventional education and placing them disproportionately in alternative educational centres and schools or units for children with 'educational and behavioural difficulties' (EBD) (Cooper *et al.*, 1991), or suspending and expelling them, more 'liberal' strategies of control were used. There were attempts, for example, to channel the supposed excess energy of black pupils/students into more physical activities such as sport. The notion that black children were 'naturally' physically well co-ordinated worked hand in hand with the idea that academically they were not able – a seemingly positive attribute coupled with a negative one (see the discussion on racism in Chapter 3, p. 44).

The issues for pupils/students of Asian origin have differed in some ways to those of black pupils/students. The 'seemingly positive' stereotype as 'ideal pupils/ students' that they have acquired masks some of the negative experiences that they have. Researchers have documented some of the overt as well as unintentional racism of teachers against pupils/students of Asian origin (Bagley, 1992; Wright, 1992b; Blair *et al.*, 1998), while others have revealed the extent of racial harassment to which they are often subjected by their peers (Kelly and Cohn, 1988).

The racializing of Asian pupils/students as 'language problems' has had a deleterious effect on their academic progress. In 1996 Gillborn and Gipps carried out an overview of the literature on the academic achievement of minority ethnic group pupils/students and reported that pupils/students of Pakistani and Bangladeshi, as well as of African-Caribbean, origin were under-performing in relation to their white peers. Indian pupils/students, on the other hand, appear to perform well in relation to all their peers, pointing to the interactions of class and ethnicity in the academic performance of Asian pupils/students. Although most schools now adopt bilingual policies which ensure that the child uses his or her first language in the acquisition of English, Blair *et al.* (1998) found that teachers were largely ill equipped to incorporate bilingual issues in their everyday classroom practice.

Discipline

Researchers have obtained evidence of some of the unfair ways in which black pupils/students have been treated. From his observations, Gillborn, for example, reported that,

> Perhaps even more significant than the frequency of criticism and controlling statements which Afro-Caribbean [sic] pupils/students received was the fact that they were often singled out for criticism even though several pupils/ students of different ethnic origins were engaged in the same behaviour . . . In sum, Afro-Caribbean pupils/students were not only criticised more often than their white peers, but the same behaviour in a white pupil might not bring about criticism at all.
>
> (Gillborn, 1990, p. 30)

The result of these kinds of interactions has been widespread antagonism between white teachers and black pupils/students because, as Wright (1987, p. 111) reported, 'pupils/students were inevitably forced into highly significant face-winning, face-retaining and face-losing contests between themselves and the teachers'.

This tendency to over-discipline black pupils/students has resulted over the years in high percentages of black pupils/students facing exclusion. The long term effects of this can at present only be a matter of speculation. However, it does not require empirical research to conclude that the disruption or curtailment of a child's education is likely to have a negative effect on their chances in life.

Ethnic and gender differentiation

There has been general criticism of studies which present minorities as single, undifferentiated groups. Mirza (1992) for example, criticized the tendency of researchers to subsume girls' experience within boys' experience, or else to present boys' experience as representative of all pupil experience. Research has shown that black girls face different forms of exclusion and marginalization in schools and also that they respond differently from boys to these experiences (Fuller, 1984; Mac an Ghaill, 1994; Mirza, 1992). For example, in interactions with male teachers, girls are more likely to face stereotypes about their sexuality, and while girls of Caribbean origin are more likely to be seen as 'bossy' and 'loud' – a supposed indicator of the matriarchal tendencies in black families – Asian girls are likely to be seen as destined for early (forced) marriage upon whom education is somewhat wasted (Brah and Minhas, 1985). This highlights that racism is not the only factor in the experience of Asian and black pupils/students and that schools are equally implicated in those institutionalized modes of social production which reproduce the subordination of women (Mac an Ghaill, 1994). Researchers have also reported the different responses of black girls to discriminatory and unfair practices. Fuller (1984), Mac an Ghaill (1988) and Mirza (1992) found that black girls present an image of co-operation but resist internally teacher assumptions and attitudes, and will attempt to succeed academically despite their negative experiences.

However, Mac an Ghaill also documented that not all girls are 'pro-school' but they are largely 'invisible' as disciplinary problems, resulting in more resources being allocated to male pupils/students who are perceived as a threat to the institution. Mirza also concluded that black girls in her study, would, if given support, have achieved their high ambitions but were often held back by the lack of, or the inadequate or inappropriate, career advice which they received, advice based on assumptions about their gender, class and 'race'.

Writers have also pointed to the complexities of ethnic identification (Blair *et al.*, 1998; Gillborn and Gipps, 1996) and the importance of breaking down labels such as 'Asian' in order to make obvious the differences in academic performances between the different 'Asian' groups. The tendency to view people of Indian, Pakistani and Bangladeshi origin as one homogenous group had disguised the different experiences of these groups within the education system.

Addressing the problems

The momentum for changing the situation of minority ethnic group pupils/students came from minority groups themselves. Parents organized 'mother-tongue' teaching for children in addition to instruction in the faith which they received at the mosque. Black parents started their own supplementary or Saturday schools. This reflected a growing frustration in black communities over the failure of the education system to produce positive results for their children. Supplementary schools were intended to counteract some of the distortions of history, the misinformation and the inadequate academic instruction which parents believed their children were receiving (Chevannes and Reeves, 1987). Through Asian and black parent and teacher associations and through community action, the disadvantaged position of black pupils/students in schools was placed on the public and educational agenda. In 1979, the government commissioned an inquiry into 'the education of West Indian children'. The Rampton Report (1981) was made available in 1981 and confirmed what black parents had been saying all along – that racism against black children was indeed a major factor in their experience of school. However, the Report was not received wholeheartedly by the government, which commissioned another study, whose brief this time was extended to cover other minority ethnic groups. The Swann Report, *Education for All*, (1985) confirmed some of the findings of the Rampton Report but also made some of the most wide-ranging suggestions for education in an ethnically diverse society. Amongst these was the suggestion that children in all schools should be educated for life in a multicultural society. One of the underlying principles of this suggestion was that if children were taught about each other and each other's cultures, this would help to reduce prejudice, especially amongst white children.

Multicultural education

The Swann Report's predominant focus on culture set the trajectory of multicultural education along a superficial line in which children learnt about the food, the clothes and the music of different countries without also understanding the structural and institutional inequalities which had been at the core of community campaigns (Troyna, 1993; Sarup, 1986).

Preceding the broadening of multicultural education to include all schools regardless of ethnic composition, schools had attempted to deal with the supposed low self-esteem of black pupils/students by including within the curriculum, subjects which were deemed to be 'ethnically relevant' and would help black pupils/students to acquire a more positive self-identity.

The broadening of multicultural education to include white pupils/students and teachers, and the recognition that racism was a factor affecting the education of black pupils/students did not, however, give rise to a radical rethinking of the curriculum or of pedagogy. What in effect took place was an extension of the 'Black Studies' approach to include white pupils/students, so that white pupils/students too could play steel drums or learn to cook Asian or Caribbean foods, and wear 'ethnic' clothes. The exoticization of minority ethnic group cultures and customs merely served to reinforce the notion that these cultures were indeed 'Other' and drew the boundary more firmly between 'Them', the 'immigrants' or 'foreigners' and 'Us', the 'real' British. Needless to say, this approach itself came under severe criticism, as a form of education that was said to be tokenistic and failed to address the real problems of schools. While multicultural education was an attempt to address the prejudices of white teachers and pupils/students, it was not appropriate for tackling and changing inequalities in society (Sarup, 1986). Sleeter, (1994), described liberal forms of multicultural education as an opportunity for white people, 'to project a positive image about groups of color without actually confronting white supremacy'.

Antiracist education

The criticism of multicultural education led to a greater awareness of personal and institutional inequalities, and to a shift from a focus on the alleged 'deficiencies' of minority pupils/students and cultures to different manifestations of racism in schools and society. There was greater stress on individual and institutional racism and on the need to educate teachers in particular to explore different teaching strategies which not only allowed for personal examination of racism, but ways in which these new understandings could be incorporated into teaching. Race Relations Advisors, and Multicultural Advisory teachers also struggled with finding ways to promote antiracist teaching in schools and were sometimes accused of adopting strategies which were damaging and counterproductive. Strategies which were based on the premise that all white people were racist, by virtue of their whiteness, induced feelings of guilt and left no room for change or transformation (see, for example, Sivanandan, 1985). A further criticism was that antiracists functioned with simplistic notions of racism and failed to recognize the complex and contradictory ways in which racism was manifest (see Chapter 3 of this volume for suggestions that we should adopt a wide definition or racism).

The twenty-first century

We should learn from these criticisms as we continue to confront racism in the twenty-first century. The differential racialization of children from minority ethnic groups continues. As far as permanent exclusion from school is concerned, for example, latest figures (23 June 2005) show that 0.29 per cent of black Caribbean, black African and black other pupils/students are in this situation as compared with 0.14 per cent of white pupils/students (http://www.dfes.gov.uk/rsgateway/DB/SFR). On leaving school, young people experience differential rates of unemployment, with those of Pakistani/Bangladeshi origin facing 11 per cent compared to 7 per cent of young white people (figures not available for young black people). In addition, a report commissioned by the London Development Agency reported that 70 per cent of African-Caribbean pupils left school with fewer than five high-grade GCSEs. It concluded that low teacher expectations played a major part in the underachievement of black children and that black pupils found they were encouraged by black teachers (Bright, 2004).

Recent research (Cole and Stuart, 2005) has shown that racism and xenophobia directed at British Asian and black and at overseas student teachers in schools in the south-east of England is endemic. This research documents a variety of racist and xenophobic incidents. Covert racism was found almost everywhere. Three of our interviewees mentioned: 'You hear them say things as you pass', or 'making animal noises', but nothing is done about it (ibid.).

We also found a considerable degree of xenophobia. Remarks such as 'we hate all foreigners' or 'go back to your own country' were directed at white, European, as well as Asian and black, student teachers (ibid.).

What also came out strongly from the case studies is that many pupils are very ignorant about the world and its people beyond their own communities. They know little about European countries and one thought polar bears came from Poland. A Sri Lankan teacher was asked what she described as 'the most amazing questions', like did she ride on elephants and were there cars in Sri Lanka? Pupils/ students regularly confused African teachers with Jamaicans, making ill-natured jokes about drug-smuggling and reggae (ibid.).

There is much 'misinformation' among pupils (cf. Gaine 1995). Some of the African teachers are deeply concerned by the image of Africa presented by the media, which focuses – sometimes in well-meaning ways – on poverty and deprivation. One consequence is that the pupils think all Africans live in mud huts, and know nothing of modern life. Two Zimbabwean teachers of food technology brought photos of their own homes in to persuade the children that they did have experience of electric stoves and microwaves. One said, comparing these pupils' stereotypes with their behaviour:

> We were teaching in civilised schools, where kids will make sure they are neat, they will fix their tie before they say 'Morning ma'am' with respect. They behave like ladies and gentlemen, but people here think we are like animals.
>
> (ibid.)

Our findings were underscored by some recent interviews with young people undertaken by a local council in the same region (East Sussex Local Education Authority, 2004). The following extracts speak for themselves:

> They were laughing behind me and joking about my name and where I come from and my country's music or something like that.

> They still think Asian people are, you know, like a bit stupid.

> I feel really uncomfortable and I really want to get out of that school as fast as I can, every time when school finished or the bell rings I say 'OK I'm pack up' and then run for the bus.

I want to leave England, I want to go back to my own country, you know, because it is so uncomfortable. I can't do nothing. I can't talk with no one, just talk with my own family.

(East Sussex LEA, 2004, p. 15)

It was horrible because I could see her at the end of the corridor, I knew she was going to say something or do something. She'd barge past and be like, 'You black bitch' and swear at me, and everything.

(ibid., p. 16)

Some of my friends they still think I'm a Muslim, like they just call me a Muslim but really I'm a Hindu. But I know they don't really understand so you've just got to live with it basically.

(ibid., p. 17)

Conclusion

We believe that, rather than racism existing in multiple unrelated forms (the postmodernist and poststructuralist position), racism is a discrete phenomenon, but one that takes different forms in different historical periods and geographical locations.[9] None of these forms can or should be viewed in isolation from economic and political factors, nor can they be understood, and dealt with, without reference to these factors. Thus in the imperial era, in order to justify the continuance of 'the strong arm and brave spirit' of the British Empire (see above), and the ongoing and relentless pursuit of expanding capital accumulation, the African subjects of the colonies were racialized, in school textbooks, as 'fierce savages' and 'brutal and stinking' (Glendenning, 1973, p. 35), while freed West Indian slaves were described as 'lazy, vicious and incapable of any serious improvement or of work except under compulsion' (Chancellor, 1970, p. 240). When the British 'race' and therefore Empire was seen to be under threat at home, foreign Jews were described at the same time, by the media, as 'semi-barbarous', unable or unwilling to 'use the latrine', depositing 'their filth' on 'the floor of their rooms' (Holmes, 1979, p. 17) and involved in world conspiracy (thus directly threatening British Imperial hegemony): 'whenever, there is trouble in Europe', the ILP paper, *Labour Leader*, put it, you may be sure a hook-nosed Rothschild is at his games' (Cohen, 1985, p. 75).

In the post-World War 2 period, not surprisingly given the aforementioned colonial history, the British Cabinet racialized many of the African-Caribbean community as 'accustomed to living in squalid conditions and have no desire to improve' (*The Observer*, 1/1/89), while their children were described, by one local education authority, as 'physically robust and boisterous, yet mentally lethargic'. At the same time, the same LEA perceived there to be 'very real problems' with the 'domestic habits and personal hygiene of the Asiatics' as well as 'the problem of [their] eating habits' (Grosvenor, 1987, pp. 34–35). Children from minority ethnic groups (not a source of cheap labour, as were their parents) were racialized as problems to be dealt with in these post-war years.

As we have seen, recent research (East Sussex Local Education Authority, 2004; Cole and Stuart, 2005) has shown that racialization continues to deform the educational institutions of the society. Whatever the shortcomings of both multi-cultural and certain forms of antiracist education, it seems clear that the lack of governments' commitment did little to encourage teachers and schools to take the issue of racism more seriously. During the Conservative era, equality issues were not only placed on the back burner, but actively demonized. Groups who attempted to restore public attention to equity issues found themselves increasingly marginalized and derided for 'political correctness', a pernicious concept invented by the Radical Right, and which, to our dismay, has become common currency.[10]

As was argued in Chapter 3, the onset of a Labour government has done little, despite the rhetoric of 'an inclusive society', to challenge the fundamental injustices and inequalities faced by Britain's minority ethnic communities. While government support for initiatives like the Index for Inclusion (Booth and Ainscow, 2002), the stress on English as an Additional Language, as well as the DfES (2003) 'Aiming High' strategy to close achievement gaps for pupils/students from minority ethnic groups, are to be welcomed, there remains a need to challenge the fundamentally racist nature of British society. At the time of writing (January 2005) the new Home Secretary, Charles Clarke has just announced an extension of ethnic monitoring right across the public services that aims to provide the first official, systematic picture of racial inequality in Britain. In education, the strategy will focus on providing help to those left behind, with aid to Bangladeshi and black African children, of whom a smaller proportion attend childcare and nursery education. This initiative will also include, where necessary, the poor white working class. This is a significant move forward.

So, what else needs to be done? The Stephen Lawrence Inquiry report acknowledged that '[r]acism, institutional or otherwise, is not the prerogative of the Police Service' (Macpherson, 1999: 6.54) and that 'other agencies including for example those dealing with housing and education also suffer from the disease [sic]' (ibid.). It went on to argue that '[i]f racism is to be eradicated there must be specific and co-ordinated action both within the agencies themselves and by society at large, *particularly through the education system*, from pre-primary school upwards and onwards' (ibid.) (our emphasis).

We have two major suggestions. First, there is an urgent need for schools to fully abide by the Race Relations (Amendment) Act (2000) and be pro-active in the pursuit of 'race' equality.

Second, we would argue for the amendment of the National Curriculum. The Stephen Lawrence Inquiry report stated that schools fear negative publicity if they adopt antiracist policies (1999, 6.56). This probably relates to the traditional association (prior to the State's acknowledgement of institutional racism) of antiracism with Radical Left politics. It may also relate to publicity given to bad forms of antiracist practice, detailed in the book, *Murder in the Playground* (Macdonald *et al*, 1989), even though the authors are at pains to emphasize that they were in favour of *constructive* antiracist education. It is our view that the way forward is to promote both antiracism and antiracist multiculturalism. This should avoid simplistic versions of 'Racist Awareness Training', practised in the past (for a critique, see Sivanandan, 1985), and patronizing and offensive 'multicultural education' (for a critique, see, for example, Cole, 1992). Using the web creatively, multicultural antiracist education should be about the importance of antiracism as an underlying principle, and about the promotion of respect and non-exploitative difference in a multicultural world. As the Inquiry put it, in order to seek to eradicate racism in society as a whole:

> The Government should consider how best to empower local education authorities to create, monitor and enforce anti-racist policies through codes of practice and by amendment of the National Curriculum, to provide education which deals with racism awareness and valuing cultural diversity in the multi-cultural and multi-ethnic society in which we live.
>
> (ibid: 6.56)

One major way of amending the National Curriculum would be to re-introduce an honest and critical analysis of imperialism, past and present (cf Cole, 2004a, p. 534, Cole and Stuart, 2005).

As conservative historian, Niall Ferguson (2003) has argued,

> Empire is as 'cutting edge' as you could wish . . . [It] has got everything: economic history, social history, cultural history, political history, military history and international history – not to mention contemporary politics (just turn on the latest news from Kabul).

The teaching of imperialism, past and present, in schools, we would argue, provides more than this. It informs us *most precisely* about the historical and contemporary nature of British society.

The full implementation of the Race Relations (Amendment) Act together with changes in the National Curriculum must be part of a much wider and concerted effort to encourage all educational (and other) institutions to view the undermining of racism, not as an irrelevance or as an encumbrance but as one of the key issues facing the world in the twenty-first century.

In the light of escalating racism, Islamophobia, xenophobia and xeno-racism, in Britain (see Chapter 3 of this volume; see also Cole, 2004c), mainland Europe and worldwide, not least Tony Blair's central role in the imperialist project of George W. Bush (Cole, 2004a, 2004d), the mandatory implementation of measures to undermine institutional racism is more urgent than ever.

Notes

1   We put 'race' in inverted commas for the reasons discussed in Chapter 3, Note 1, of this volume.
2   For an in-depth discussion of racism and racialization, see Chapter 3 pp. 44–6 of this volume.
3   In concentrating on the experiences of Asian and black pupils/pupils/students, we fully

accept that those who do not fall into this category also experience racism (for a discussion of nomenclature, see Chapter 3, Note 8 of this volume).

4   Fryer cites evidence of a large percentage of skeletons of black Africans found among 350 skeletons excavated in 1951, dating back to Roman times (Fryer 1984, cited in Brandt, 1986, p. 7).

5   For a more in-depth analysis of the Imperial curriculum, see Cole, 2004a, pp. 526–30.

6   One of the authors of this chapter (Maud Blair) worked as an advisor for multicultural education, and as late as 1989 was helping schools identify books with outdated colonial theories and racist views and images. Not only were there history and geography books, but story books and well-intentioned books by NGOs such as Oxfam, even published in the 1970s, which still presented images that were demeaning to Asian and black peoples.

7   This epitomizes the assimilationist or monocultural approach to education, a form of intentional or sometimes unintentional racism, and the dominant and traditional approach to education in multicultural Britain.

8   Cashmore and Troyna (1982) went so far as to claim that 'there is a penchant for violence within the West Indian culture' (p. 32). For a critique, see Cole, 1986, pp. 128–33. Ironically, Troyna went on to totally abandon such notions and to become one of Britain's leading antiracist educators.

9   For an expansion of this critique of the postmodernist/poststructuralist position, see Cole, 2004b, p. 52, Note 15. For a discussion of the theoretical differences between postmodernism and poststructuralism, see Cole, 2003, pp. 494–5.

10 The term 'political correctness' was coined to imply that there exist (left-wing) political demagogues who seek to impose their views on equality issues, in particular appropriate terminology, on the majority. In reality, nomenclature changes over time. Thus, in the twenty-first century, terms such as 'negress' or 'negro' or 'coloured', nomenclatures which at one time were considered quite acceptable, are now considered offensive. Antiracists are concerned with *respect* for others and, therefore, are careful to acknowledge changes in nomenclature, changes which are decided by oppressed groups themselves, bearing in mind that there can be differences of opinion among such oppressed groups. The same applies to other equality issues. Thus, for example, it has become common practice to use 'working class' rather than 'lower class'; 'lesbian, gay, bisexual and transgender' rather than 'sexually deviant'; 'disability' rather than 'handicap', 'gender equality' rather than 'a woman's place'. Using current and acceptable nomenclature is about the fostering of a caring and inclusive society, not about 'political correctness'. The term has recently been extended to include anything that the Radical Right finds not to its liking. Thus, for ex-leader of the British Conservative Party, Michael Howard, 'political correctness' has blurred the difference between 'right' and 'wrong'. As he puts it, '[t]he clear distinction between right and wrong has been lost in sociological mumbo-jumbo and politically correct nonsense'. (http://politics.guardian.co.uk/conservatives/story/0,9061,1280083,00.html). Is Howard aware that the origin of 'mumbo jumbo' is 'the protective spirit of the Khassonkee tribe of Senegal' (Green, 1998, p. 815)?

References

Armytage, W.H.G. (1981) 'Issues at stake: the biosocial background of the 1902 Education Act', *History of Education*, 10, (3).

Bagley, C. (1992), 'In-service provision and teacher resistance to whole-school Change', in D. Gill, D.B. Mayor, and M. Blair (eds) *Racism and Education: Structures and Strategies*, London: Sage.

Blair, M. (1994) 'Black teachers, black pupils/students and education markets', *Cambridge Journal of Education*, 24, pp. 277–91.

Blair, M. and Bourne, J. with Coffin, C, Creese, A, and Kenner, C. (1998) *Making the Difference: Teaching and Learning Strategies in Successful Multi-ethnic Schools*, London: DfEE.

Brah, A. and Minhas, R. (1985) 'structural racism or cultural differences: schooling for Asian girls', in: G. Weiner (ed.) *Just a Bunch of Girls*, Milton Keynes: Open University Press.

Brandt, G.(1986) *The Realization of Anti-Racist Teaching*, Lewes: Falmer.

Bright, M. (2004) 'Gangsta culture a deadly virus, says top TV presenter', *The Observer*, 12 September: http://observer.guardian.co.uk/uk_news/story/0,,1302814,00.html

Bryan, B., Dadzie, S. and Scafe, S. (1985) *The Heart of the Race: Black Women's Lives in Britain*, London: Virago.

Cashmore, E. and Troyna, B. (eds) (1982) *Black Youth In Crisis*, London: George Allen and Unwin.

Chancellor, V. (1970) *History for their Masters*, Bath: Adams and Dart.

Chevannes, M. and Reeves, F. (1987) 'The black voluntary school movement: definition, context and prospects', in B. Troyna (ed.) *Racial Inequality in Education*, London: Tavistock.

Coard, B. (1971) *How the West Indian Child is made Educationally Sub-Normal in the British School System*, London: New Beacon Books.

Cohen, S. (1985) 'Anti-semitism, immigration controls and the welfare state', *Critical Social Policy*, 13, Summer.

Cole, M. (1986) 'Teaching and learning about racism: a critique of multicultural education in Britain', in S. Modgil, G. Verma, K. Mallik and C. Modgil (eds) *Multicultural Education: the Interminable Debate*, Lewes: The Falmer Press.

Cole, M. (1992) 'British values, liberal values or values of justice and equality: three approaches to education in multicultural Britain', in J. Lynch, C. Modgil and S. Modgil (eds) *Cultural Diversity and the Schools: Vol. 3: Equity or Excellence? Education and Cultural Reproduction*, London: The Falmer Press.

Cole, M. (2003) 'Might it be in the practice that it fails to succeed? A Marxist critique of claims for postmodernism and poststructuralism as forces for social change and social justice, *British Journal of Sociology of Education* 24 (4) pp. 485–98.

Cole, M. (2004a) '"Rule Britannia" and the new American Empire: a Marxist analysis of the teaching of imperialism, actual and potential, in the English school curriculum', *Policy Futures in Education*, 2 (3), pp. 523–38.

Cole, M. (2004b) '"Brutal and stinking" and "difficult to handle": the historical and contemporary manifestations of racialisation, institutional racism, and schooling in Britain', *Race, Ethnicity and Education*, 7 (1), pp. 35–56.

Cole, M. (2004c) 'F*** you – human sewage: contemporary global capitalism and the xeno-racialization of asylum seekers', *Contemporary Politics* 22, 10 (2) June 2004, pp. 159–65.

Cole, M. (2004d) 'US imperialism, transmodernism and education: a Marxist critique', *Policy Futures in Education*, 2 (3 and 4), pp. 633–43.

Cole, M. and Stuart, J.M. (2005) '"Do you ride on elephants" and "never tell them you're German": the experiences of British Asian and black, and overseas student teachers in south-east England', *British Educational Research Journal*, 31 (3), pp. 349–66.

Connolly, P. (1995) 'Boys will be boys? Racism, sexuality and the construction of masculine identities amongst infant children', in M. Blair and J. Holland (eds) *Equality and Difference: Debates and Issues in Feminist Research and Pedagogy*, Clevedon: Multilingual Matters.

Cooper, P., Upton, G., Smith, C. (1991) 'Ethnic minority and gender distribution among staff and pupils/students in facilities for pupils/students with emotional and behavioural difficulties in England and Wales', *British Journal of Sociology of Education*, 12, 1, pp. 77–94.

Department for Education and Skills (DfES) (2003) *Aiming High*, London: DfES.

East Sussex Local Education Authority (2004) *One of Us*, Brighton: East Sussex Local Education Authority.

Ferguson, N. (2003) 'Prince and empire are the key to history', *The Sunday Times*, 6 July.

Fryer, P. (1984) *Staying Power: The History of Black People in Britain*, London: Pluto Press.

Fuller, M. (1984) 'Black girls in a London Comprehensive School', in M. Hammersley and P. Woods (eds) *Life in School: The Sociology of Pupil Culture*, Milton Keynes: Open University Press.

Gaine, C. (1995) *Still No Problem Here*, Stoke-on-Trent: Trentham Books.

Gillborn, D. (1990) *"Race" Ethnicity and Education*, London: Unwin Hyman.

Gillborn, D. and Gipps, C. (1996) *Recent Research on the Achievement of Ethnic Minority Pupils/students*, London: HMSO.

Glendenning, F.J. (1973) 'History textbooks and racial attitudes: 1804–1969', *Journal of Educational Administration and History*, 5, pp. 35–44.

Grosvenor, I. (1987) 'A different reality: education and the racialisation of the black child', *History of Education*, 16 (4).

Grosvenor, I. (1989) 'Teacher racism and the construction of black underachievement' in R. Lowe (ed.) *The Changing Secondary School*, Lewes: The Falmer Press.

Green, J. (1998) *The Cassell Dictionary of Slang*, London: Cassell.

Hiro, D. (1971) *Black British, White British*, London: Pelican.

Hendrick, H. (1980) 'A race of intelligent unskilled labourers: the adolescent worker and the debate on compulsory part-time day continuation schools, 1900–1922', *History of Education*, 9, (2), pp. 159–73.

Hobsbawm, E. (1964) *Labouring Men*, New York: Basic Books.

Holmes, C. (1979) *Anti-Semitism in British Society 1876–1939*, London: Edward Arnold.

Humphries, S. (1981) *Hooligans or Rebels? An Oral History of Working-Class Childhood and Youth 1889–1939*, Oxford: Basil Blackwell.

Inner London Education Authority (ILEA) (1981) 'ISSUES in Race and Education', 34 Autumn, London: ILEA.

Kelly, E. and Cohn, T. (eds) *Racism in Schools – New Research Evidence*, Stoke-on-Trent: Trentham Books.

Lawrence, E. (1982) 'Just plain common sense: the "roots" of racism', in Centre for Contemporary Cultural Studies, *The Empire Strikes Back: Race and Racism in 70s Britain*, London: Hutchinson.

Macdonald, I., Kahn, L., Joh, G. and Bhavani, R. (1989) *Murder in the Playground: The Burnage Report*, London: Longsight Press.

Mac an Ghaill, M. (1988), *Young Gifted and Black: Student–Teacher Relations in the Schooling of Black Youth*, Milton Keynes: Open University Press.

Mac an Ghaill, M. (1994), *The Making of Men: Masculinities, Sexualities and Schooling*, Buckingham: Open University Press.

MacKenzie, J.M. (1984) *Propaganda and Empire: The Manipulation of British Public Opinion 1880–1960*, Manchester: Manchester University Press.

Maclure, J.S. (1979) *Educational Documents: England and Wales 1816 to the Present Day*, London: Methuen.

Macpherson, W. (1999) *The Stephen Lawrence Enquiry, Report of an Enquiry by S. William*, London: The Stationary Office.

Mangan, J.A. (1986) 'The grit of our forefathers: invented traditions, propaganda and imperialism, in J.M. Mackenzie (ed.) *Propaganda and Empire: the Manipulation of British Public Opinion, 1880–1960*, Manchester: Manchester University Press.

Mirza, H. (1992) *Young Female and Black*, London: Routledge.

Mortimore, P. Sammons, P. Stoll, P. Lewis, D. Ecob, R. (1988) *School Matters: the Junior Years*, Wells: Open Books.

Rampton Report (1981) *West Indian Children in Our Schools*, Cmnd 8723, London: HMSO.

Sarup, M. (1986) *The Politics Of Multicultural Education*, London: Routledge and Kegan Paul.

Scarman, Lord (1981) *The Brixton Disorders 10–12 April 1981, Report of an Inquiry by the Rt Hon Lord Scarman OBE*, London: HMSO.

Semmel, B. (1960) *Imperialism and Social Reform*, London: George Allen and Unwin.

Sewell, T. (1997) *Black Masculinity and Schooling*, Stoke-on-Trent: Trentham Books.

Shannon, R. (1976) *The Crisis of Imperialism 1865–1915*, London: Paladin.

Simon, B. (1974) *Education and the Labour Movement 1870–1920*, London: Lawrence and Wishart.

Sivanandan, A. (1985) 'RAT and the degradation of black struggle', *Race and Class*, 25 (4), pp. 1–33.

Sleeter, C. (1994), *White Racism, Multicultural Education* 1 (4), pp. 5–8.

Swann Report (1985) *Education for All: Report of the Committee of Inquiry into the Education of Children from Minority Ethnic Groups*, London: HMSO.

Tizzard, B., Blatchford, P., Burke, J., Farquhar, C, and Plewis, I., (1988) *Young children at School in the Inner City*, Hove: Lawrence Erlbaum Associates.

Tomlinson, S. (1984) *Home And School In Multicultural Britain*, London: Batsford.

Troyna, B. (1993) *Racism and Education*, Buckingham: Open University Press.

Visram, R. (1986) *Ayahs, Lascars and Princes*, London: Pluto Press.

Walvin, J. (1973) *Black and White: the Negro and English society 1555–1945*, London: Allen Lane.

Webb, S. (1896) *The Difficulties of Individualism*, Fabian Tract, 69, London.

Wright, C. (1987) 'Black pupils/students-white teachers', in B. Troyna (ed.) *Racial Inequality in Education*, London: Routledge.

Wright, C. (1992a) 'Early education: multiracial primary school classrooms', in D. Gill, B. Mayor and M. Blair *Racism in Education, Structures and Strategies*, London: Sage.

Wright, C. (1992b) *Race Relations in the Primary School*, London: David Fulton Publishers.

5 The making of sexualities

Sexuality, identity and equality

Simon Forrest and Viv Ellis

Introduction

> The forces of inhumanity are overwhelming, but only one's continued oppo-
> sition can make any other order possible, can give an added strength for all
> those who desire freedom and equality to break at last those fetters that seem
> now so unbreakable.
>
> (R. Duncan in Blasius and Phelan, 1997, p. 233)

This quotation, from an essay written in the 1940s by the American poet Robert
Duncan, is an apposite epigraph for this chapter. It is indicative, in a number of
ways, of the content of the chapter, and comes from an essay to which we will
return in our discussion of the key issue of sexuality and identity. First, it identifies
a struggle for human rights, equality and freedom on the part of those oppressed
because of their sexuality. Second, Duncan's speculation on the possibility of 'any
other order' draws attention to a definition of sexuality as a cultural field which is
subject to both construction and reconstruction as part of a historical process.
Third, decontextualized as it is, the quotation appears to allow for diversity of
sexual potential rather than delimiting categories such as heterosexual, homosexual, bisexual or transgendered. Finally, the epigraph actually comes from
an essay by a homosexual male which demonstrates that, even with categories
based on sexual behaviour, there is no single or simple identity across the category,
neither no one homosexuality nor heterosexuality. Duncan was arguing against
such separate identities. It is this reading which provides for the context for this
chapter in which we aim to trace some of the history of the oppression of sexualities other than heterosexuality and consider the implications of recent events
and campaigns for the progress of the struggle for equality of lesbian, gay, bisexual
and trangendered (LGBT) people. Within this enterprise we will consider attempts
to define and represent sexuality, particularly in the modern era, moving towards
a discussion in which we focus on conceptions of sexuality *per se* rather than
individual categories, these categories being relatively recent cultural effects. So
although we may try in this chapter to generalize about sexuality as a cultural field,
yet self-consciously hang our comments on a history of categories, especially (but
not exclusively) the male homosexual, we will inevitably come back to the very

problematic nature of the production of these separate (and multiple) identities (and communities) based on sexual behaviour.

Defining sexualities

Definitions of sexuality medical, legal and otherwise abound. Some, like Oscar Wilde's famously expedient misreading of Plato in the dock, 'It is that deep, spiritual affection that is as pure as it is perfect. It is intellectual' (Wilde, 1895, p. 111) have attempted to side-step the issue of difference in sexual practices. Wilde's 'love that dare not speak its name' also, of course, involved sexual acts, criminalized by the Victorians as 'gross indecency', a crime of which Wilde and his co-defendant, Alfred Taylor (the keeper of a male homosexual brothel), were eventually convicted. The conversion of sexuality to sexual acts subject initially to religious codification, then to the pathologies of medicine and the jurisdiction of the law, is one on which we will focus in our 'history'.

One of the earliest and most detailed attempts at categorizing sexualities was made by the nineteenth-century German sexologist Karl Heinrich Ulrichs. He was a legal official who took a campaigning position against what he saw as repressive laws against male homosexuals, exemplified by Paragraph 175 of the German Imperial Code: 'Unnatural vice committed between two persons of the male sex or by people with animals is to be punished by imprisonment; the verdict may also include the loss of civil rights' (Ulrichs cited in Blasius and Phelan, 1997, p. 63). From the early 1860s, Ulrichs produced many short publications designed to challenge such legislation, based on conversations and correspondence with individuals throughout Europe. Alluding to Plato's terminology in *The Symposium*, Ulrichs devised a series of categories and sub-categories which set the boundaries for what he thought to be all the possibilities for sexual behaviour. These included: 'Men' and 'Women', whose sexual object-choice lay exclusively in the opposite sex; 'Urnings', or male homosexuals, who could be 'Mannlings' (virile), 'Weiblings' (effeminate) or 'Intermediaries' (a mixed sub-category); through to 'Urningins' (lesbians), 'Uranodionings' (male bisexuals), 'Uranodioningins' (female bisexuals) and 'Hermaphrodites' (sharing the physical characteristics of both sexes). Ulrichs (1994, p. 314) actually defined a range of twelve sexual types if we include all his sub-categories.

Although his intentions were progressive, Ulrich's project lay the ground for the subsequent pathologizing of sexual behaviour in the discourses of medicine and psychiatry which is still powerful today. The tensions between this progressive intention and the pathologizing effect can be seen in this extract from an appeal to the regional governments of North Germany and Austria in 1870:

> That an actual man would feel sexual love for a man is impossible. The urning is not a true man. He is a mixture of man and woman. He is man only in terms of bodily build. The urning too is a human being. He, too, therefore has natural human rights. The urning is also a citizen of the state. He, too, therefore has civil rights: and correspondingly, the state has duties to fulfil vis-à-vis him as

well. The state is not entitled to treat the urning as a man without rights, as it has up to now.

(Ulrichs cited in Blasius and Phelan, 1997, p. 65)

The drive to pathologize sexual behaviour was intensified throughout the nineteenth century by, for example, Karoly Maria Benkert (said to be the person who invented the term 'homosexual'), Richard von Krafft-Ebing and, of course, Sigmund Freud. By the middle of the twentieth century, the proposition that sexual behaviour that had been diagnosed as deviant could be treated was commonplace. Aversion therapies based upon a malign behaviourist psychology became part of the medical/psychiatric repertoire and led to the institutional abuse of countless homosexuals, transvestites, transgendered and transsexual people and others. It was comparatively recently that homosexuality was removed from some catalogues of mental disorders, and only then after a considerable struggle. The anthropologist Gayle Rubin (1993) has shown how medicine and psychiatry multiplied these pathologies in a hierarchy of (deviant) sexual behaviour that continues to be pervasive but, talking of the relative successes of homosexuals in establishing some human rights in some places and in coming out of the medical textbook, notes that '[s]exualities keep marching out of the *Diagnostic and Statistical Manual* and on to the pages of social history' (Rubin, 1993, p. 416).

The work of Alfred Kinsey (Kinsey *et al.*, 1948; 1953) on human sexual behaviour represents a watershed in the modern understanding and definition of sexuality. Kinsey set out to describe and catalogue the sexual behaviour of human beings by interviewing American men and women about their sexual lives and experiences and by observing sexual behaviour in the laboratory. A major achievement of his studies was to show that contemporary preconceptions about the mutual exclusivity of sexual identities were erroneous. Many of the men and women participating in his study reported both heterosexual and homosexual contacts, leading Kinsey to develop an analytic scale on which sexual behaviour could be described in terms of one of six points, ranging from exclusively homosexual with no heterosexual contacts to exclusively heterosexual with no homosexual contacts, with grades reflecting more or less homosexual and heterosexual behaviour respectively in between. By looking over study participants' sexual histories Kinsey was able to assign them a place on the scale. Although he found that most of the men and women participating in the study reported exclusively heterosexual contacts, and a relatively small number (a few per cent) reported exclusively homosexual contacts, up to 37 per cent of the men in his sample had experienced a same-sex sexual experience to the point of orgasm in their lifetime. While the findings of Kinsey's work challenged previously held notions of the exclusivity of homosexual and heterosexual sexual behaviour it did so from within the paradigm of existing essentialist beliefs about sex and, as such, was not as progressive as it might at first appear. The focus on sexual acts rather than any idea of sexual identities did nothing to challenge critical perceptions of homosexuality as a deviancy. The discovery that apparently heterosexual men reported homosexual contacts in their youth could be dismissed as either evidence of a periodic 'arrested development' (à la Freud), or of a mature heterosexuality overcoming immature homosexual tendencies.

The fallout of essentialist investigations of sexuality via studies of sexual behaviour is still being felt. Most recently, attention has focused on the search for a genetic basis for homosexuality (and presumably, therefore, heterosexuality). This search is hampered by the inability of genetic science to explain ideas of a sexual identity any more satisfactorily than Kinsey's studies. Consequently, evidence from essentialist studies tends to become hostage to the ideologies of its commentators. Homophobic commentators have latched on to the potential existence of a gay gene as offering the possibility of genetic correction of a perceived sexual deviancy. However, some gay lobbyists have welcomed the 'gay gene' as biological proof that they are essentially biologically different from heterosexuals and have not created a deviant social identity for themselves. Between these lines, factions cross sides and, illustrating the political utility of essentialist findings, some gay lobbyists have argued for the rejection of Kinsey's work because it seems to provide too small an account of exclusive homosexuality. Some 'libertarian' right-wing ideologues draw the conclusion that, if homosexuality is genetically determined, then it is a natural state and should be decriminalized. For Kinsey, the reading of his work by the McCarthy-influenced US government at the time was sufficiently negative that funding was withdrawn from his studies.

While sexological surveys continue, the chief development of thinking about definitions of sexuality comes from fields outside the laboratory. Gagnon and Simon (1973) make the significant contribution to the sociology of sexuality by describing sex as a socio-cultural phenomenon rather than a natural act. This means that if sex is a social construct, subject to various meanings and deemed to have different functions at different times and in different places, it can be reconstructed according to social, cultural and political trends, needs and pressures. This paved the way for the work of Foucault (1978, 1984) who developed an analysis of sexualities as products of cultures and defined by the interaction of the personal with social norms, scientific knowledge, religious and legal doctrine and authority. Subsequently, feminist thinkers and activists have sought to destabilize patriarchal values and practices by challenging the cultural, social and political hegemony of male heterosexuality. By questioning the orthodoxies of gender, its roles and meanings, feminist authors like MacKinnon (1989) have concluded that sexuality is a cultural effect dependent upon constructions of gender. From this analysis flows a critique of the essentialist paradigm which sets up heterosexuality, and all the associated baggage about gendered sexual roles, as the dominant discourse and other sexualities as subordinate varieties.

We might conclude by observing that in setting out a paradigm of particular sexualities through essentialist studies earlier in the century, academics and activists provided the framework and evidence which has made it possible latterly to deconstruct that paradigm. Definitions of sexuality have moved from previously fairly solid ground on which a simple mutual exclusivity of heterosexuality and homosexuality seemed adequate to describe human experience to a shifting terrain on which sexuality appears as a fluid, discursive phenomenon. A contemporary definition would have to acknowledge the complex interplay of social, cultural and intrapersonal factors in the production of a changing identity. We might describe sexuality as that element of identity which contains a sense of a self in which sexual feelings, ideologies, desires and needs are integrated with one another and reconciled with modes of sexual expression and behaviour. Bringing together our feelings, values and desires may be difficult, as may reconciling these with modes of expression and behaviour acceptable to ourselves and others. Without some reconciliation between these aspects of our internal world and ways of acting and interacting, we are vulnerable to feelings of dislocation between who we are and how we live. Reconciling feelings and actions does not take place only at a psychological level but in the context of the social world in which expressions of sexuality are differently valued. The inevitable consequence of this differentiation is that people who cannot reconcile their sexuality with those who are most socially valued can feel they themselves are less valued.

While on the one hand the weakening of prescriptive definitions opens the field for powerful legal arguments for the equalization of treatment of different sexualities, it also has the potential to undermine the resources available to minorities who feel a strong impulse to congregate around one identity label. In short, what is to be the relationship between sexual acts and identity? Can a gay man be gay in thought and not deed (as the Anglican Episcopal Church would seem to allow)? Can a heterosexual woman have a homosexual relationship and still feel herself to be heterosexual or ought she now regard herself as bisexual? At one level, the invention of a sexual identity which depends heavily on represen-tation of the self has reinvigorated the sexual act as a defining idea. As we shall see, history and the contemporary media have both striven to reinject sexual acts into representations of sexuality in order to keep the lines of distinction clear and position us still on the fringes of either reaction or revolution.

Representations of sexuality

Representations of sexuality are a central feature of contemporary popular culture. However, the possibilities for representation have been contested in a number of areas by special interest groups, and by the state in the manipulation of obscenity laws by police 'vice' squads and, paradoxically, given its daily content in terms of features, photographs, advertising and readers' letters, the tabloid press has often seen one of its most important editorial functions to be upholding notional standards of sexual morality.

As Epstein and Johnson have pointed out, grasping the influence of the media, especially the tabloid press is critical in the formulation of an understanding of how the wider sexual culture is constructed and what kinds of tools and resources we are supplied with to help us make sense of this environment (Epstein and Johnson, 1998). Part of their attempt to theorize about the links between politics, culture, schooling and sexuality charts a series of high profile outbursts of outrage in the tabloid press in the mid-1990s at the way that sexuality and sexual diversity has been represented to children and young people in schools. As Epstein and Johnson demonstrate in their unpicking of a series of 'scandals' surrounding the provision of sex education, the self-appointment of the tabloid press as a arbitrator on matters of sex and sexuality relies primarily on two constructs. First, the envisaging of a hierarchial arrangement of sexualities which implies both the primacy of one over others (heterosexuality over other sexualities) and the need for vigilance, resistance and even active action to suppress shifts within the hierarchy which threaten that dominance. Second, the identification of schools as particularly important sites in this struggle because young, innocent and ignorant minds are vulnerable to subversion and even corruption by teaching which lacks an explicit endorsement of heterosexuality as normative or 'natural'.

While, in general, tabloid coverage of the education of children and young people about sex and sexuality is presented as a straightforward issue of maintaining prescribed morals and morality, identities and behaviours against the insurgencies and challenges of alternatives, the tabloid press tends to adopt a slightly different approach to the coverage of adult sexuality. The overtly prudish moral tone is often turned down, perhaps in part, in reaction to the need to square the basically negative position on non-heterosexual sex and sexualities with perceived changes in public opinion and the political climate which no longer tolerate the rehearsal of explicit homophobia and prejudice against 'alternative' lifestyles and sexual identities. Tabloid coverage of 'Big Brother', the television series which pitches 'ordinary' people into a sealed community, subjects them to round the clock scrutiny via closed circuit cameras and invites the viewing public to vote them out one at time until a winner emerges, provides an interesting example of the way that media coverage negotiates the potential contradictions between acceptance of sexual difference and diversity and the maintenance of the basic moral framework which privileges heterosexuality.

The tabloid press expended a significant amount of effort in corralling the sexuality of one eventual winner, Nadia, a transsexual, in ways that did not explicitly denigrate it but which maintained its status as 'other'. In fact, her sexual identity became the chief focus of writing about her. Her previous life as a man was reported in *The Sun* on 2 June 2004 under the headline, 'Nadia before her sex swap – When he had a beard and was called Carlos'. Latterly, her father, who had not had contact with Nadia for some years, was sought out in South America and told about her sex change and his reactions (which were largely positive) reported. In general, the tabloid press focused on two specific aspects of identity; her appearance and her sexual proclivities and ambitions.

When Nadia's sexual identity was revealed to the other housemates by a member of the public, the press reported their reactions primarily in terms of their assessment of her physical appearance and their comments about how convincing Nadia was as a woman. They were reported as commenting on her 'great breasts' and the fact that, 'you would never have known that she was a he'. Interviewed after winning the competition, both *The Sunday Mirror* and *The People* of 8 August 2004, wrote about Nadia's sexual ambitions under the headlines, 'Transsexual TV show winner in Britain sets sights on first sex' and, 'Big Brother

Nadia: I want 3 in a bed rock', respectively. The headline in *The People* referring to Nadia's assertion that she wanted to celebrate her victory by, 'bagging two blokes for raunchy sex. The sex-swap brunette wants to bed a Fred Flintstone-style caveman lover AND a sensitive millionaire'. Both types of stories can be seen as shoring up heteronormativity by repeatedly drawing our attention to how Nadia's sexual identity both inhabits and departs from it. References to Nadia as the 'Portugeezer' serve to remind us over and again that 'she' was once 'he'.

For the tabloid press 'Big Brother' provides a particularly rich resource for this process of 'othering' sexuality. Press coverage can inhabit the discourses within which the program situates itself: the pseudo-scientific rubric of 'people-watching' which, in this case, is used to legitimate subjecting others to invasive surveillance, and manipulation of groups and individuals. In this context we are permitted to pry into the 'housemates' pasts and presents, to expose and unravel the components of their identities, including their sexualities, in order that we might understand them, and ultimately ourselves.

While Nadia seems to have settled for the positions offered to her by these discourses which set her up as a person defined primarily by her sexual identity she also, in interviews after winning the competition, signalled something more was at stake for her. Buried in the middle of coverage in *The People* on 8 August she 'revealed' that while 'sex is top of her priorities, Jason [a fellow house-mate] was top of her bonking hit-list when she met him; a second boob job is on the cards', that, 'public acceptance means more to her than any prize money'. Rejecting both the competitive element in the program and the attempts to maintain her 'other' status as a she/he she concluded, 'If you asked me to choose what is more important – the [prize] money for winning or the public loving me – it is the public, there is no contest. The whole reason for going into the house was so I could believe myself that I am a woman rather than be categorized as something else'.

This discussion of some of the media representations of sexuality and sexual identity within 'Big Brother' highlights some of the particularly rich contradictions in modern Western culture's definitions of sexuality. In her influential book *Epistemology of the Closet*, Eve Kosofsky Sedgwick (1994, p. 1) describes these contradictions as extremely powerful 'nodes of thought and knowledge' across 'twentieth century Western culture as a whole'. In tabloid media coverage of 'Big Brother', we see what Sedgwick describes as the 'minoritising view'. What Sedgwick says about homosexuality would apply equally to transsexuality: that it is only a matter for 'a small, distinct, relatively fixed . . . minority'. Nadia had been identified as one of 'them', and the question of identity is only an issue for 'them'. None of the heterosexual 'housemates' sexualities were subjected to such intense and sustained scrutiny and discussion. As the public, we have shared in both the prurient interest of the tabloid press in Nadia's past sexual identity within the context of fixed conceptions of gender, primarily and determinatively associated with particular sexual behaviours and desires. It is only in Nadia's own words about her hopes for acceptance that the possibilities for change to narrow and confining conceptualizations of sexuality and gender are aired. These are competing discourses which, Sedgwick argues, both structure and fragment our ways of knowing ourselves and the world.

Although Nadia did not come out as gay, her sexuality was uncovered through a process which parallels 'being outed'. But far from being a simple transliteration of the metaphor of 'coming out of the closet' as a wider and more general signifier that can be commonly used in everyday conversation produced in an enormous range of contexts, Sedgwick argues that:

> exactly the opposite is true. I think that a whole cluster of the most crucial sites for the contestation of meaning in twentieth century Western culture are consequentially and quite indelibly marked with the historical specificity of homosocial/homosexual definition.
>
> (Sedgwick, 1994, p. 72)

In this context we understand the tensions between secrecy, disclosure and private and public which Nadia experiences as an effect of an attempt at sexual and individual definition. We are able to recognize that our efforts to understand our own identities take place in the realm of competing yet co-existing discourses.

Even for those women and men who acknowledge their sexual attraction to people of the same sex, the question of identity is not simple. 'Dykes' or 'queens', 'butch/femme', 'straight-acting' or 'scene' are just some of the possibilities for self-identification that are open to homosexuals. There is not one homosexual identity but many. However, they all establish their meaning in a relationship with the 'other', whether that be a generic heterosexual other or another homosexuality. To this extent, they are all products of a minoritizing discourse. In his essay 'The Homosexual in Society', Robert Duncan argued against minoritizing discourses which produce a 'ghetto' or 'cult' of homosexual 'superiority'. He criticized what he saw as the triviality and vapidity of a developing homosexual subculture which sought to keep itself separate, secret and in some ways superior to a notional general population. In doing so, he created a simple opposition between being 'human' and being 'homosexual' which could potentially, in some readers' eyes, assign him to the category of self-hating gay man: 'It is hard . . . to say that this cult plays any other than an evil role in society' (Duncan cited in Blasius and Phelan, 1997, p. 231).

Duncan was actually arguing for the as-yet-unnamed act of 'coming out' to the whole of society rather than seeking a 'sense of sanctuary such as the Medieval Jew must have found in the ghetto' (Duncan cited in Blasius and Phelan, 1997, p. 232). He was regretting his own experience of being silent on the political issues and using the 'group language' of the cult. In his final paragraph he does ameliorate his criticism of members of the cult, yet at times his own language particularly in his comments on camp, tone and 'self-ridicule' foreshadows that of members of the 'anti-gay' movement in the 1990s (e.g. Simpson, 1996). Nevertheless, the final sentence of his argument (used as the epigraph to this chapter) encapsulates the sense of political responsibility every individual must recognize in the struggle for equality, and the importance of self-disclosure, that remains at the heart of radical campaigning organizations such as Outrage.

Sex has no history

In this section, we will attempt to give an overview of some key events in a history of sexuality and sexual identity. Like any history, it is inevitably partial and the narrative structured from one perspective. The context for our brief discussion is Western societies and cultures, particularly Britain: we will not attempt to consider sexuality in other cultures or anywhere else on the other side of this epistemological border.[1] The history from which we draw most heavily is largely one of legal prohibitions on same-sex activity, most often directed at male homosexuals, and the struggle by oppressed groups for some degree of equality in the eyes of the law. We have chosen to focus on three significant moments in this history, each separated from the preceding by nearly one thousand years. The purpose is not to dismiss the intervening stretches of time but rather to illustrate vividly how mutable are the social conventions around homosexuality. Throughout, we will view sexuality not as some essential expression of biological drives but as a cultural effect produced and changed by different discourses. The subheading to this section, taken from David Halperin's work, draws attention to this difference between sex ('a natural fact, grounded in the functioning of the body') and sexuality ('the appropriation of the human body and of its physiological capacities by an ideological discourse') (Halperin, 1993, p. 416). By looking at the shifting position of homosexuality in the eyes of the Christian Church, government, science and the law it is clear the extent to which sexuality is solicited by capital in the establishment and maintenance of particular kinds of social relationships between citizens/subjects and of particular kinds of social/moral order. In general, this has meant differentiating homosexuality from heterosexuality and privileging the latter in certain ways. In fact, heterosexuality has become the central resource of the capitalist, nationalist order as conservative visions of the heterosexual, 'nuclear' family as the basic building block of society imply. It provides the means for managing rights of succession and the transfer of capital and power, and the foundation for creating a belief in a natural national family. What our history shows us, in part, is the struggle to control that capital.

Although authors like Taylor (1997), have recently begun to explore the prehistory of sex through the study of early representations of the human being and body on artefacts and in paintings, studies of sexuality in history usually start with a number of observations about the supposed predilection of men in ancient Greece to bugger adolescent boys and the apparent acceptance of these 'homosexual', cross-generational relationships. This is either meant to show that homosexuality is the choice of educated and civilized people (one reading of Plato's *Symposium*, where the context for such relationships is educational in intent) or that it is an unspeakable, foreign vice (another reading of the same text by translators and editors of various historical periods who expunged the offending passages in Plato's original). It is clear, however, that the sexual activities which appear to be described in some classical Greek texts were not seen as an expression of any kind of 'sexual identity' that could be defined as homosexual. They were simply acts that took place in a completely different kind of relationship altogether. David Halperin has said that, '[s]ex is portrayed in Athenian documents not as a mutual enterprise in which two or more persons jointly engage but as an action performed by a social superior upon a social inferior' (Halperin, 1993, p. 418). Halperin presents the sexual dynamic of classical Athens as a relationship between a citizen 'penetrator' (male) and 'penetrated' minors. These 'minors' included women, post-pubertal 'free' males not old enough to be citizens and slaves. The penetrator and the penetrated each had separate 'identities' and the participation in the sexual act did not in any way bring them together in any shared identity based upon an identifiable 'sexuality'. Their personal, physical desires were real but 'their very desires had already been shaped by the shared cultural definition of sex as an activity that generally occurred only between a citizen and a non-citizen' (ibid., p. 419).

In his definitive study of Greek homosexuality, Kenneth Dover (1978) describes how Greek society, particularly between 480 BC and 146 BC, revolved around presumptions of the authority of adult male citizens and that sexual relations between men became overt and acceptable. However, these relationships took on a peculiarly stylized form and emotional tone and were largely confined to men of the higher social classes who mixed in more or less segregated groups as part of military and educational training. The central focus was on the development of a bond between an older man, an *erastes* (lover), and a younger man or boy, an *eromenos* (the loved). The older man, it was expected, would feel strong sexual attraction to the younger man, admiring his beauty, agility and physical attributes, and courting him with gifts. The younger man, rather than experience any emotional reciprocity, was expected to admire the older man for his wisdom and experience and look upon him as a model of masculinity. Over time it was anticipated that the relationship would alter as the younger man grew up, all emotional and sexual overtones would dim and the relationship would become one of friends.

The conventions about the emotional nature of the connection between the men in these relationships percolated through to influence the nature of their sexual intimacies. Officially at least, buggery was taboo, and in theory attracted the penalty of being stripped of one's citizenship. Hence, the usual method of intercourse was intercrural, the *erastes* being the active sexual partner. Sexual relationships between men of equal ages were frowned on, as was penetration of the *erastes*. The strict ideals about the nature of the relationship between men and the nature of Greek masculinity would be violated by such actions. As it stands, masculinity was associated with adult male status and sexual licence to be the penetrative and active partner. Another crucial aspect of Greek attitudes to homosexuality is the emphasis placed on restraint. The Platonic stress on transcending the real world and entering the world of Forms, where the universal essence of objects and ideas is arrayed, canonized restraint and emotional control. So, while Plato, and Socrates before him, accept and venerate homosexual feelings and relationships, their consummation is condemned since it shows passion blinding reason. Towards the end of his life, Plato was driven by inexorable logic, profoundly influential on later thinkers, to describe homosexual behaviour as unnatural. In Dover's translation, he writes:

> Anyone, who, in conformity with nature proposes to re-establish the law as it was before Laios, declaring that it was right not to join with men and boys in sexual intercourse as with females, adducing as evidence the nature of animals could, I think, make a very strong case.
>
> (Plato, *Laws*, 836c–e, (trans. in Dover, 1978, p. 166)

In the Roman Empire, as in the Greek, people were not categorized as hetero-sexual or homosexual. While prostitution, both male and female, flourished under official licence, emphasis was placed on the maintenance of culturally and socially sanctioned ideals of masculinity and femininity which resulted in a continuation of the Greek proscriptions of penetrative and penetrated sexual roles. The 'gender-bending' antics of the imperial classes attracted particular opprobrium from the Roman chattering classes. The satirist Juvenal, in his vitriolic *Second Satire*, turns his anger several times on effeminacy among the ruling classes. He castigates the Emperor Domitian for reintroducing tough laws on sexual activity while indulging in incest and sodomy, reserving his harshest judgements for the soldier Emperor Otho, whom, he suggests, betrays ideals of Roman masculinity through his effeminacy:

> Another queen or queer, even nastier/holds a hand mirror his face to show/the very spectre of the pathic Otho/in which he admired his uniform/while sounding the charge at Bedriacum./Is this the lesson of Rome's recent story/'The path of beauty is the path to glory?'
>
> (Juvenal, *Satire II*, 98–103 (trans. Plumb, 1968, p. 36)

Clearly, while censorious attitudes towards certain types of sexuality emerge in Hellenistic cultures the focus falls on twisting and breaking gender roles and not on sexual identity as a separate entity. A new and peculiar moral sensibility is added to these attitudes by the construction of sexuality emerging with early Judaeo-Christian doctrine and finding full voice in the teaching of the Christian Church in medieval Europe (Richards, 1990). Sexual feeling and experience became synonymous with sin. As St Anselm, Archbishop of Canterbury at the end of the eleventh century, wrote:

> There is one evil, an evil above all other evils, that I am aware is always with me, that grievously and piteously lacerates and afflicts my soul. The evil is sexual desire, carnal delight, the storm of lust that has smashed and battered my unhappy soul, drained it of all strength and left it weak and empty.
>
> (cited in Richards, 1990)

As the teaching of St Paul stressed, celibacy was therefore the highest achievable ideal and reproductive sex in the context of marriage an acceptable second best. The Church's control of sexual behaviour was extended principally through the establishment of a legal, sacred marriage service which celebrated, sanctified and moralized about the complementary roles of men and women exemplified by the biblical story of Adam and Eve. For women, this resulted in typification as at once inferior, as the product of Adam's body, and evil, for succumbing to the serpent's temptation. This connection between female sexuality and sinfulness made it logical to sanction wife-beating, as a measure for instilling discipline and the forbidding of women from holding public office or undertaking any military service.

The Church's view of the role of sex inside and outside of marriage is illustrated by accounts of confessions and penances for sexual acts. Payer's (1984) work on the penitentials (books guiding priests in determining the gravity of various sins and the consequent scale of penance) shows a broadly consistent religious attitude towards sexual activity. Sexual matters formed the largest single category of offences in most penitentials. Although the details of penances varied, they were generally based on fasting on bread and water and avoiding sex for a number of consecutive days in multiples of ten. The Church pronounced the proper form of intercourse within marriage as penetrative vaginal sex with the man lying on top of the woman. Dorsal intercourse, with the woman on top, would earn three years' penance; anal intercourse seven years'. Sex was encouraged only at night and then partially clothed. Burchard of Worms (d. 1025) graded penitentials as follows: ten days on bread and water for male masturbation by hand, twenty days if it involved a perforated piece of wood. Interestingly, sexual intercourse with a female servant attracted the same penalty, illustrating the indulgence extended to young men and the social position and relative (un)importance of women. Highest penalties were reserved for incest, sodomy and bestiality. Burchard also proscribed the telling of dirty jokes, mixed bathing and fondling.

Medieval theology has no definition of homosexuality as such, only of homosexual acts. In fact, the terms used by St Paul to condemn homosexual sexual acts imply their occurrence only among heterosexual people. The line was very clear. Drawing on the Book of Leviticus (18:22 and 20:13), homosexual sex was ranked alongside incest, adultery and bestiality as the most serious sin. While the Church dealt in sexual acts, there is evidence to suggest that a homosexual subculture centred on male brothels in barbers' shops and bath-houses sprung up in some French and Italian cities in the twelfth century (Boswell, 1980). Along with the emergence of poetry and song extolling the virtues of erotic love between men, an argot is recorded which refers to young gay men as 'Ganymedes', sex as 'The Game', and cruising as 'Hunting'. Perhaps partially in reaction to this emergent subculture, theologians began to conceptualize homosexuality as an insidious inversion of 'natural', God-given laws. They opined that it was inconceivable that God should have been perverse enough to create sexual activities which undermined His own law, so homosexuality must be the product of a deviant, unnatural and ungodly mind. Consequently, consent to homosexual sex was no defence. By the end of the twelfth century, monarchies in England, France and Spain decreed death as a suitable punishment for those convicted of homosexual acts.

A state of illegality effectively lasted for a further 700 years. In the years following the trial, conviction and jailing of Oscar Wilde in 1895, although there was no concerted attempt to force a liberalization of the law in Great Britain, homosexuality became more visible at the fringes of artistic society. The repression seemed to have been irretrievably undermined by the world wars in which sexual liberalism spread among the ranks of civilians and the armed forces alike. With the advent of peace in 1945, however, sexual morals were supposed to be restored. The prosecution of gay men rose to new heights. In a climate of political retrenchment, the numbers of men arrested by the police and convicted rose threefold. A series of high-profile cases reached a peak early in 1954 with the conviction of Lord Montagu of Beaulieu, Peter Wildeblood, the diplomatic correspondent of the *Daily Mail* and Michael Pitt-Rivers, a wealthy land-owner, for conspiring to incite two RAF men to 'commit unnatural offences'. The case achieved notoriety, not only because of the social status of the defendants but because the prosecution painted a lurid scene of debauchery in a beach hut on the Beaulieu estate. Regardless of the fact that all the men were consenting adults and the discovery that both Montagu's and Wildeblood's homes were burgled in suspicious circumstances during the course of the trial, the defendants were convicted and sentenced to custody. They found themselves at the centre of a public debate about homosexual rights. A popular limerick of the time ridiculed the law:

An aircraftsman named McNally
Was caught with a lord in a chalet
The judge said my dears
They're patently queers
Give them two years
For being too pally.

Pressure built for a reassessment of the law fuelled by the Church of England's Moral Welfare Council's publication of *The Problem of Homosexuality: An Interim Report*, which stated that although sex between men was undoubtedly a sin, so too were adultery and fornication, neither of which attracted legal censure. A notable Tory MP, Sir Robert Boothby, lobbied the Home Secretary, Maxwell Fyfe, for a Royal Commission on the matter. Contemporaneously, the Hardwicke Society, a senior debating forum for barristers, carried the motion 'The penal laws relating to homosexual offences are outmoded and should be changed'.

Succumbing to the inevitable, the Home Secretary relented to mounting pressure and established the Departmental Committee on Homosexual Offences and Prostitution under the aegis of John Wolfenden, the Vice-Chancellor of Reading University. This committee sat for the first time on 4 August 1954 and heard evidence from over 200 individuals and groups in the course of more than sixty meetings before publishing its report in September 1957. The committee quickly reached the conclusion that while homosexuality might be morally unacceptable, it could not be stamped out by legislation and continued criminalization was legally untenable since it exposed homosexual men to blackmail and represented an indefensible intrusion into personal privacy. Consequently, Wolfenden's report concluded with the recommendation that homosexual behaviour in private between consenting adults (over twenty-one) should be decriminalized. Wolfenden added that it was not the business of law to 'settle questions of morality, to interfere in the private lives of the citizens; it is only when public decency is offended that the law is entitled to step in and institute criminal proceedings'.

The report received blanket coverage in the press. Seven national newspapers with a combined readership of over 60 per cent of the public gave the report favourable coverage; only two condemned it. However, as Wilde observed of the Labouchere Act, it was not public opinion but politicians' fear for their seats which determines what passes to the statute book. As if to prove the veracity of Wilde's observation that, 'It is not so much public opinion as public officials that need educating,' H. Montgomery Hyde was the first, but not the last, MP to be deselected by his constituency committee in the run-up to the 1959 election for supporting the adoption of Wolfenden's recommendations into law. It was observed, 'We cannot have as our member one who condones unnatural vice.' It took seven parliamentary debates on the Wolfenden Report between 1958 and 1967 before the recommendations were adopted into law, and only then by passing initially through the House of Lords where members could vote freely without having to concern themselves with constituency committees.

It would be disingenuous to interpret these historical events as evidence of the forces of reaction carving out a homosexual identity rather than any gay identity emerging through the activities of people themselves. The process of the invention of sexuality *per se*, and of a stigmatized gay identity in particular, is a complex interaction of action and reaction. However, authority has managed successfully to corral sexual acts into an identity which contains implications of ungodliness, unnaturalness and even potentially sedition. These themes reappear in near-contemporary inventions of HIV/AIDS as a 'gay plague', and, between 1997 and 1999, British newspaper, *The Sun* expressed fears about a gay cabal at the heart of the New Labour government. A result of the politicization of sexuality by the state, the Church and the law has been to harden political activism among those affected by such moralizing and sermonizing. The modern gay rights movement has come to focus its attention on deficits in human rights which can only be addressed by the state. In the penultimate section of this chapter we look at three particular instances of contestation about equality of sexualities which illustrate these contemporary concerns.

Sexuality and equality: some current issues

With the emergence of HIV in the United Kingdom in the early 1980s gay men were subjected to a backlash of stigmatization. Partly fuelled by perceptions that gay men were responsible for the spread of HIV, surveys of British social attitudes throughout the 1980s showed a rising disapproval of homosexuality among a large section of the public. The Conservative government saw an opportunity to capitalize on these negative attitudes and embarrass Labour-led local authorities (many of which supported lesbian, gay and bisexual organizations) by introducing legislation which made it illegal for local authorities to, 'intentionally [to] promote homosexuality or publish material with the intention of promoting homosexuality', or to 'promote the teaching in any maintained school of the acceptability of homosexuality as a pretended family relationship'. The amendment to Local Government Act (1988), widely known as Section 28, in reference to the number which denoted its location within the statute, was, despite vague wording and widespread lack of clarity about its legal standing, effective in signalling an intention to return to the position prior to 1967 in which gay men and lesbians were not to behave as if their relationships were valid or as if they merited equal rights with heterosexuals. As recent research by Viv Ellis (Ellis with High, 2004, Ellis, 2005) has demonstrated, Section 28 may have led directly to the increases in the proportion of students reporting problems in school associated with their sexuality, particularly in relation to isolation, verbal abuse, teasing, physical abuse, ostracization and pressure to conform. Section 28 may have contributed to the marginalization of lesbian, gay and bisexual young people and fuelled some teachers' sense of their authority to broadcast moral judgements about their pupils.

The Labour administration which came to power in 1997 was committed to repeal but cautious both about public opinion and entering into a protracted and bitter struggle with the House of Lords which might obstruct its attempts at constitutional reform. It was only in 2003 that the Act was finally repealed and, then as we shall see, not without the institution of other legislation which replaced some of the proscriptions of Section 28. Similarly, legislation to equalize the age of consent at sixteen (previously young men could only consent to sex with another man once they were aged eighteen) was coupled with the establishment of proscriptive legislation elsewhere in the Statute book. The reform of the laws relating to age of consent was precipitated directly by the actions of Chris Morris, at the time a sixteen-year-old student, and Euan Sutherland who took their case for equal treatment under the law on sexual consent to the European Court of Human Rights. Earlier that year the Court had handed down a preliminary ruling in favour of Lisa Grant, an employee of South-West Trains who had sought equal access to travel and pension rights for her female partner to those extended to heterosexual employees' partners. While the European Court was clearly keen to support equalization of gay rights and public opinion seemed to be untroubled and even supportive, the British Parliament initially stalled on the important issue of forcing a Bill through the Lords.

Again deadlock seemed to be broken by shoring up the law of consent elsewhere. So, in 2003 a new Sexual Offences Act (2003) came into force which forbids any sexual activity between under 16s, ranging from touching to sexual intercourse. Although the government maintained the Act was put in place to protect children from inappropriate sexual attention and that it would instruct the Crown Prosecution Service (the organization which decides whether cases presented to it by the police should go to court) not to prosecute under-16s for consensual sexual activity, was to send the net effect of a strong message about sex and sexuality remaining the preserve of adulthood.

The reaction to the bitter debates about effect of repeal of Section 28 on the education of young people was deflected by introducing a passage to an Education Act which placed a responsibility on the Secretary of State for Education] to ensure that pupils at state-maintained schools

> (a) . . . learn the nature of marriage and its importance for family life and the bringing up of children, and,
>
> (b) . . . are protected from teaching and materials which are inappropriate having regard to the age and the religious and cultural background of the pupils concerned.
>
> (Learning and Skills Act, 2000, Section 148)

This has ensured that despite the repeal of Section 28, there is still scope for parents or others to challenge activities in schools in the context of sex education which they deem offensive. While it is clearly not unreasonable to provide parents and carers with some power to act in matters relating to their children, in this context, the institution of this Act was clearly, in part, intended to signal to teachers that their activities in relation to teaching about sexuality would still be subject to regulation.

Common bonds? LGBT equality, 'race', class and gender

The relationship between the history for the struggle for equality in terms of sexuality and the struggle for equality in terms of 'race', class and gender is, at times, contradictory and conflicting. There is insufficient space to enter into this debate fully here but we will make brief comments on some of the problematic areas. First, the possibilities for representations of sexuality have been challenged at times not only by reactionary self-appointed guardians of morality and the state, but by feminists committed to the anti-pornography and lesbian-feminism movements whose starting point has been the exploitation of female subjects by a 'phallocracy' (Frye, 1981; Rubin, 1993). Feminists have also criticized some male homosexuals for appropriating a stereotypical female gender identity which is bound up with notions of 'effeminacy' at the one end of the spectrum and 'camp' at the other.[2] There have also been criticisms of the black community in Britain and North America (from within those communities) for a perceived, endemic homophobia that is, at times, celebrated publicly in popular cultural representations (Harper, 1991).[3] And, often, the emergence of the homosexual, and of homosexuality leading to an identity choice, is seen as a consequence of a process that began with the rise of capitalism and the formation of the working class. Some commentators have explicitly identified an association between the increasing influence of capitalism and the opening up of possibilities for diverse sexual expression. The historian John D'Emilio has said that:

> gay men and lesbians have not always existed. Their emergence is associated with the relations of capitalism; it has been the historical development of capitalism – more specifically the free labour system that has allowed large numbers of men and women in the late twentieth century to call themselves gay, to see themselves as part of a community of similar men and women, and to organise politically on the basis of that identity.
>
> (D'Emilio, 1983, p. 468)

D'Emilio argues that it was the changes in the nature and role of the family produced by the free-labour market under capitalism that created the possibilities for diversity of sexual expression and the formation of sexual identities. To oversimplify his argument, he believes that, as the family was no longer 'an independent unit of production' (ibid., p. 469), there was no need to produce many children to labour in this unit. It became possible for individuals to live outside the family unit and to realize erotic lives that did not need to find their expression in reproductive sex. Capitalism allows the possibility for individuals to be economically independent, whereas the former model of family-based units of production made this virtually impossible. However, D'Emilio also recognizes that while capitalism makes this independence a possibility, it also values the family highly as a social structure that can, to some extent, guarantee continuity of production and the maintenance of the status quo. Capitalism, he says, forces individuals into families 'at least long enough to reproduce the next generation of workers' and, simultaneously, into the discourses of heterosexism and homophobia (ibid., p. 474).

But it is not possible to say that these discourses are simply a product of capitalism or that the oppression of dissident sexualties is one of its functions. For example, Marxism itself has been appropriated in such a way as to become implicated in pathologizing sexual behaviour. The boast made by groups such as the Socialist Workers Party that Bolshevik Russia abolished anti-homosexual laws is, albeit to be understood to be made in the context of a critique of Stalinism, profoundly misleading: all Tsarist laws were abolished shortly after the revolution, effectively legalizing murder (Edge, 1995, pp. 37–9). Indeed, later Stalinist legislation and public health documents pathologized homosexuality and made it subject to 'treatment' in state hospitals (ibid., p. 41). Edge goes on to outline a relationship between homosexuals and revolutionary socialists in the latter half of the twentieth century in which issues of class equality are consistently put above those of equality in terms of sexuality to the extent that violent homophobia is put to one side.[4] The very problem with sexuality for the revolutionary left, according to Edge, is that it makes sexual identity inequality an issue in itself rather than assimilating it into the common struggle against capitalist social class inequalities. The notion of a 'gay "identity" or "community" [becomes] a separatist diversion' (ibid., p. 47) to the 'greater' fight against capitalism.

Edge argues instead for the continued development of an autonomous lesbian and gay community on the political left which is able to fight for equality on its own terms, cutting across other categories of social injustice. In doing so, he is echoing Gayle Rubin, who argued for a 'radical theory' of resistance to the discourses of oppression that was not solely based on feminism:

> Sex is a vector of oppression. The system of sexual oppression cuts across other codes of social inequality, sorting out individuals and groups according to its own intrinsic dynamics. Its is not reducible to, or understandable in terms of, class, race, ethnicity, or gender . . . even the most privileged are not immune to sexual oppression.
>
> (Rubin, 1993, p. 22)

The difficulties with locating and assimilating the struggle for lesbian and gay equality within a wider political struggle for equality, focused on inequalities of distributions of wealth and power, are illustrated in the debate between Nancy Fraser and Judith Butler in the *New Left Review* (Fraser, 1997, 1998; Butler, 1998).

Both authors seek, in Fraser's words, to 'combine an egalitarian politics of redistribution with an emancipatory politics of recognition' with regard to lesbian and gay equality. Both identify the rise of so-called cultural politics as problematic in that it seems to position some issues, like lesbian and gay equality, as ones of 'cultural misrecognition' rather than the social politics of redistribution. But where Fraser identifies difficulties with (re)appropriating lesbian and gay equality within the redistributive struggle because it might mean some loss of the sense of solidarity and the power that lesbians and gays derive from a culturally differentiated identity, Butler is confident that there is no potential for a loss of this kind since the politics of distribution can only be understood in terms of the reproduction of gender relationships which lead to heteronormativity and feed homophobic prejudices and discrimination.

Some socialist activists seem to have made sense of the difficulties exposed in this debate by making a link between the establishment of political and social equality and an end to the misrecognition of all sexual minorities. Identifying Section 28 of the Local Government Act (see the following chapter for a fuller discussion) and the inequality in ages of consent for heterosexual and homosexual men, as particular targets, Vallee *et al.* (1992), in a *Militant* publication on gay rights, identified the Thatcherite legal and rhetorical bolstering of the 'family' as a tactic for scape-goating a whole raft of minorities and blaming them for the failings of capitalism.

In this chapter we have illustrated that, in our view, there are inextricable links between struggles for cultural recognition and wider struggles for fairer social and economic distribution. And where the struggle seems, at first, to be solely about cultural recognition, we are of the view that it is always potentially about a political and economic freedom too, because invisibility can and does impede equal gay and lesbian participation in social actions and institutions.

Conclusion

There is some evidence of a steady, if not inexorable, shift in British political and social life in relation to equality for LGBT people. A recent survey of British Social Attitudes (National Centre for Social Research, 2000) shows a decreasing proportion of the population, particularly among the young, who think that, 'two adults of the same sex having sexual relations' is 'always wrong' (a 12 per cent decrease among both men and women from 56 per cent to 44 per cent and 44 per cent to 32 per cent respectively). The Conservative party leadership has recently convened a 'summit' with gay groups, dropped its support for the restoration of Section 28 and has promised to offer Tory MPs a free vote on proposals to allow civil partnerships for lesbian and gay couples. But, these changes are not uncontested from within the Right. Some Conservative MPs have condemned the 'summit' as a cynical attempt to attract the 'pink' vote and others see it as an attempt to marginalize the 'family'. Meantime, as Ellis's research has suggested (Ellis with High, 2004), the quality of the educational experience for young lesbian, gay and bisexual people shows no sign of improving and may, in fact be worse than ever. They identify a need to shift the content of sex education from essentialist approaches to sexuality to those which acknowledge it as an aspect of culture and identity. They also point to 'issue-driven' curricula which contribute to the marginalization of homosexuality, its representation as a 'controversial' issue, the continued pathologization of homosexuality as either a mental illness or indication of vulnerability to HIV, and the explicitly homophobic remarks and discriminatory actions on the part of teachers which they note, '. . . as reported by our respondents – had no compunction about demonstrating a form of prejudice that could have led to disciplinary action in the case of gender or "race"' (ibid.: 222) as essential contextual components in redressing inequalities in ways that will concretely improve young people's lives.

The issue of the role of schools in educating young people about sexualities is one we will return to in the next chapter in this book, but what we have attempted here is to explore the ways in which homosexuality has been constructed as a negative, subordinate collection of activities and identities in relation to heterosexuality. We have demonstrated how the contemporary invention of sexualities has evolved, in part, through the struggles of the repressed, principally gay men and women, against reaction and social authority which has denied them equal rights with straight men. Ellis's research illustrates the extent to which an embittered and hostile heterosexuality still succeeds in driving to the periphery alternative sexual lifestyles and identities. The message is clear that sexuality represents a cultural field in which the personal and private have been made political. Sexuality has been commodified by the interest of the press and made a legitimate concern of the state. As citizens and subjects, we are all implicated in a struggle to make sexual identities for ourselves, and defend those of others. As teachers, it is inevitable that engagement with young people will mean engagement with the political reality of sexualities. To realize the legitimacy of that engagement is only to reflect an awareness that young people are particularly vulnerable to the play of negative constructions of sexualities. And to begin, we must, as Halperin (1993, p. 426) notes:

> train ourselves to recognise conventions of feeling as well as conventions of behaviour and to interpret the intricate texture of personal life as an artefact, as the determinate outcome, of a complex and arbitrary constellation of cultural processes. We must, in short, be willing to admit that what seem to be our most inward, authentic, and private experiences are actually, in Adrienne Rich's admirable phrase, 'shared, unnecessary/and political'.

Notes

1   The anthropologist Gilbert Herdt offers an interesting comparative study of sexualities in different cultural contexts in *Same Sex, Different Cultures* (Oxford: Westview, 1997).
2   These beliefs are reflected in the journalism of popular British feminists such as Julie Burchill.
3   See also the coverage in the black British weekly, *The Voice*, following the footballer Justin Fashanu's coming out as a gay man and also following his suicide in 1998.
4   Edge quotes the SWP writer Mark Brown: 'Homophobia divides working class people. Only the working class can destroy the homophobic capitalist system. There can be no gay liberation without socialism' ('Socialism or Separatism?', *Rouge*, 18, London, 1994; Edge, 1995, p. 11).

References

Act of Parliament (2000) Learning and Skills Act, London: HMSO
Act of Parliament (2003) Sexual Offences Act, London: HMSO
Blasius, M. and Phelan, S. (eds) (1997) *We Are Everywhere: A Historical Sourcebook of Gay and Lesbian Politics*, London: Routledge
Boswell, J. (1980) *Christianity, Homosexuality and Social Tolerance*, Chicago: Chicago University Press
Butler, J. (1998) 'Merely Cultural', *New Left Review*, 227, 33–45
D'Emilio, J. (1983) 'Capitalism and Gay Identity', in Snitow, A., Stansell, C. and Thompson, S. (eds), *Powers of Desire: The Politics of Sexuality*; reprinted in Abelove, H., Barale, M.A. and Halperin, D.M. (eds), *The Lesbian and Gay Studies Reader*, London: Routledge, 1993, pp. 467–78
Dover, K.J. (1978) *Greek Homosexuality*, Cambridge, MA: Harvard University Press
Duncan, R. (1944) 'The Homosexual in Society', *Politics* (August); reprinted in Blasius, M. and Phelan, S. (eds), *We Are Everywhere: A Historical Sourcebook of Gay and Lesbian Politics*, London: Routledge, 1997, pp. 230–3
Edge, S. (1995) *With Friends Like These*, Marxism and Gay Politics, London: Cassell
Ellis, V. (2005) 'Sexuality, strategic essentialism and the high school curriculum; or, 'how to be a particular non-contradictory person within a consistent story line'; paper presented at the American Educational Research Association Annual Meeting, Montreal, 11–15 April, 2005
Ellis, V. with High, S. (2004) Something to Tell You: Gay, Lesbian or Bisexual Young

People's Experiences of Secondary Schooling, *British Educational Research Journal*, 30(2), 213–25

Epstein, D. and Johnson, R. (1998) *Schooling Sexualities*, Buckingham: Open University Press

Foucault, M. (1978) *History of Sexuality*, Vol. 1, New York: Pantheon

Foucault, M. (1984) *The Use of Pleasure: Volume Two of The History of Sexuality* (trans. R. Hurley), Harmondsworth: Penguin

Fraser, N. (1997) 'Comment: A Rejoinder to Iris Young', *New Left Review*, 223, pp. 126–9

Fraser, N. (1998) 'Comment: Heterosexism, Misrecognition and Capitalism: A Response to Judith Butler', *New Left Review*, 228, 140–9

Frye, M. (1981) 'Lesbian Feminism and the Gay Rights Movement'; reprinted in Blasius, M. and Phelan, S. (eds), *We Are Everywhere: A Historical Sourcebook of Gay and Lesbian Politics*, London: Routledge, 1997

Gagnon, J. and Simon, W. (1973) *Sexual Conduct: The Social Sources of Human Sexuality*, London: Hutchinson

Halperin, D.M. (1989) 'Is There a History of Sexuality?', *History and Theory* 28, pp. 257–74; reprinted in Abelove, H., Barale, M.A. and Halperin, D.M. (eds), *The Lesbian and Gay Studies Reader*, London: Routledge, 1993, pp. 416–31

Harper, P.B. (1991) 'Eloquence and Epitaph: Black Nationalism and the Homophobic Impulse in Responses to the Death of Max Robinson', *Social Text* 28, 68–86; reprinted in Abelove, H., Barale, M.A. and Halperin, D.M. (eds), *The Lesbian and Gay Studies Reader*, London: Routledge, 1993, pp. 159–75

Herdt, G. (1997) *Same Sex, Different Cultures*, Oxford: Westview

Kinsey, A.C., Pomeroy, W.B. and Martin, C.E. (1948) *Sexual Behavior in the Human Male*, Philadelphia: W.B. Saunders

Kinsey, A.C., Pomeroy, W.B., Martin, C.E. and Gebhard, P.H. (1953) *Sexual Behavior in the Human Female*, Philadelphia: W.B. Saunders

MacKinnon, C. (1989) *Towards a Feminist Theory of the State*, Cambridge, MA: Harvard University Press

National Centre for Social Research (2000) *British Social Attitudes: Focusing on Diversity*, London: Sage

Payer, P. (1984) *Sex and the Penitentials*, Toronto: Toronto University Press

Plumb, C. (1968) *Juvenal: The Satires*, London: Panther Books

Richards, J. (1990) *Sex, Dissidence and Damnation: Minority Groups in the Middle Ages*, London: Routledge

Rubin, G.S. (1993) 'Thinking Sex: Notes for a Radical Theory of the Politics of Sexuality'; revised edition reprinted in Abelove, H., Barale, M.A. and Halperin, D.M. (eds), *The Lesbian and Gay Studies Reader*, London: Routledge, 1993, pp. 3–44

Sedgwick, E.K. (1994) *Epistemology of the Closet*, London: Penguin

Simpson, M. (ed.) (1996) *Anti-Gay*, London: Freedom Books

Taylor, T. (1997) *The Prehistory of Sex: Four Million Years of Human Sexual Culture*, London: Fourth Estate

Ulrichs, K.H. (1994) *The Riddle of 'Man-manly' Love: The Pioneering Work on Male Homosexuality* (trans. Michael A. Lombardi-Nash), Buffalo, NY: Prometheus Books

Ulrichs, K.H. (1997) *Araxe5: Appeal for the Liberation of the Urnings's Nature from Penal Law* (trans. James Steakley); new translation of extract in Blasius, M. and Phelan, S. (eds), *We Are Everywhere: A Historical Sourcebook of Gay and Lesbian Politics*, London: Routledge, 1997

Vallee, M., Redwood, H. and Evenden, M. (1992) *Out, Proud and Militant: The Fight for Lesbian and Gay Rights and the Fight for Socialism*, London: Militant Publications

Wilde, O. (1895) Extract from the trial transcript; reprinted in Blasius, M. and Phelan, S. (eds), *We Are Everywhere: A Historical Sourcebook of Gay and Lesbian Politics*, London: Routledge, 1997, pp. 111–12

6   Straight talking
Challenges in teaching and learning about sexuality and homophobia in schools

Simon Forrest

Introduction

Things that could have made a difference:

- open discussion of homosexuality in class (not discussed as a problem);
- open discussion of the oppression of lesbians and gays;
- role models;
- talks by ex-students;
- plays;
- books;
- teachers standing up for you;
- being taken seriously.

(Young lesbian, reported in Rogers, 1994, p. 64)

To learn about homosexualities would be helpful. What is masturbation on the feminine side? To understand what it is like when going through (and having) sexual intercourse would be information. To explore female genitalia deeper would be interesting. What is a period? IN DETAIL

(Anonymous questions in a 'suggestion box' on sex education from a boy in Year 9)

Why has teaching about sex and sexuality in schools failed to satisfy the evident needs of these young people? What has prevented teachers from affirming young lesbian, gay, bisexual and transgendered (LGBT) people's identity? Why do teachers steer clear of answering questions like those on the boy's list? What is the effect of not dealing with these concerns? What issue of equality is at stake here? This chapter sets out to address these questions by exploring the phenomenon of homophobia in English secondary schools. My aim is first to provide some illustrative accounts of how sexuality is imbricated in teaching, learning and extra-curricula aspects of schooling; second, to give a brief description of the statutory requirements and guidance to schools in relation to young people, sex and sexuality; third, to suggest some practical strategies for dealing with questions and concerns like those raised above; and, fourth, to suggest how tackling homophobia within schools addresses a deficit in equal rights.

Young people, sexuality and school

Schools can be a particular focus when we think about how and what young people learn about sexuality. This no doubt reflects the combined effects of the spotlight thrown onto school-based sex education by the largely prurient media attention and the high degree of governmental policy activity in the area. These two interests generally spiral round each other in 'feeding-frenzies' with fairly predictable ideological positions occupied by the government and the tabloid press. As a long-term media mapping exercise by Patricia Kingori *et al.* (2004) has shown, these 'frenzies' lead to the production of coverage which is often both distorted, hyperbolic, and in which the story is used primarily as a means to rehearse the ideological position of the paper. In recent years the UK has seen headlines like, 'Scandal of sex lessons for kids aged 7' (*Daily Express*, 27.02.2002), 'Pill plan for schoolgirls gets furious response', (*The News* (Portsmouth), 26.02.2000) and '900 pupils given sex aids at school' (*Bicester Advertiser*, 05.06.2002). All of which conspire to form the impression that schools are both very active and the most important site of learning about sexuality for young people.

However, much of what young people learn comes from outside the school. The ever-expanding corpus of strategy, policy and practice work by international organisations acknowledges that it is through the family, community and media that young people first learn about sexuality, and, moreover, that these sources, like the content and practice schooling itself, are shaped by the norms, the values and resources made available by the wider socio-cultural context. For example, in a recent report on conceptions and births to teenagers living in rich nations, UNICEF, identified a wide range of factors which influence sexuality, sexual behaviour and, the focus in the case of this report, conceptions:

> . . . includ[ing] the spread of cheap, safe and effective contraception, the liberalization of abortion law, the progress made by women towards educational and career equality, the widespread rejection of traditional sexual codes, and the emergence of a more sexualised society as old taboos have fallen away and the sexual imagery and messages have permeated the information environment.
>
> (UNICEF, 2001: 8)

As well as sketching the breadth and depth of influences on sexuality, the UNICEF report is also valuable for identifying the role that values and beliefs play in constructing the 'problem' and circumscribing the potential solutions. This meta-analytical observation, that taking up a particular paradigmatic approach will *de facto* define both the 'problem' and limit the epistemological and ethical possibilities available to address it, holds as well for issues about homophobia and the exclusion of LGBT issues from most sex education. So, how is the 'problem' defined?

Looking again, initially to International bodies, the 'problem' of non-heterosexual relationships and sexualities is usually defined in terms of human rights. For example, the World Health Organisation argues that existing International Human Right documents already include sexual rights. For the WHO, the right,

> ... of all persons, free of coercion, discrimination and violence, to: the highest attainable standard of health in relation to sexuality, including access to sexual and reproductive health care services; seek, receive and impart information in relation to sexuality; sexuality education; respect for bodily integrity; choice of partner; decide to be sexually active or not; consensual sexual relations; consensual marriage; decide whether or not, and when to have children; and to pursue a satisfying, safe and pleasurable sexual life, is self-evidently part of their wider human rights.
>
> (WHO, 2003a)

In this reading, the 'problem' lies not with people who chose to form relationships with people of the same sex, for this is their human right, but with those who would seek to stigmatise, discriminate or act against them for it. In this context, homophobia is assigned the same status as racial and sexist discrimination and, moreover, linked by WHO to poorer health outcomes. As the WHO submission to the fifty-ninth Session of the UN Commission on Human Rights stated (WHO, 2003b),

> ... Discrimination causes and magnifies poverty and ill health. In other words, overt or implicit discrimination can lie at the root of poor health status. The link between health and discrimination leads to the conclusion that the respect, protection, and fulfilment of human rights can reduce vulnerability to, and impact of, ill health. Societies that address racism, sexism, xenophobia, and homophobia also tend to provide for better health.

So, what do young people learn about sexuality and how? Learning about sexuality starts in infancy and goes on throughout a person's life. There is good empirical evidence which shows that children from age 5 can identify aspects of sexuality and how it relates to adult relationships and, furthermore, articulate how sexuality is gendered. For example, Janus and Bess (1976) found children from Grade 2 telling stories about how kissing is what girls and boys do together, by the fourth and fifth grade, the following themes were predominant: touching and its association with sex, bodily shapes and personal tastes, awareness of intimate sexual activity, and privacy with the opposite sex. Similarly, Terry Brown's work with 6/7 and 10/11 year olds has shown the formation of strong perceived connections between sexual behaviour, sexuality, gender and relationships, and, furthermore, demonstrated the degree to which heteronormativity has permeated children's worlds with all images and accounts of sexuality pairing women and men and showing men in dominant and women in submissive sexual roles (Brown, 1995). The pervasiveness of the gendering of sexuality which takes place in childhood, and its consequent casual, almost unnoticed collusion with heteronormativity has been elegantly described through accounts of playground and classroom activities (Epstein, 1995; 1997a; 1997b).

The development attitudes, beliefs and narrativisations of sexuality are coupled with and supplemented by the accumulation of sexual experience throughout childhood. The work of Larsson and Svedin (2002), for example, involving the gathering of retrospective accounts from teenagers of their experiences prior to 13 years old shows massive majorities have explored their own bodies, kissed, cuddled and talked about sex with other children and a significant proportion of boys have looked at pornography. This work and others confirms high levels of sexual curiosity among primary-school aged children, tracks emergent gender differences reflecting socialisation processes which construct masculine and feminine sexuality as complementary parts of a dominant and normative hetero-sexuality (Haugarrd, 1996; Greenwald and Leitenberg, 1989).

Notwithstanding the evident importance of these early childhood experiences to the formation of sexual identity, adolescence tends to be regarded as a particularly significant period in this process and is frequently dramatised as a time of intense physical and psychological development coupled with emergent emotional and social independence from the family as young people wrestle with the needs to understand dominant social context, norms and proscriptions about sexuality and to reconcile and integrate these with the development of an independent and unique identity (Moore and Rosenthal, 1993). Becoming successfully and healthily sexual, feeling confident and secure about one's sexual identity, feelings and experiences, is critical in feeling positive about one's whole self.

For young LGBT people, heteronormativity is particularly repressive and oppressive. They are very likely to experience profound emotional and psychological tension and feelings of isolation. Some of the accounts reported in Simon Blake's little book recording recent experiences of young gay men in Britain reflect this:

> There was this group of them in the year above me and they called me names and stuff for about two years. It was queer, backs to the wall, all those sorts of things, sometimes they would whistle at me and blow me kisses. I would just dread seeing them in the corridor or at lunch times, so I learnt to go to places where they would not be. Looking back, I probably spent half my time looking for places to hide and the other half waiting for them to say something.
>
> (cited in Blake, 2003: 21)

And others graphically illustrate the costs in terms of psychological and physical health and happiness:

> I just felt so low and I couldn't ever imagine feeling any different, any better, and so I planned it all out. I was going to take pills, but in the end I couldn't do it, that scared me more than being gay.
>
> (cited in Blake, 2003: 47)

For these young gay men it is their treatment which is deeply troubling; for other young people it is finding appropriate and meaningful labels for their identity, feelings and experiences which proves difficult. The hundreds of letters sent to the problem pages of teenage magazines every week demonstrate the conceptual and emotional difficulties they face in fitting the complexities of their identities within social proscriptions of sexuality into simple dualities: masculine or feminine, straight or gay (Forrest, 1997).

> She Had Sex with a Girl
> I was at a party when I saw my best friend go upstairs with another girl. A little while later I went upstairs into the room where they were and caught them having sex with each other. I freaked out and ran downstairs. I haven't spoken to her since. Will she always be like this?
>   Rachel, 15, East Anglia. (in Forrest, Biddle and Clift, 1997, p. 9)

For both girls and boys, being in step with the physical, emotional, attitudinal and experiential development of their peers, and balancing their development with perceived social and parental expectations, makes an important contribution to their feelings of normalcy and confidence. School represents an important arena where this process of 'working out' sexuality takes place. Alongside the taught curriculum there are many rituals associated with schooling which project powerful messages about how and 'what' sexuality ought to be experienced (Epstein and Johnson, 1998).

For example, menarche, a defining element of feminine sexuality, can be a traumatic experience for many girls who experience difficulty in getting hold of sanitary towels or tampons, find there is no soap or hot water in school toilets or locks on the doors. They soon learn that menstruation is a 'secret' and a potentially unpleasant and shameful fact of life as a woman (Prendergast, 1994). In addition, through sports and school uniform, for example, boys and girls find their bodies subject to forms of regulation which seek to confine them within strict stereotypes of gendered sexuality. These stereotypes effectively condemn alternative sexualities as inversions or deviance. School-based rituals often demonstrate both patterns of 'identity-work' which both collude with these regulations and subvert them. For boys, sport, particularly football, is a powerful medium for learning about male sexuality. At breaks and lunchtimes school playing fields are usually dominated by groups of boys playing football. These games can be rough, physical contests in which social status off the field can be enhanced by success on it. In observing games of football it is apparent that some of the ritualized encounters between boys are primarily about the body and not the football. Prendergast and Forrest (1998, p. 161), in their work on boys' experiences of school, describe a daily ritual:

> Every lunchtime a group of small boys played football on the school fields. They, like other groups of boys, had their particular patch, their place in the occupation of the school space. A group of bigger boys often joined in with

their game and took pleasure in getting the ball and keeping it from the smaller boys, who were unable to push them off or catch them when they ran away. In the game the big boys slid into tackles on the smaller boys, knocking them over. Some of the smaller boys slid into the big boys in return. The big boys laughed and got up. But sometimes the big boys then tackled the smaller boys with real viciousness, intending to hurt them.

Through these encounters boys are learning that size matters. The bodily capital of the male depends on his size and strength, and display of immunity from physical pain. The big boys indulge their smaller peers, initially knocking them over playfully, showing restraint, saving their bodily capital, but when they have had enough of the smaller boys' playfulness they use their added weight and height to hurt them. The account shows how boys engage with each other in games which are about physical hierarchies in which bigger is better. These rituals and their significance do not grow up spontaneously. They are a product of schooling which celebrates sporting prowess as manly. By pitting bigger boys against smaller boys they endorse cultures of male physicality which demean the masculinity of smaller boys.

Uniform rules are another vector through which schooling impresses orthodoxies about gendered sexualities on young people. This account, from field notes collected while researching gender in schools, illustrates how a headteacher responds to calls from the school council for girls to be allowed to wear trousers. The headteacher seems not to see that making girls wear skirts makes them constantly sexually vulnerable, placing an onus on them to think about how they sit, stand and play so that boys cannot tease them.

> The Head tells us that the School Council is always complaining about uniform rules. They want girls to have the right to wear trousers instead of skirts. He says he thinks it is rather a trivial point which the Council meetings always get bogged down by. Last year he suggested to the Council that if it was really a matter of equal rights then they ought to lobby for boys to wear skirts too.

A final example vividly illustrates how discourses and practices which bind the sexual and gendered body are inhabited and reworked by young people is provided by this extract from *P'tang, Yang, Kipperbang and Other TV Plays* (Rosenthal, 1984, p. 21) where physical intimacy is shorn of its sexual meaning and the rules of heterosexual engagement inverted. Eunice, is not the target of the boys' sexual interest, but performs as though she is and the boys for their part go through a performance of conventional masculine sexuality.

> A couple of girls are stuffing homework into their satchels and making for the door. They completely ignore the end-of-day routine which is being carried out across the room by the windows.

The routine is this: Eunice stands with her back to the wall, blowing bubble-gum, as the boys, their homework in their satchels, form a queue in front of her. Each boy, in turn, then presses his body against Eunice's for a moment with complete absence of passion, then wanders from the room to go home.

As each boy presses against her, Eunice – automatically and unconvincingly – complains: 'Honestly, you're terrible. You boys really! A girl just isn't safe! You're horrible . . . it's every night, the same? I'm disgusted with you, I am truly.'

It is evident that the way the body is treated in school carries strong messages about sexuality and about gender. Even where young people inhabit discourses and take on cultural practices associated with 'doing' sexuality and gender in ways that superficially challenge the dogmas of female v. male, gay v. straight, they have to do so through engagement with them which always acknowledges their privileged position as the dominant discourse. This is the discourse which demands that human sexuality is patterned in line with two genders, circling each other in complementary roles and capacities, and that other sexualities and genders must therefore fall outside.

Homophobia

In 1994 Stonewall (the UK national organisation lobbying for lesbian, gay and bisexual civil rights) undertook a survey of lesbian, gay and bisexual experiences of violence, harassment, verbal abuse and avoidance strategies (Mason and Palmer, 1995). Forty-eight per cent of people under eighteen responding to the survey reported experiencing a violent attack, and 22 per cent had been 'beaten up'. Of the violent attacks, 40 per cent had taken place in school and in half the cases the perpetrators of the attacks had been other students. Forty-four per cent of under-eighteens had been harassed by fellow students and 79 per cent had been called names. A young lesbian described her experiences as follows:

> I was 'outed' at school when I was fourteen by some 'friends' who thought I shouldn't need to hide my sexuality . . . People tried to push me off my bicycle in local parks, I had sandbags thrown at me in one science lesson. Fortunately myself and my partner decided to tell some teachers . . . The group of boys who were doing the bullying were given a warning . . . and did eventually stop. However, the girls in my year who I was not close friends with continued to make remarks about us fancying them, and they acted very strangely (embarrassed) when changing for PE lessons.
>
> (cited in Mason and Palmer, 1995, p. 61)

Through detailed qualitative research, Rivers (1995, 1996) drew four conclusions about homophobic bullying in school. First, that the majority of homophobic bullying takes the form of non-physical attacks, including being given nasty stares and looks, vandalism of personal property and being 'sent to Coventry'. Second, that some of the main environments in which bullying takes place are unavoidable, public areas of school including, classrooms, corridors, school yards and playing fields. Third, only the minority of bullying attacks are reported and in even fewer cases (about 6 per cent) did the victimisation end as a result. Finally, Rivers identified the most frequent perpetrators of bullying as groups of boys, then boys and girls together, followed by groups of girls. Significantly, in half the cases teachers had colluded with the bullying by making snide remarks or failing to challenge homophobic remarks made in class. The work of Douglas *et al.*, illustrates not only the endemic nature of homophobic bullying, but also indicates high levels of awareness of it among school staff (Douglas *et al.*, 1998). In their study of homophobic bullying, support of lesbian, gay and bisexual students, HIV/AIDS education they found that 82 per cent of responding teachers were aware of verbal and 26 per cent of physical homophobic bullying among students. The majority of teachers reported between one and six incidents in the last term. Both Stonewall and Douglas *et al.*, point out that while homophobic bullying focuses on young gay people, it also affects young people perceived by their peers to be gay and those expressing tolerant views about homosexuality. These studies indicate some of the characteristics of homophobic bullying in schools. It is principally perpetrated by groups of boys, generally takes the form of verbal abuse and is focused on young people who are 'different' because they have a particularly close friendship with someone of the same sex, support gay rights or are openly gay. While a substantial proportion of teachers are aware of homophobia their responses to it are not perceived by young people as particularly effective. There is, in fact, a marked reluctance to report homophobic bullying and assaults. The Stonewall survey found that only 18 per cent of the young respondents reported violent attacks to the police. It is suggested that it is difficult, particularly for gay men under sixteen, to disclose their sexual orientation in reporting attacks upon them in the light of concerns about implying a breach of the law on age of consent. Research also highlights the profound effects of homophobic bullying. Rivers reports truanting as a strategy to avoid the worst situations in school, but respondents in his study often found it hard to avoid school without facing difficult questions at home. Other young people avoid confrontation by concentrating on academic schoolwork with the hope that success will lead to opportunities to escape to safer, more tolerant learning and working environments. Where these strategies prove insufficient to deflect or make homophobic bullying tolerable, Remafedi (1991) shows that experience can be linked to drug use, self-harm and suicide among young LGBT people.

Homophobia has no unitary cause however, research reviewed by Stephen Clift (1988) has identified some association between holding negative attitudes towards homosexuality and having no homosexual experiences or feelings, little or no contact with gay people, and negative attitudes towards sexual relationships outside marriage. Homophobia also strongly correlated with adherence to religious convictions which disapprove of sex and/or homosexuality and lower social and educational class. Homophobia also seems to be more overtly, aggressively and frequently displayed by boys than girls and may be associated with rigidity of models of masculinity (Forrest, 1997b).

Contemporary homophobia also revitalised long-standing beliefs that homosexuality is morally deviant and represents either a source or vector for disease. Modern beliefs that gay men are both more susceptible to and responsible for the HIV/Aids pandemic in the Northwestern world simply reproduce, for example, admonishments handed down to boys for over a century. Baden-Powell, the founder of the worldwide scouting movement, mounted an attack on masturbation and homosexuality threatening over seventy years ago which linked them to sexual and moral dissipation and degeneracy and, ultimately, diminution of the national blood-stock (Baden-Powell, 1930).

The role of heteronormativity in providing a legitimation for homophobia is also clear, for example, in implying that boys who show their feelings or who are too intimate with other boys are either 'girls' or 'poofs'. Equally, girls who are deemed to be too tomboyish run the risk of being called 'dykes' or 'lesbians'. The threat of victimisation which arises from failure to conform to gender role stereotypes actually produces homophobia as a means of showing off heterosexual one's credentials.

Ideological and political frameworks of school sex education

In the UK, the legislative context for sex education is complex. Since 1986 there has been a steady stream of policy level activity manifest in the handing down on several volumes of guidance to state-maintained schools (which make up 90 per cent of all education providers), a number of education Acts which have re-organised or oriented sex education in relation to a national curriculum, and a number of relevant policy developments and Acts of Parliament dealing with sexual health.

The increasing involvement of government since the 1980s in describing the aims, limits and content of school sex education has to be seen in the context of an evolving political interest in bringing under increased control the whole system of maintained education. The restructuring of the financial management of schools under, first, local management and, latterly, grant maintenance, and the imposition of a national curriculum represent the two main mechanisms through which the autonomy of teachers and schools has been brought under the dual authority of central government and parents in the form of school governing bodies. The establishment of the Office for Standards in Education (Ofsted) and the gearing up of the parental right to choose have placed increased pressure on schools to be seen to perform successfully in relation to one another.

One effect of these changes has been to encourage schools to concentrate on populist measures which are perceived to increase their appeal to parents of potential pupils. Alongside activity within the taught curriculum, schools have often resorted to clamping down on unruliness, suspected, real or imagined drug use, and the imposition of rigid rules in order to present an orderly face to the outside world thus implying firm leadership and through firm leadership, success.

Such reactionary educational attitudes are, for the most part, supported by parents. A subsidiary effect of the dual focus on academic standards (measured through student successes in public examinations) and orderliness has been to further squeeze the time available for aspects of social education within the taught curriculum and marginalise their importance. Not only is social education often perceived to have no bearing on a school's standing in the exam league tables (despite emergent evidence to the contrary, for example, (Weare, 2000), but emphasising social education may be perceived by parents as a reaction to some neediness of the part of students or weakness on the part of schools to combat misbehaviour or unruliness. Providing social education, particularly on sex and drugs, can also attract negative press and parental attention, as a series of highly publicised scandals has illustrated (see, for example, the review of media coverage of sex education in schools in Epstein and Johnson, 1998). Consequently, schools may be reluctant to foreground curriculum activity in relation to social education and teachers may be nervous about tackling the subject and may adopt repressive positions, providing only the basic facts about sexual behaviour as part of science teaching.

Alongside the development of education policy the UK Government Department of Health has also provided impetus to school-based sex education through a number of policy directives and strategic initiatives focusing on or referring to young people and sexual health. In 1992, the then Conservative administration launched a strategy for national health, *The Health of the Nation* (Department of Health (DoH), 1992) which set a target for a 50 per cent reduction in the rate of pregnancies in girls under sixteen years old by 2000. A revised version of the target was latterly set by the New Labour administration which took office in 1997.

Although the target, albeit subject to some revision of detail rather than in substance, neatly passed from government of one hue to government of another, the motives behind deploying it, and the mechanisms for achieving it diverged in ways that were predictable given the ideological leanings of the administrations. For Conservative administrations the driving concern was welfare spending associated with single parenthood. In a series of highly publicised speeches, a succession of Conservative government ministers characterised absent fathers as irresponsible for failing to provide for the maintenance of their female partners and children, and young single mothers as feckless scroungers who got pregnant in order to jump housing queues and whose intention was to live off benefits (for example, see *Independent on Sunday*, 10 October 1993). This moralistic ideological thrust found specific form and definition in the Thatcherite rallying call to the post-1987 election Conservative Party conference for a return to 'family values'. The sexual behaviour of young people was characterised as a threat to traditional moral values and their attitude towards state benefits and welfare was cited as evidence of the decline. Schools were positioned on the front line in the attempt to counter the creeping moral decay.

Consequently, guidance to schools on sex education formulated under Conservative administration emphasised a framework of values which sought to, 'encourage [pupils] to appreciate the value of stable family life, marriage and the responsibilities of parenthood' (DfE, 1994) within the wider aims of the then current Education Act which articulated the aim of education as the, 'promot[ion of] the spiritual, moral, cultural, mental and physical development of pupils at the school and of society; and . . . prepares such pupils for the opportunities, responsibilities and experiences of adult life' (DfE, 1993).

The New Labour administration which came into office in 1997 established an initiative under the auspices of the Home Office aiming to formulate responses to social exclusion which turned quickly its attention to teenage pregnancy and developed an overarching teenage pregnancy strategy (SEU, 1999). This strategy forms the major plank underpinning subsequent policy development with regard to sex education. The SEU (Social Exclusion Unit) report reconfigured the 'problem' of teenage sexuality in accordance with New Labour ideological inclinations. Although the economic costs of young parenthood still figured in the analysis, a wider brief also drew attention to the costs and disbenefits of early parenthood to teenagers themselves and to their children. Early parenthood was equated with the loss of educational and hence employment opportunities and increased risk of adverse health and social outcomes for children. The strategy recommended so called 'joined-up' activity across government departments and areas of the public sector to address primary prevention of unplanned and unwanted pregnancies through sex education and improved sexual health services, especially facilitating access to contraception, to establish or enhance care and support to young parents and their children through the provision of continuing education to young parents (mothers in particular) and childcare. Notably, the teenage pregnancy strategy also identified socio-cultural attitudes towards young people and sexuality and 'mixed' media messages as important influences on sexual behaviour. This more liberal understanding of the 'problem' and contingent measures were coupled with more coercive actions including hiking up the pressure on young people to enter training or employment and increasing the powers of the state to pursue absent fathers for financial contribution to the costs of caring for their children.

The values and policy implications of the teenage pregnancy strategy heavily influenced the new guidance to schools on what became known as 'sex and relationships education' (SRE) handed down in 2000. This has been accompanied by a raft of other guidance documentation on the provision of sexual health services for young people, confidentiality and the needs of specific groups of young people which has mainly flowed from the cross-Departmental Teenage Pregnancy Unit set up to implement, fund and monitor the strategy.

Despite this strategic reconfiguration and directing of significant public monies towards teenage pregnancy (and young people and sexual health in general), SRE still has a marginal status with schools. Even with the restructuring of the national curriculum to incorporate a new subject in portfolio of social education in the form of 'citizenship', nothing beyond the requirements of the national curriculum for science, which include the biological aspects of sex education, is mandatory. The current legislative requirements on schools and the content of guidance documents relating to SRE are, arguable therefore, substantively unchanged over the course of fifteen years.

The guidance to schools defines SRE as, '. . . lifelong learning about physical, moral and emotional development. It is about the understanding of the importance of marriage for family life, stable and loving relationships, respect, love and care. It is also about the teaching of sex, sexuality, and sexual health'. In addition, on a point to which we return, it notes that, '. . . It is not about the promotion of sexual orientation or sexual activity – this would be inappropriate teaching' (DfEE, 2000: 5).

SRE is to be delivered through science and also across the curriculum in personal, social, health and citizenship education (PSHCE) and bound by each school, in a clear policy statement which details what will be taught, by whom, to whom and when. In terms of specifying the content of SRE programmes the guidance states that by the end of the primary school years (aged 11), under Science provision, children should know,

> . . . that animals including humans, move, feed, grow, use their sense and reproduce . . . recognise and compare the main external parts of the bodies of humans . . . that humans and animals can produce offspring and these grow into adults . . . recognise similarities and differences between themselves and others and treat others with sensitivity . . . that the life processes common to humans and other animals include nutrition, growth and reproduction . . . about the main stages of the human life cycle.
>
> (DfEE, 2000: 20)

In addition, provision through PSHE and citizenship will ensure that all children, '. . . develop confidence in talking, listening and thinking about feelings and relationships; are able to name parts of the body and describe how their bodies work; can protect themselves and ask for help and support, and; are prepared for puberty' (DfEE, 2000: 19).

With regard to the secondary school years (by the age of 16) the guidance notes that provision through science should mean that children know,

> . . . that fertilization in humans . . . is the fusion of a male and female cell . . . about the physical and emotional changes that take place during adolescence . . . about the human reproductive system, including the menstrual cycle and fertilization . . . how the foetus develops in the uterus . . . how the growth and reproduction of bacteria and the replication of viruses can affect health . . . the way in which hormonal control occurs, including the effects of sex hormones . . . some medical uses of hormones including the control and promotion of fertility . . . the defence mechanisms of the body . . . how sex is determined in humans.
>
> (DfEE, 2000: 21)

In addition, provision through PSHE and citizenship will ensure that all children are,

... prepared for an adult life in which they can: develop positive values and a moral framework that will guide their decisions, judgments and behaviour; be aware of their sexuality and understand human sexuality; understand the arguments for delaying sexual activity; understand the reasons for having protected sex; understand the consequences of their actions and behave responsibly within sexual and pastoral relationships; have the confidence and self-esteem to value themselves and others and respect for individual conscience and the skills to judge what kind of relationship they want; communicate effectively; have sufficient information and skills to protect themselves and, where they have one, their partner from unintended/ unwanted conceptions, and sexually transmitted infections including HIV; avoid being exploited or exploiting others; avoid being pressured into unwanted or unprotected sex; access confidential sexual health advice, support and if necessary treatment; and, know how the law applies to sexual relationships.

(DfEE, 2000: 20–21)

The guidance goes on to suggest some appropriate teaching strategies including detailing how to set and maintain ground rules with a group of students, deal with difficult questions and use active, participatory and project-based learning to maximum effect. Moreover, the guidance dedicates several pages to outlining the way in which schools should approach and deal with several specific issues within policy and practice including puberty, menstruation, contraception, abortion, safer sex, HIV/Aids and sexually transmitted infections, being sensitive to and inclusive of the needs of boys and young men, young people from ethnic minorities and those with special educational needs and learning difficulties.

Although these detailed sections are a departure from previous guidance documents, as noted the substantive position of SRE within the curriculum, its aims and content have remained unchanged despite the change in political administration. However, it is with regard to the explicit references to homosexuality and sexual orientation that a difference in tenor is striking suiting the more inclusive and liberal social agenda set out by the New Labour government.

Despite the resolutely negative reference to 'sexual orientation' in the opening definition of SRE provided by the guidance document, there are several other places where a more positive tone is evident, much more congruent with the rights-based statements by the WHO cited at the beginning of this chapter. For example, in the fifth paragraph of the introduction the guidance states, 'Pupils need also to be given accurate information and helped to develop skills to enable them to understand difference and respect themselves and others and for the purpose also of preventing and removing prejudice' (DfEE, 2000: 4). This veiled reference is followed by this, from the section of specific issues to be addressed SRE policy: '. . . It is up to schools to make sure that the needs of all pupils are met in their programmes. Young people, whatever their developing sexuality, need to feel that sex and relationships education is relevant to them and sensitive to their needs', and becoming, finally, completely clear that what is being referred to is that the needs of young LGBT people it reads, 'The Secretary of State for Education and Employment is clear that teachers should be able to deal honestly and sensitively with sexual orientation, answer appropriate questions and offer support' (DfEE, 2000: 13). The guidance goes on to acknowledge that parental concerns about what this comprises will need to be met through liaison and consultation but caps it by noting that schools have a duty to address homophobic bullying (thus offering teachers a ready argument for including these issues in their provision) because of the, '. . . unacceptability of and emotional distress and harm caused by bullying in whatever form – be it racial, as result of a pupil's appearance, related to sexual orientation or for any other reason' (DfEE, 2000:13).

Under both Conservative and New Labour policy-makers the debate about the specific form the legislation and guidance to schools on sex education should take was heated. Recurrent themes have been balancing the rights of the child to SRE and the right of their parents to withdraw them from any part which lies outside the national curriculum (in other words the basic reproductive science), identifying (or often fudging) the teacher's position in relation to giving contraceptive advice to young people and when at what age SRE should be provided.

Both administrations struggled, in similar ways with the needs to act pragmatically and on the basis of the best available scientific evidence (which has always pointed towards the provision of early, comprehensive SRE and free, easily accessible sexual health services) to address disease epidemics and silence the siren voices of moralists arguing for retrenchment.

So for the Conservative administrations from the mid-1980s the advent of HIV, the virus which causes AIDS, demanded a response which included the provision of school-based sex education about HIV since all the available evidence, then as now, specified it (Wight, 1993; HEA, 1998; Collins *et al.*, 2002). However, moralistic approaches to sex education are not congruent with effective educational interventions in HIV/AIDS prevention. They cannot accommodate, for example, the need to challenge the stigmatisation of gay men, which contributes to their vulnerability to infection, since any tacit acceptance of homosexuality undermines the prescriptions of sexuality involved in promoting a narrow heterosexual preconception of 'family values'.

To some extent, similar problems have haunted New Labour which has seen STIs rise exponentially among young people and needed on the one hand to silence the voices of the right-wing press and advocates for 'family groups' which argue that this is evidence of a failed analysis and wrong-headed response (they predictably prefer moral-retrenchment) and on the other, to implement ever more radical solutions including making emergency contraception more easily and widely available and bringing sexual health services into schools and colleges in line with the body of effectiveness research.

Section 28

In 1988, under the Local Government Act, Margaret Thatcher's government, responding both to tabloid claims that young people were at risk of being corrupted in SRE lessons, and seeing an opportunity to make political capital from hardening public attitudes towards homosexuality in the light of the emerging HIV epidemic (Jivani, 1997) by accusing Labour-led local authorities of sponsoring gay and lesbian groups passed an amendment to the Local Government Act 1986 which stated that

> a local authority shall not–
> (a) intentionally promote homosexuality or publish material with the intention of promoting homosexuality
> (b) promote the teaching in any maintained school of the acceptability of homosexuality as a pretended family relationship.
>
> (Local Government Act, 1988)

The deleterious effects on school-based SRE are evident. Confusion in the classroom and the deterrence of teachers from responding to the needs of young LGBT people (Frost, 1997) and worse still, an active endorsement of their own homophobia (Buston and Hart, 2001) and the provision of a twisted legitimation for victimisation and assaults of young LGBT people (Mason and Palmer, 1995). New Labour, finally, fulfilled a commitment to the repeal of this statute first in Scotland in 2000 and then more recently in England and Wales in 2003.

Despite its repeal the effects are still felt through, for example, the phrase within the DfEE guidance on SRE which warns against '. . . direct promotion of sexual orientation' and the admonishment that that sex education 'is not about the promotion of sexual orientation' (see above). In addition, there have been moves at the level of local government to reintroduce versions of Section 28. For example, in the case of Kent County Council (KCC), which agreed that it would not 'publish, purchase or distribute material with the intention of promoting homosexuality' (Gillan, 2003) and statements from within the Conservative party that Section 28 should be expanded to include other areas of the public sector rather than repealed (Willets and Streeter, 2002). As Peter Cumper, a human rights lawyer with an interest in SRE has noted it is important to examine why this provision is incompatible with Britain's domestic and international human rights obligations in case any future administration should seek to reintroduce it (Cumper, 2004: 129). He concludes that it is incompatible with the freedom of expression enshrined in the European Convention on Human Rights, Article 8 which provides that, '. . . Everyone has the right to respect for his private and family life' since it stigmatises homosexuality breaching principles of non-discrimination and suppresses the, '. . . pluralistic treatment of homosexuality with the use of the pejorative term "pretended family relationship" (Cumper, 2004: 131).

Notwithstanding its repeal, Section 28 still seems to exercise some degree of hold over teachers' practice within SRE. As Buston and Hart (2001) note (post-repeal in Scotland) although few teachers in their study explicitly referred to Section 28, they did seek recourse to the language constructions within the Act which refer to 'promotion of homosexuality' in explicating their reluctance and difficulties with discussing lesbian, gay and bisexual issues in the classroom.

Similarly, Ellis and High (2004), in researching young lesbian, gay and bisexual people's experiences of coverage of homosexuality in schools assert that contrary to some propositions that Section 28 silenced discussion of homosexuality in schools, it may actually have contributed to the marginalisation of LGBT young people and been interpreted by some teachers as a legitimation of their authority to broadcast moral judgements about their pupils. For Ellis and High, the repeal of the Act, while removing its symbolic authority, will have little impact on young people's lives, arguing that its deleterious effects will only be mitigated by shifting the pedagogical ground from essentialist approaches to sexuality to approaches which locate it as an, '. . . aspect of culture and identity' (2004: 223).

Addressing sexuality in school

Despite the extent of political interest in school-based sex education, provision may still be patchy and inconsistent. Teachers are under-trained and under-resourced and lack confidence and conviction about the utility of addressing gender, sexuality, relationships and emotional and attitudinal aspects of sex education which lie outside the National Curriculum Orders for Science. A combination of these doubts and the weak structural position occupied by sex education provision outside the national curriculum in English and Welsh Schools seem to be chief culprits.

SRE provision which lies outside the National Curriculum Orders for Science and within personal, health and social education and citizenship involves an aggregation of social subjects within which SRE may be more or less marginal depending on the prejudices and interests of individual teachers, school management and governance. Its non-examinable status may make it comparatively unimportant to teachers focused on subject specialisms being taught towards public examination. PHSCE may also be organised in a variety of ways which disperse responsibility and accountability for its provision. The role of PHSCE co-ordination in schools often brings with it no budget, and added with the low status of the subject may not seem to have equally high status as other co-ordinating roles. It is difficult not to agree with Stears *et al.* (1995, pp. 181–2), who described the position of the social subjects within school in the light of a threefold strategy resulting in the,

> . . . censoring a critical social perspective within National Curriculum core and foundation subjects . . . by excluding social subjects from the National Curriculum and . . . by garrisoning social subjects into a variety of cross-curricular themes which suggests they lack the credibility of 'real' subjects within the curriculum proper.

A recent School Inspectorate survey of SRE provision identified many of these weaknesses noting, in particular, the benefits of having a specialist team of SRE teachers, the need for clear learning objectives (the absence of which is reflective of the non-examinable status of SRE/PSHCE), and the need to focus on the development of attitudes and values as well as the transmission of knowledge about sexual matters (Ofsted, 2002). Ofsted even go so far as to imply that this should embrace issues about sexuality in quoting a student commenting on coverage of attitudes and values who said,

> We never talked about homosexuality. There are over a thousand boys in this school and it must be an issue for some of them. But the staff seem scared to talk about it.
>
> (Year 10 boy in an all-boys school) (Ofsted, 2002: 17, para. 44)

Analysis of the structural status of PSHE/SRE within the curriculum will only, however, take us so far in generating a thorough understanding of the problems with SRE. In addition to these weaknesses, SRE/PSHCE provision also suffers because of teachers' lack of confidence which is partly a product of the tendency of published resources to recommend a participative, child-centred approach to learning which is currently out of favour with educational orthodoxies. The marginal nature of PHSCE, the sensitivity of the subjects, and the lack of interest of teachers may all conspire with students' sometimes volatile reactions in the classroom to deter teachers from starting or continuing to provide social education. The tendency of boys in particular to exploit their own and the teacher's embarrassment by misbehaving during sex education within PHSCE is well documented (see, for example, Measor *et al.*, 1996).

In addition, Buston and Hart (2001) suggest that SRE is premised on a basis which privileges heterosexuality by placing human reproduction and pregnancy prevention centre stage. Through questionnaire surveys and interviews with teachers and classroom observations they conclude that a significant minority of teachers are overtly homophobic. This took the form of complicity in student homophobia such as laughing along at homophobic comments and jokes and the active problematisation of homosexuality through the dissemination of myths and stereotypes or categorical comments. These teachers tended to frame homosexuality as being solely about sexual behaviour and this colludes with its pathologisation and the stigmatism of LGBT sexualities. In an equal number of lessons LGBT sexualities were rendered 'invisible' through the discussion of sexual intercourse entirely in terms of vaginal penetration and reference to relationships as being solely between male and females.

When it came to exploring the constraints under which teachers felt they were operating in relation to delivering inclusive, non-heterosexist sex education Buston and Hart identified discomfort with teaching about homosexuality as a general principle or in relation to their own attitudes and beliefs, lack of support from within senior echelons of their schools and wider concerns about local, regional and governmental policy and fear of adverse media exposure as major factors. They conclude that the factors which militate against 'good practice' are various and operate at a number of levels including the personal, institutional and cultural. At the personal/practice level they identify a lack of positive language and discourses which teachers can access, so homosexuality is often referred to as 'it' or 'that issue'. In terms of squaring these findings with pupil responses, which indicated a fairly tolerant attitude towards sexual and relational diversity, they conclude that homophobic behaviour may be 'mobbing' in the classroom and that attitudes and that the behaviour of a vocal few are distorting teacher perceptions of the views of the many. They also note that teachers suggest that pupils may be more tolerant of the principle of homosexuality than they are about the, '. . . possibility of their peers being gay or lesbian' (2001: 108). Similar findings emerged from a study by Ellis and High (Ellis and High, 2004) which identified the treatment of homosexuality as an 'issue', and that teachers' own views served both to pathologise and problematise the topic.

Looking more closely at the heteronomativity imposed by ways of talking about sex and sexuality it is apparent that the dominant imagery of heterosexual vaginal intercourse interacts with ideals about masculinity and femininity to inform and reinforce homophobia in a particularly pernicious way. Male sexuality is characterised as thrusting, active, urgent and penetrating; female, conversely, as passive, receptive and penetrated (Reiss, 1998). As a result young people can reach the conclusion that same-sex sexual relationships must be pseudo-heterosexual and involve penetration and the partners in roles which mimic heterosexual gender roles. This may reinforce the stereotyping of gay men as effeminate and lesbian women as butch.

The centrality of the vagina and penis as penetrated and penetrating sexual organs effectively delegitimises some sexual acts. As Jewitt (1996) has pointed out, some sex education material describing human sexual organs fails to label the anus at all, thus making anal sex invisible. An effect of the conflation of sexual acts with heterosexual gender and sex roles is that gender role behaviour is used by young people both to explain and understand sexuality. The body itself can become suspect. For example, bigger, heavier girls, who do not conform to masculine stereotypes of feminine body shape, can often find themselves labelled lesbian. Finally, since same-sex sexual activity is characterised as a substitute for heterosexual sexual behaviour, it is often portrayed as though it were an arrested sexual development, an immature or displaced heterosexuality. This may lie at the root of preconceptions that LGBT young people are failed heterosexuals who have either never had proper heterosexual sex or else were turned away by bad heterosexual experiences.

Overall, it is apparent that policy level activity around SRE has not been backed up by the establishment of the 'subject' on a firm and equal footing to other traditional academic subjects. It is also apparent that although there has been an increasing willingness, within policy, to 'talk' equality and action to address the most gross offensives of oppression of non-heterosexual young people through bullying this has not been coupled to the development of a thorough understanding of the heteronormativity of SRE itself or the role of wider aspects of schooling as described elsewhere in this chapter in marginalising lesbian, gay and bisexual identities and sexualities. Moreover, policy has not found a way to direct practice to engage with aspects of the socio-cultural context, particularly media representations of sex and sexuality which continue to largely portray homosexuality in terms of stereotypes of camp gay men, butch or lipstick lesbian women and mixed up bisexual and transgendered people.

The tendency in schools is still towards a lowest common denominator of providing 'hard' facts about human reproduction seasoned with stern warnings about the moral risks of teenage sexual behaviour which has relegated dealing with sexuality critically, as a political and social phenomenon, to the educational sidelines. At the centre of policy and provision lie heterosexual reproduction and the reproduction of heterosexuality, and sexual diversity, feelings and pleasures are at the edge.

It has been said that sexuality is 'everywhere and nowhere' in school (Redman, 1994). This combination of pervasiveness and elusiveness may seem, initially, a deterrent to teachers looking for somewhere to start addressing issues like homophobia and heterosexism. Teachers' priority will, rightly, always fall on what can be done directly in relation to young people. However, in addressing sexuality it may be better to begin at the level of staff training and policy-making. A first step is to achieve some agreement on the need and motives for raising awareness of sexuality within the school. These might include any of the following:

- Young people have a right to accurate information about sexuality. Since sexualities are diverse and not limited to concerns about disease or repro-duction, sex education which does not address the diversity of sexualities is not accurate.
- Students frequently discuss and play about sexuality among themselves. To exclude it from the formal curriculum is to collude with the inevitable perpetuation of misinformation which may cause some young people anxiety.
- Attempts to tackle bullying which exclude explicit reference to challenging homophobia and sexism are unlikely to succeed.
- Partly as a result of homophobic bullying, LGBT young people need extra support in school.
- The wider school community, including some parents and governors, may welcome attempts on the part of a school to alter sexist and homophobic attitudes among young people.
- The stigmatisation of young gay men and the exclusion of relevant information about safer sex from school sex education increases their vulnerability to HIV infection and may also decrease young heterosexual people's awareness of their vulnerability to sexually transmitted infections, including HIV.

A positive step is to assess these motives in relation to existing policy in a relevant area: for example, considering whether anti-bullying policy contains a sufficiently explicit commitment to challenging homophobic remarks; also, whether the way homophobic bullying is dealt with is likely to encourage disclosures from other victims. Within sex education and elsewhere in the curriculum opportunities exist for opening up sexuality for discussion. Teachers can establish sufficiently safe classroom environments for discussion of gender or attitudes towards sexuality in the course of drama, English and history lessons. Harris (1990) provides a detailed guide to suitable resources available to the English teacher. Accounts are readily to hand in the works of Jeanette Winterson (1985) and extracts from *The Diary of Anne Frank* (Frank, 1997) and among collections of gay and lesbian stories and histories (Jivani, 1997). Leaflets which contain accounts of the experiences of young gay men are available from such organisations as the AIDS Education and Research Trust (AVERT) and the Terrence Higgins Trust (THT).

A useful activity for staff may be to collect a selection of leaflets from local and national lesbian, gay and bisexual help and advice services and to use them as prompts to discussion about what information should be made available to students on noticeboards in the school. These same materials can be used by students, along with other service information, within a sex education lesson in order to make a poster or flyer detailing local agencies available to young people. Most materials of this kind are available free in small quantities from the relevant agencies.

Sexuality, education and equality

The previous chapter described the 'invention' of sexuality and showed how there has been a movement towards depathologising and politicising homosexuality in recent years. Sexual practices have become to a lesser extent the domain of the medical and legal establishment as people have demanded the right to their own sexual identity and to engage in whatever sexual practices they choose. The tendency to liberalisation has not, however, been uncontested. Reactionary political and moral forces have sought to champion institutions like 'the family', and establish a strong link between homosexuality and disease, and homosexuality and moral decline. However, the increasing visibility of LGBT people, and the 'outing' of historical figures, makes these positions untenable.

Within education, however, as a result of the combined pressures to scale down social education (seen by the political right as a transgression on personal freedom and the role of the family), to avoid offending parents and making the school vulnerable in the educational market-place and prurient media interest in sex education, the conservative tendency has not been fully reversed. A gulf has opened between young people's experience of the wider world, in which sexuality is seen as more fluid and pleasure-orientated, and schooling, where it remains fixed to traditional gender-role stereotypes and focused on policing reproductive sex. Currently, young people are being denied a right to an education which equips them for adult life. For young LBGT people, their enforced invisibility and the denial of equal access to basic relevant sex education is a breach of a human right (in transgression of both the ECHR and the government's SRE guidance). The equalisation of the ages of sexual consent and the repeal of Section 28 is welcome, but until schools take up the issues in the classroom, changes in the law are unlikely to have much impact on knowledge, attitudes and behaviour.

References

Act of Parliament (1988) *Local Government Act 1988*, London: HMSO

Baden-Powell, R.S.S. (1930) *Rovering to Success: A Book of Life-sport for Young Men* (fifteenth edition), London: Herbert Jenkins Ltd

Blake, S. (ed.) *Young Gay Men Talking: Key Issues and Ideas for Action*. London: Working With Men

Brown, T. (1995) Girls have long hair. *Health Education* 2, 23–9

Buston, K. and Hart, G. (2001) Heterosexism and homophobia in Scottish school sex education: exploring the nature of the problem. *Journal of Adolescence*, 24: 95–109

Clift, S.M. (1988) Lesbian and gay issues in education: a study of first year students in a college of higher education. *British Educational Research*, 14 (1): 31–50

Collins J., Robin, L., Wooley, S., Fenley, D., Hunt, P., Taylor, J., Haber, D., Kolbe, L. (2002) Programs-that-work: CDC's guide to effective programs that reduce health-risk behaviour or youth. *Journal of School Health*, 72(3): 93–9

Cumper, P. (2004) Sex Education and human rights – a lawyer's perspective. *Sex Education*, 4(2) 125–36

Department for Education (1993) *Education Act 1993*, London: HMSO

Department for Education (1994) *Education Act 1993: Sex Education in Schools*. Circular 5194, London: HMSO

Department for Education and Employment (2000) *Sex and Relationships Education Guidance*, London: HMSO

Department of Health (1992) *The Health of the Nation*. London: HMSO

Douglas, N., Warwick, I., Kemp, S. and Whitty, G. (1998) *Playing it Safe: Responses of Secondary School Teachers to Lesbian, Gay and Bisexual Pupils, Bullying, HIV and AIDS Education and Section 28*. London: Health and Education Research Unit, University of London

Ellis, V. and High, S. (2004) Something to tell you: gay, lesbian or bisexual young people's experiences of secondary schooling. *British Educational Research Journal*, 30(2): 213–25

Epstein, D. (1995) 'Girls don't do bricks': gender and sexuality in the primary classroom', in J. Siraj-Blatchford and I. Siraj-Blatchford (eds) *Educating the Whole Child: Cross-Curricular Skills, Themes and Dimensions*. Buckingham: Open University Press, pp. 56–69

Epstein, D. (1997a) Cultures of schooling/cultures of sexuality. *Journal of Inclusive Education* 1(1): 37–53

Epstein, D. (1997b) Boyz' Own Stories: Masculinities and Sexualities in Schools. *Gender and Education* 9, 105–15

Epstein, D. and Johnson, R. (1998) *Schooling Sexualities*. Buckingham: Open University Press

Forrest, S. (1997) Confessions of a Middle shelf shopper. *The Journal of Contemporary Health*, 5: 10–14

Forrest, S., Biddle, G. and Clift, S. (1997) *Talking about Homosexuality in the Secondary School*, Horsham: AVERT

Frank, A. (1997) *The Diary of a Young Girl: The Definitive Edition* (trans. O. Frank and M. Pressler). London: Penguin

Frost, N. (1997) The (Lack of) provision of sex education for young gay men. *Childright*, 142

Gillan, A. (2003) Section 28 gone . . . but not forgotten. *The Guardian*, November 17.

Greenwald, E. and Leitenberg, H. (1989) Long-term effects of sexual experiences with siblings and non-siblings during childhood. *Archives of Sexual Behaviour* 18, 389–99

Haugaard, J.J. (1996) Sexual behaviours between children: professionals' opinions and undergraduates' recollections. *Families in Society: Journal of Contemporary Human Services* 77: 81–9

Harris, S. (1990) *Lesbian and Gay Issues in the English Classroom*. Milton Keynes: Open University Press

Health Education Authority (1998) *Reducing the Rate of Teenage Pregnancies: An Overview of the Effectiveness of Interventions and Programmes Aimed at Reducing Unintended Conceptions in Young People*. London: HEA

Janus, S.S. and Bess, B.E. (1976) Latency: fact or fiction. *The American Journal of Psychoanalysis* 36: 339–46

Jewitt, C. (1996) *Forum Factsheet 11: Supporting the Needs of Boys and Young Men in Sex and Relationships Education*. London: Sex Education Forum

Jivani, A. (1997) *It's Not Unusual: A History of Lesbian and Gay Britain in the Twentieth century*. London: Micheal O'Mara Books

Kingori, P., Wellings, K., French, R., Kane, R., Gerrusu, M. and Stephenson, J. (2004) Sex and relationship education and the media: an analysis of national and regional newspaper coverage in England. *Sex Education*, 4(2) (July) 111–24

Larsson, I. and Svedin, C. (2002) Sexual experiences in childhood; young adults' recollections. *Archives of Sexual Behaviour* 31: 263–73

Mason, A. and Palmer, A. (1995) *Queerbashing: A National Survey of Hate Crimes against Lesbians and Gay Men*. London: Stonewall

Measor, L., Coralie, T. and Fry, K. (1996) Gender and sex education: a study of adolescent responses. *Gender and Education*, 8 (3): 275–88

Moore, S. and Rosenthal, D. (1993) *Sexuality in Adolescence*. London: Routledge

National Curriculum Council (1990) *Curriculum Guidance 5: Health Education*. York: The National Curriculum Council

Ofsted (2002) *Sex and Relationships Education in Schools*, London: Office for Standards in Education

Prendergast, S. (1994) *This Is the Time to Grow up: Girls' Experiences of Menstruation in School*. Family Planning Association

Prendergast, S. and Forrest, S. (1998) 'Shorties, low-lifers, hardnuts and kings': boys, emotions and embodiment in school, in G. Bendelow and S. Williams (eds), *Emotions in Social Life: Criticial Themes and Contemporary Issues*. London: Routledge

Redman, P. (1994) Shifting ground: rethinking sexuality education, in D. Epstein (ed.), *Challenging Lesbian and Gay Inequalities in Education*. Buckingham: Open University Press

Reiss, M. (1998) The representation of human sexuality in some science textbooks for 14–16 year olds. *Research in Science and Technology Education*, 16: 137–49

Remafedi, G. (1991) Risk factors for attempted suicide in gay and bisexual youth. *Paediatrics*, 87: 869–75

Rivers, I. (1995) The victimisation of gay teenagers in schools: homophobia in education. *Pastoral Care*, 3: 35–41

Rivers, I. (1996) Young gay and bullied. *Young People Now*, 18–19 January 1996

Rogers, M. (1994) Growing up lesbian: the role of the school, in D. Epstein (ed.), *Challenging Lesbian and Gay Inequalities in Education*. Buckingham: Open University Press

Rosenthal, J. (1984) *P'tang, Yang, Kipperbang and Other TV Plays*. Harlow: Longman

Stears, D., Clift, S. and Blackman, S.J. (1995) Health, sex and drugs education: rhetoric and reality, in J. Ahier and A. Ross (eds), *The Social Subjects within the Curriculum: Children's Social Learning within the National Curriculum*. London: Falmer Press

Social Exclusion Unit (1999) *Teenage Pregnancy*. London: HMSO

UNICEF (2001) *A League Table of Teenage Births in Rich Countries Innocenti Report Card No. 3*, July 2001. Florence, Italy: UNICEF Innocenti Research Centre

Weare, K. (2000) *Promoting Mental, Emotional and Social Health: A Whole School Approach*. Routledge, London

Wight, D. (1993) A reassessment of health education on HIV/AIDS for young heterosexuals. *Health Education Research*, 8 (4): 473–83

Willetts, D. and Streeter, G. (eds) (2002) *Renewing One Nation*. London: Politics Publishing.

Winterson, J. (1985) *Oranges Are Not the Only Fruit*. London: Pandora Press

World Health Organisation (2003a) UN Commission on Human Rights Agenda item 6, Racism, Racial Discrimination, Xenophobia, and all Forms of Discrimination Statement by the World Health Organization, Geneva, 24 March 2003. http://www. who.int/reproductive-health/gender/sexual_health.html (accessed, 20.04.05)

World Health Organisation (2003b) WHO statement to the fifty-ninth Session of the UN Commission on Human Rights, 17 March–24 April 2003, http://66.102.9.104/u/who? q=cache:0NCN8HquTj8J:www.who.int/entity/hhr/information/en/item6_final.pdf+ho mophobia&hl=en&ie=UTF-8 (accessed, 20.04.05)

7 Disability equality

Confronting the oppression of the past

Richard Rieser

Introduction

At least 10 per cent of the world's people have a significant, long-term, physical or mental impairment which can and usually does disable them from taking part in the usual educational, social and economic activity in their community. This is due to barriers in attitudes, in the built environment and in the way society is organized, which prevent us from participating on an equal level with others. The reason why most of these barriers exist is because societies have until very recently not recognized that the systematic way in which they discriminate against disabled people when backed by discriminatory laws and practices of the state, often amounts to oppression. Barnes (1991) gives a full account of the discrimination disabled people encounter in all areas of life. This oppression has developed from our history, from myths and beliefs that attribute characteristics to disabled people which are unrelated to the reality of disabled people's lives. Such collections of attitudes often determine how non-disabled people respond to the 'different' in their midst; how they form stereotypes of the disabled person as saint, sinner, super-hero, freak, fiend, victim, obsessive avenger, isolationist, the butt of jokes, just a burden, or someone to be pitied. The particular form of stereotyped thinking depends on the society's history, its explanation of how it has come to be and the resultant culture.

The dimensions of inequality to do with gender, sexual orientation, 'race' and class all interact with disablement to create additional oppressions for those with one or more of these oppressions. However, until very recently, the arguments for disability equality have often been ignored in the development of thinking about equal opportunities. In this chapter, therefore, I will begin by looking at how disablement is defined and modelled. I will then look at the extent of disability, world-wide and in the UK. Next, I will give a brief history of disablement, including the growth of the Disabled People's Movement and our struggle for civil rights. I will conclude with an examination of stereotypes in the media – images that are continually recycled to maintain prejudice – and what is being done to counter this.

Two ways of viewing disablement: the 'medical model' and the 'social model'

The 'medical model' of disability

The 'medical model' sees the disabled person as the problem. We are to be adapted to fit into the world as it is. If this is not possible, then we are shut away in some specialized institution or isolated at home, where only our most basic needs are met. The emphasis is on dependence, backed up by the stereotypes of disability that call forth pity, fear and patronizing attitudes. Rather than on the needs of the person, the focus is usually on the impairment. With the medical and associated professions' discourse of cures, normalization and science, the power to change us lies within them. Often our lives are handed over to them.

Other people's (usually non-disabled professionals') assessments of us are used to determine where we go to school; what support we get; what type of education; where we live; whether or not we can work and what type of work we can do; and indeed whether we are even born at all, or are allowed to procreate. Similar control is exercised over us by the design of the built environment, presenting us with many barriers, thereby making it difficult or impossible for our needs to be met and curtailing our life chances. Whether it is in work, school, leisure and entertainment facilities, transport, training and higher education, housing or in personal, family and social life, practices and attitudes disable us.

Powerful and pervasive views of us are reinforced in language, and in the media, books, films, comics and art. Many disabled people internalize negative views of ourselves which create feelings of low self-esteem and achievement, further reinforcing non-disabled people's assessment of our worth. The 'medical model' view of us creates a cycle of dependency and exclusion which is difficult to break.

'Medical model' thinking about us predominates in schools where special educational needs are thought of as emanating from the individual who is seen as different, faulty and needing to be assessed and made as normal as possible (see Figure 7.1).

The 'Social Model' of Disability

If, instead of focusing on differentness within the individual, the focus were on, for example, all children's right to belong and to be valued in their local school, then we would be asking 'what is wrong' with the school and looking at the strengths of the child. This second approach is based on the 'social model' of disability. This model views the barriers that prevent disabled people from participating in any situation as being what disables them. The social model makes a fundamental distinction between impairment and disability. *Impairment* is defined as 'the loss or limitation of physical, mental or sensory function on a long-term, or permanent basis', whereas *disability* is 'the loss or limitation of opportunities to take part in the normal life of the community on an equal level with others due to physical and social barriers' (Disabled People's International, 1981, in Dreiger, 1989).

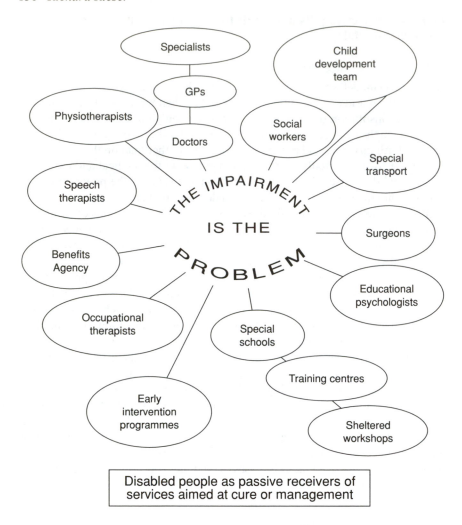

Figure 7.1 The medical model

The Disability Movement, which consists of organizations controlled by disabled people, comprises those disabled people and their supporters who understand
that they are, regardless of their particular impairment, subjected to a common
oppression by the non-disabled world. We are of the view that the position of
disabled people and the discrimination against us are socially created. This has
little to do with our impairments. As disabled people, we are often made to feel
that it is our own fault that we are different. The difference is that some part, or
parts, of our bodies or minds are limited in their functioning. This is an impairment.
This does not make us any less human. But most people have not been brought
up to accept us as we are. Through fear, ignorance and prejudice, barriers and

discriminatory practices develop which disable us. This understanding of the process of disablement allows disabled people to feel good about ourselves and empowers us to fight for our human rights (Oliver, 1990; Morris, 1991; Mason and Rieser, 1994).[1]

I will illustrate the two models of disability, with reference to my own history. I had polio in 1949 which led to the loss of muscle in my left leg, right arm and back. My impairment by the time I was six years old was not major – I could walk, swim, ride a bicycle and so on – but I walked with a limp. However, when I expressed the desire to attend the local primary school, which was all built on one level, the headteacher refused to have me, claiming that I was a fire risk. I was accordingly sent to a school for 'the physically handicapped'. This was my first experience of disablement. The school smelled like a hospital and I did not want to go there. So my parents kept me off school until the London County Council (LCC) agreed to pay for me to attend a private 'progressive' school which was not very good. There I was diagnosed as having 'learning difficulties' and 'behaviour problems'. Seven years later, I chose to leave and went to the local secondary modern, a year below my age group. Again I was disabled by not being allowed to use the lift in the six-storey building, by being bullied and being made to feel bad about myself in PE. Despite this, I did get the necessary O and A levels to enter university, though at some considerable cost to my self-esteem. In all these situations people were disabling me by presenting barriers to my equal participation (see Figure 7.2).

The Disabled People's Movement

The Disabled People's Movement represents the view that the 'cure' to the problem of disability lies in the restructuring of society. Unlike medically based 'cures', which focus on the individual and their impairment, this is an achievable goal and to the benefit of everyone. This approach, referred to as the 'social model', suggests that disabled people's individual and collective disadvantage is due to a complex form of institutional discrimination as fundamental to our society as social-class exploitation, sexism, racism or heterosexism. This leads to discrimination and the internalized oppression we experience. This is not to deny or devalue the discomfort and pain we often experience as a result of having an impairment. Recently a number of disabled writers (Morris, 1993; Crow, 1996; Shakespeare, 1992; Oliver, 1996; Shakespeare and Watson, 1997) have argued that the 'social model' of impairment must include these experiences – for example, pain, discomfort and dying – and that the Disabled People's Movement will only attract larger numbers of disabled people if it takes these ideas and practices on board. There has been understandable resistance from those who experienced their lives as dominated by the 'medical model' and the real problem is that our current 'social model' has not been developed to encompass our experience of impairment and so to develop our own responses to it.

In addition to this, the obsession with finding medically based cures distracts us from looking at causes of either impairment or disablement. In a world-wide sense,

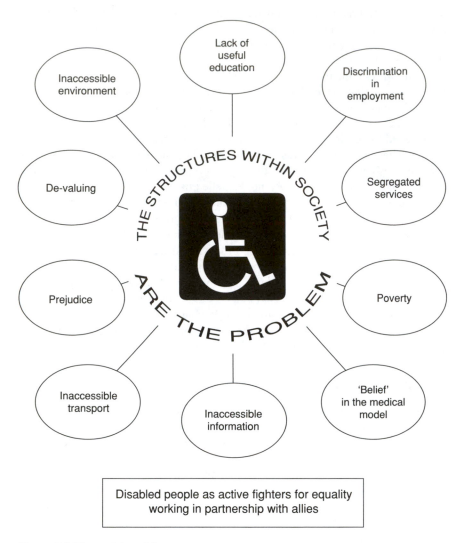

Figure 7.2 The social model

most impairments are created by oppressive systems – hunger, lack of clean water, exploitation of labour, lack of safety, child abuse and wars (see below).

Clearly, the 'social model' has important implications for our education system – particularly with reference to primary and secondary schools. Prejudicial attitudes towards disabled people and indeed against all minority groups are not inherited. They are learned through contact with the prejudice and ignorance of others. Therefore, to challenge discrimination against disabled people, we must begin in our schools.

Our fight for the inclusion of all children, however 'severely' impaired, in one mainstream education system will not make sense unless the difference between the 'social' and the 'medical' model of disability is understood (see Chapter 8 of this volume for a discussion of disability and education).

The 'social model' has empowered many disabled people and been important in uniting previously disparate, often impairment-based organizations. The self-representation of disabled people has been important in a situation where organizations 'for' disabled people, but run by non-disabled people, have sought to do things in our name, but without finding out what disabled people want. The British Council of Disabled People, made up of 129 organizations of disabled people that are run by disabled people, has had a long battle over the last twenty-one years to establish itself. This has been particularly hard when large charities 'for' disabled people such as the Royal National Institute for the Blind (RNIB), the Royal National Institute for the Deaf (RNID), the Royal Association for Disability and Rehabilitation (RADAR), SCOPE (for people with cerebral palsy) and MENCAP (Royal Society for Mentally Handicapped Children and Adults) get large amounts of government funding to provide services for disabled people, have influence, but do not represent disabled people and are not controlled by them. This was very apparent when the 1995 Disability Discrimination Act passed through Parliament and these organizations welcomed the new law in the face of opposition from disabled people's organizations.

The Disability Discrimination Act was seen by the Disabled People's Movement as weak and full of 'get-out' clauses, such as a 'reasonable' discrimination. In addition, the Act did not create a commission to enforce and support disabled complainants although a Disability Rights Commission was subsequently established in 2000. Transport and Education were largely left out of the Act's provisions, and the legislation only applied to employers with twenty or more employees – thus exempting 96 per cent of employers (after pressure, this was reduced to fifteen or more employees and from October 2004 to 5 or more, as a result of new European Legislation). The split in the Rights Now Coalition (a group campaigning for civil rights legislation) between the factions 'of' and 'for' us was patched up, with the establishment of the Disability Rights Task Force.

The Labour government did not honour its manifesto commitment to introduce enforceable civil rights legislation for disabled people, but it has introduced, in 2001, the Special Educational Needs and Disability Act. This extended the DDA to cover the provision for the whole education system. Currently, (August 2004) a new Disability Bill is awaited which will implement the remainder of the Task Force recommendations and introduce a new duty on all public bodies (including schools and colleges) to promote disability equality. This follows the introduction of the Race Relations (Amendment) Act 2000, which following the enquiry into the death of Stephen Lawrence, introduced a duty to promote race equality on all public bodies. None of these developments would have occurred without pressure from the trade unions, community groups and disabled peoples' organizations.

What is disablement?

World figures

Disablement, then, is a social process, but many of the attempts to enumerate disabled people do not take account of this; instead, they view it as a medical problem or personal tragedy. In 1996, the United Nations estimated there were at least 500 million disabled people in the world. This was made up of people with the following impairments: 55 million visually impaired (11 per cent), 70 million hearing impaired (14 per cent), 130 million with severe intellectual impairment (26 per cent), 20 million with epilepsy (4 per cent) and 160 million with some sort of mobility impairment (Disability Awareness in Action, 1995, p. 7). Many poor countries do not have information on disability. In some, cultural taboos lead to disabled people being hidden away. In addition, major categories of impairment, such as mental distress, facial disfigurements and deformities, cancer, HIV/AIDS, hidden impairments like diabetes, sickle-cell anaemia, acute asthma and many other conditions which affect physical or mental functioning on a long-term basis, are not included in these figures. If all these groups were to be added, the number would certainly increase significantly to at least 850 million or one in eight. The World Health Organization estimates 10 per cent (Coleridge, 1993, p. 108).

The UN figures also reveal the major causes of impairment. These include: malnutrition (100 million (20 per cent)); accident, war and trauma (including 20 million injured by land mines; 78 million (15.6 per cent)); infectious diseases, such as TB, polio and leprosy (all of which are preventable) (56 million (11.2 per cent)); non-infectious diseases (100 million (20 per cent)); and congenital diseases (100 million (20 per cent)). It has been estimated that 80 per cent of the impairments in the world are preventable as they are caused by poverty, war, hunger and disease. The report gives many examples of self-help projects from around the world, where disabled people have managed to dismantle barriers to their inclusion (Disability Awareness in Action, 1995, p. 9).

It is also clear that the number of people counted as 'disabled' increases as the standard of living increases, showing it to be a social construct. The proportion of disabled people in Austria, for example, is twenty times higher than that in Peru (Coleridge, 1993, p. 105). Local perception, barriers, survival rates and longevity vary considerably from rich to poor countries and will help to explain such variations.

UK figures

A DfEE Workforce Survey (Winter 1994–5) showed that only 40 per cent of disabled adults of working age (sixteen to sixty-five years old) were working or registered unemployed. The rest – 60 per cent or 2.2 million disabled people – were on benefit and not looking for work. It also showed that, of the 3.7 million disabled working age adults (up by 1.2 million on the OPCS survey eight years earlier), 41 per cent had no educational qualifications. This compared to the whole working population very poorly, where only 18 per cent had no educational qualifications (cited in Sly *et al.*, 1995). 2002 figures put this at 48 per cent, but there has been an increase in the number of disabled people of working age of 1 million (Smith and Twomey, 2002).

These figures follow on from a ground-breaking sample survey in the mid-1980s by the Office of Population Census (*6 Reports Survey of Disability in Great Britain*, cited in Martin *et al.* 1988) that sought to enumerate the number of disabled people in the United Kingdom. This showed that there were at least 6.5 million disabled people in Britain. Of these, 6.2 million were adults (14.2 per cent of the adult population); 41.8 per cent or 2.59 million of these were aged sixteen to sixty-five and 360,000 were five- to sixteen-year-olds. More recent surveys show increases in all categories. The survey did not include under-fives who, given the rise in the birth rate and improved medical techniques, would number at least another 300,000. This is borne out by the 1991 Census which recorded 6.9 million people who were disabled or long-term sick.

To be classed as disabled in this Office of Population Census (OPCS) survey, one had to have a significant impairment that 'restricted or led to a lack of ability to perform normal activities, which has resulted from the impairment of a structure or function of body or mind' (OPCS, 1988, p. xi). Thresholds were set on ten scales such as mobility, hearing, sight, incontinence, lifting, mental ability. Panels of judges developed the scales by examining the responses to narrowly based questions. People were interviewed and asked 'what they normally can do'. Anyone who is disabled has had to learn to do things in an environment and with objects that are not designed for us to use. Second, the questions asked were individualized rather than socialized and did not examine people's impairments against a background of the social and environmental contexts of disabled people's lives.

Criticizing the survey method and the ideology that lies behind it, Mike Oliver (1990) makes the different orientations clear. From the OPCS survey (1986–8), he examines questions that were drawn from the face-to face interviews. The questions were:

1   Can you tell me what is wrong with you?
2   What complaint causes you difficulty in holding, gripping or turning things?
3   Do you have a scar, blemish or deformity which limits your daily activity?
4   Have you attended a special school because of a long-term health problem or disability?
5   Does your health problem/disability affect your work in any way at present?
6   Do your health problems/disability make it difficult for you to travel by bus?

These questions clearly see disability as individualized and are based on 'medical model' thinking. They could have been put in an alternative way that draws on a 'social model':

1   Can you tell me what is wrong with society?
2   What defects in design of everyday equipment like jars, bottles and lids causes you difficulty in holding, gripping or turning things?

3   Do other people's reactions to any scar, blemish or deformity you have limit your daily activity?
4   Have you attended a special school because of your education authority's policy of sending people with your long-term health problem or disability to such places?
5   Do you have problems at work as a result of the physical environment or the attitudes of others?
6   Do poorly designed buses make it difficult for someone with your health problem/disability to use them?

(Oliver, 1990, pp. 7–8)

Abberley (1992, p. 154), in criticizing the surveys, has this to say:

> It is a matter of political choice that OPCS surveys were designed in terms of an individualistic 'personal tragedy' approach to disability, rather than to devote significant resources to an exploration of the ways in which it is society that disables impaired people. Whilst there are ways in which we may utilise OPCS data, we must not in doing so lose sight of this most fundamental flaw. Information gathered on the basis of an oppressive theory, unless handled with circumspection, is itself one of the mechanisms of oppression.

Anyone who has followed the pronouncements of the New Labour government in the UK on disability benefits can see the dangers of this oppressive theory. Despite announcing a task force to recommend full civil rights legislation for disabled people, the government allowed the Benefits Integrity Project to whip up pressure generally to cut back on the non-means-tested Disability Living Allowance (DLA) by producing false figures that one in five claimants was bogus. When this was shown to be false they claimed that if everyone who was entitled to claim Disability Living Allowance did, then 8.6 million people would be eligible on the current criteria, thus creating a climate for cut-backs. This time a huge outcry from disabled people and their allies prevented any threat to DLA. The allowance was the one positive thing that came out of the OPCS surveys which showed definitively that disabled people lived in poverty and needed extra money to participate in society. *OPCS Report 2* (Morris and White, 1988) established that disabled people were poorer than any other section of UK society. Now DLA is under threat because the government fails to understand that the barriers in society disable us and until they have been removed we need to be compensated for the extra cost of being disabled. These statistics are shifting sands. Using the DDA definition the 2001 Census identified 10.5 million adults who are long term sick or disabled – that is 22 per cent of the adult population. In addition, the DfES in 2004 identified 700,000 young people under 16 who are disabled.

The history of disablement

The continuing inequality we face will not be rectified by ramps, lifts and accessible communications, or the outlawing of discriminatory behaviour, welcome as these may be. The well-spring of our oppression comprises deeply held social attitudes that reflect generations of prejudice, fear and discrimination towards disabled people in education, work and social life. The main reasons are negative attitudes and stereotypes which are based on untrue ideas that have been around for thousands of years and which are amazingly persistent.

We can, at any time, all become disabled – develop a physical or mental impairment. Perhaps the need to distance ourselves from this reality makes it convenient to rely on negative attitudes and stereotypes of disability. They are less troubling than accepting the individuality, the joy, the pain, the appearance, the behaviour and the *rights* of disabled people.

Work by anthropologists (Hanks and Hanks, 1948) has established that there is no one way that disabled people are viewed across a wide range of societies. Views ranged from high status to outcast. There appears to be an underlying economic basis, so in societies with more surplus produce, such as agricultural rather than nomadic or hunter-gatherer, there was more acceptance of disabled members of those societies. There was more chance of their being supported as there was surplus food. However, there were exceptions, and some evidence exists that hunter-gatherers have valued disabled members of their societies. A band of Northern Territory Aborigines carried a member of their band who could not walk with them on their wanderings for sixty years (Davis, 1989). Where an impairment was more commonly occurring, such as blindness in a Mexican village (Gwaltney, 1970), or on Martha's Vineyard, an island off the New England coast with an unusually high proportion of deaf people (Groce, 1985) the whole culture changed to accommodate guiding and signing, respectively. Though no systematic cross-cultural study of the position of disabled people has yet been carried out, it is clear that the individualized tragic view of disability prevalent in modern Western society is not universal.

The ancient world

To understand the development of this particular view of disabled people, we must go back to ancient Greece, to the beginning of 'Western civilization'. In Greek mythology Zeus and Hera had a child, Hyphaistos, God of Fire, who was born with a 'club-foot'. He was thrown off Mount Olympus into the sea, but, being a god, he survived to return and become the butt of jokes of all the other gods (Garland, 1995). He was a forger of metal and as he grew up his sexual relations with women were frequently fraught with difficulty because of the attitudes of the other gods. His wife, according to Homer, was the beautiful Aphrodite, who deceived him by having an affair with Ares. Here, we witness one of the most pernicious myths about disabled adults – that they are incapable of adult sexual relations.

The Greek and Roman attitude was to worship and adore the body beautiful. This is exemplified by the many perfectly proportioned sculptures of the human body, bodies with 'beautiful' symmetrical features. In representations on vases, tablets, sculptures and so on, there are very few disabled people. The Olympic ideal was to aspire to be like the gods in physique, intellect and morals. This is still often apparent in the Olympic Games, where the Para Olympics and Games for People with Learning Difficulties still segregate disabled athletes, although some sensory-impaired people have recently competed in the main Games.

The cult of the body beautiful was put into practice, particularly among the patrician or ruling classes in ancient Greece and Rome. Aristotle wrote 'that you should take your child off if they are imperfect and get rid of them' (Garland, 1995, p. 15). The status of 'child' was not conferred until seven days after birth, so there was time to dispose of unwanted babies legally. In militaristic Sparta, children were the property of the state and inspected at birth. 'If the child be ill-born or ill-formed', the father was required to expose it at a chasm-like place called Apothetai or the Place of Exposure (ibid., p. 14). In Rome disabled infants were meant to be drowned in the Tiber and the games at the Coliseum put on to entertain and pacify the 'mob' included disabled children being thrown under horses' hooves, blind gladiators fighting each other and 'dwarves' fighting women. The rest of the ancient world was not as proscriptive, but nevertheless exposure was widespread. Those with less significant impairments who survived generally led a half-life, disdained and ridiculed, often having to rely on begging. There were exceptions. Even in Sparta, King Agesilaos was afflicted with 'congenital lameness' but this acted as a spur to his ambition and he desired to be first in all things (ibid., p. 40). Clearly, then, exposure did not always occur, as parents do tend to love their children, and many disabled people survived infancy. In Rome, despite the dislike of and cruelty towards people with impairments, there is evidence that at least one emperor was disabled: Claudius may well have had cerebral palsy (*clauditas* in Latin means lameness). Claudius' mother, Antonia, described him 'as a monster of a man, not finished by nature but only half done' (ibid., pp. 40–2). Echoed in Shakespeare's Richard III, this develops into an abiding stereotype as the evil and avenging man/monster.

The Judaeo-Christian tradition

Another seminal source of thinking about disabled people was the Judaeo-Christian tradition that fundamentally disability is a punishment for evil – 'if humans are immoral they will be blinded by God' (Deutoronomy, 27:27); in Exodus (20:5) God tells Moses that retribution for sin will be inflicted on the offspring of the sinners for many generations. In the books of Exodus, Numbers and Deuteronomy, the people of Israel are repeatedly punished for their sinful ways through physical impairment (Rose, 1997).

The Jewish faith, however, has a more complex position, with some parts of the Talmud advocating disability as a holy state and a means of getting to heaven. Similar sentiments are expressed towards those who help disabled people. Some of this is reflected in the parables of the New Testament, but usually with Christ performing miracle cures. Rarely are disabled people accepted as themselves.

The Book of Leviticus (21:16–20) has a clear message that impairment is unclean and polluting, and prevents disabled people from receiving sacraments:

And the Lord said to Moses none of your descendants throughout the generations who has a blemish shall draw near, a man blind or lame or one who has a mutilated face or a limb too long, or a man who has an injured foot or an injured hand or a hunchback or a dwarf, or a man with defective sight or itching disease or scabs or crushed testicles. He may eat the bread of his God, both of the most holy and of holy things, but he shall not come near the veil or approach the altar, because he has a blemish, that he has a blemish, that he may not profane my sanctuaries.

This message was taken seriously. Until the 1950s people with learning difficulties were not allowed to receive certain sacraments in the Roman Catholic Church.

The medieval period

Disabled people were treated in medieval Europe as both saints and sinners. On the one hand, they were 'innocents unstained by normal and sinful human characteristics' (Barnes, 1991, p. 12) who should be offered asylum and alms; on the other, they were evil changelings – the work of the devil (Haffter, 1968).

Martin Luther, the architect of the Reformation, believed that changelings had no soul and advocated that children so 'afflicted' should be taken to the river and drowned. Nevertheless, the bulk of disabled people born into feudal villages or acquiring impairments would have been accepted and did what they could, while those with more severe impairments may have been subject to infanticide.

Veterans of war were often treated better. The first record of a sheltered workshop in Europe was the Congregation of Three Hundred, established in France in 1254 for 300 crusaders who had had their eyes gouged out by Saracens (Ford, 1981).

At times of crisis disabled people were likely to be scapegoated as superstition took over – for example, during the Plague or during the Great Witchhunt of 1480–1680. The 'Malleus Maleficarum' – 'the Hammer of Witches', 1487, written by two priests – was a bestseller in Europe and went to seventy editions in fourteen languages. It includes whole sections on how you can identify witches by their impairments or by their creation of impairments in others; or giving birth to a disabled child. Between 8 million and 20 million people, mainly women, were put to death across Europe and a good proportion were disabled. Three witches were recorded as hanged after an Oxford trial in 1613, one of whom was put on trial because she was a disabled person using crutches (Rieser, 1995, p. 6). Recent research on the treatment of people with learning difficulties, however, suggests that naturalistic accounts of learning difficulties and mental illness were accepted, rather than the disabled people being demonized (Neugebauer, 1996).

The 'disabled witch' comes through in the folklore of Britain and Europe. The Brothers Grimm collected the oral stories of northern Europe and made them into their fairy tales. The witch in *Hansel and Gretel* is deformed, blind, ugly, disabled and carries a stick (this book has been adapted for use with children as young as two years old). There are also storybooks which feature evil imps swapping healthy babies for disabled ones – changelings (Rieser, 1995, p. 5).

There are many pictures and stories from medieval times of penitent sinners. Groups of penitent 'cripples' are depicted trying to get alms and, if they wandered around long enough, feeling humble enough, then maybe they would make it in the next life. A very strong message therefore came across. Disabled people were often scapegoated for the ills of society, as in Brueghel's painting *The Cripples*, where the fox tails denote wrongdoing. Outside any medieval church are the deformed ones, the gargoyles; and on the inside are the 'perfectly formed' pictures around the crypt.

Until the seventeenth century those disabled people rejected by their families relied upon the haphazard and often ineffectual tradition of Christian charity and alms – gifts for subsistence (Barnes, 1991, Chapter 2). During the sixteenth century the wealth and power of the Church was greatly reduced due to the confrontation between Church and state in England. There was also a growth in those seeking alms due to a rise in population, poor harvests, the beginning of the commercialization of agriculture and immigration from Ireland and Scotland (Stone, 1985). To secure the allegiance of local gentry and magistrates, the Tudor monarchs were forced to make economic provision for people dependent upon charity. The 1601 Poor Law marks the first recognition of the need for the state to intervene in the lives of disabled people. Some two hundred years earlier, the Peasants' Revolt of 1381 had led to a mandate to local officials to distinguish the 'deserving poor' from the 'undeserving poor'. The bulk of relief went to the deserving poor in the form of 'household relief' to people in their homes. Segregation did not really emerge until the nineteenth century (Barnes, 1991, pp. 14–19).

Close examination of Rembrandt's sketches reveals that the beggars are often wearing white head bands. This is because in seventeenth-century Holland the bacillus-leprosy, brought inadvertently on the back of the 'spice trade' from colonies in the tropics, spread quickly around urban areas. An edict was passed by the state that all those who contracted it had to report to The Hague, and once their condition was confirmed they had all their worldly goods confiscated, had to wear a white head band and they and their families had to rely on alms as penitent sinners. Those with leprosy had to live in segregated colonies and their only reward for penance was rehabilitation in heaven (Toth-Ubbens, 1987).[2]

The eighteenth and nineteenth centuries

The development of industrial capitalism and its inherent requirement for workers to sell their labour power meant that those with significant impairments were excluded from the labour market. Those disabled people who were able to work were forced to the bottom rungs of the labour market ladder (Morris, 1969, p. 9). As a result, disabled people came to be regarded as a social and educational problem, and increasingly were segregated out of the mainstream, in institutions of various kinds: workhouses, asylums, colonies and special schools (Oliver, 1990, p. 28). According to Finkelstein (1980), this is Phase Two of disabled people's development, the phase when we were separated from our class origins and became a special segregated group, with disability seen as an impairment, requiring segregation from the labour market as well as social restriction.[3]

Throughout the eighteenth and nineteenth centuries the policy of segregating severely impaired people into institutional settings slowly spread. The main impetus was the change from working as groups or families on the land, down the mines or as cottage industry to factory work. The latter required set rates of working on repetitive tasks for long hours; time was money. By 1834, Poor Law household relief was abolished for the 'non-deserving poor' – the unemployed. The deserving poor were categorized – children, the sick, the insane, defectives and the aged and infirm, the last four being categories of impairment – and provision was uniform across the country. Deterrence was built into relief as a principle of 'least eligibility' was introduced. This meant that those on relief would be less comfortable than an 'independent labourer of the lowest class' before benefits would be granted (Barnes, 1991, p. 16). Charles Dickens and others have vividly described the horrors of the workhouse. Charities increasingly set up asylums for the insane and then special schools for blind and deaf children. This role was taken over by the state from the 1890s (Hurt, 1988).

The 'insane', which included 'idiots', 'lunatics' and the mentally infirm, were, after the 1845 Lunacy Act, able to be detained on the certification of a doctor. This was based on a theory advanced by the medical profession that mental illness had physiological causes that were treatable. This marked the beginning of the medical profession's state-endorsed involvement in the lives of disabled people (Barnes, 1991). This power is still exercised today; as a disabled person, if you want an blue (parking privileges) badge, Disability Living Allowance or Incapacity Benefit you have to be examined by a doctor. Disabled people are not trusted in general and there is always a belief that people will pretend to be disabled to get benefits fraudulently, but this does not explain the continual checking of our impairments even when medical science has no solutions and our conditions are stable or deteriorating. Far more disabled people who are entitled to benefits don't claim them than the bogus claims from non-disabled people that are made; the latter, in reality, being rarities. This symbolic treatment of disabled people who are at the margins of the workforce very much defined who was part of the workforce and who was not (Oliver, 1990).

In the last quarter of the nineteenth century, another strand of thought became highly influential – the eugenics movement. This had and continues to have a disastrous effect on the lives of disabled people. Drawn from the ideas of Aristotle, eugenics thinking first wrongly applied Darwin's theories of natural selection to ideas about racial degeneration and was then applied to disabled people. The birth of disabled children, it was claimed, would weaken the gene pool and out-breed non-disabled people. This, in turn, would weaken the European population in its task of colonizing and controlling the rest of the world (see Chapters 3 and 4 of this volume for a discussion of racism and imperialism).

The twentieth century

Traditional myths that there were genetic links between physical and mental impairments, crime, unemployment and other social evils were constantly proposed by the likes of Galton (1883, 1909), Dugdale (1895) and Goddard (1913), and many others. They wished to improve the British and American 'races' by preventing the reproduction of 'defectives' by means of sterilization and segregation. In the UK in the 1920s pressure from eugenicists for 'voluntary' sterilization increased (Ryan with Thomas, 1987) (see the website, www.eugenicsarchive.org for much more detail).

These ideas spread quickly to intellectuals of all political complexions as the century of science got under way: H.G. Wells, Sidney and Beatrice Webb, Bernard Shaw and D.H. Lawrence, W.B. Yeats, J.M. Keynes, Winston Churchill and Aldous Huxley to name but a few.

> If I had my way, I would build a lethal chamber as big as Crystal Palace, with a military band playing softly, and a Cinematograph working brightly; then I'd go out in the back streets and the main streets and bring them in, all the sick, the halt and the maimed; I would lead them gently, and they would smile me a weary thanks; and the band would softly bubble out the 'Hallelujah Chorus'.

So wrote D.H. Lawrence in 1908 in a letter to Blanche Jennings (Boulton, 1979, p. 81). This was part of an élitist intellectual culture, which included a dislike for the industrial world and the social disorder it had spawned, and eugenicist views towards disabled people (Carey, 1992).

The Mental Deficiency Act of 1913 was the result of eugenicist agitation and it led to the incarceration of 'idiots', 'imbeciles', 'the feeble minded' and 'moral imbeciles', the last category usually referring to young people who had had illegitimate children. Many were incarcerated for life in sex-segregated institutions to prevent them from reproducing. At first it was argued that units or extra classes attached to ordinary schools were best, but soon the eugenicist view prevailed and the early part of the century saw large numbers of segregated schools for 'crippled children, epileptics, educable morons and feeble minded children' (Copeland, 1997, p. 714; see also Hurt, 1988).

A great wave of building ensued after the First World War with large institutions and colonies being erected on the outskirts of towns. Simon and Binet's false science of IQ testing, refined by supporters such as Cyril Burt (1977), was developed to distinguish the educable from the ineducable. An IQ of less than 50 meant you were destined for a mental deficiency institution as a child and probably for life. It is estimated that 50,000 children with no mental deficiency were sent to these institutions prior to 1950, on the false diagnosis of doctors who, at this time, subscribed to bogus theories, such as that someone's intelligency could be determined by their head shape and size (Humphries and Gordon, 1992).

Children perceived to be ineducable, including many with cerebral palsy, Down's syndrome and speech impairments, went to junior training establishments right up to 1972. At that time, some 60,000 children joined the education system in severe learning difficulty schools. Today, many with the same conditions successfully attend ordinary schools.

In the USA, compulsory sterilization was in wide use by the 1930s. Forty-one states had provision for the sterilization of the insane and feeble minded, and seventeen states prohibited people with epilepsy from marrying. In many states women born deaf were sterilized. Twenty-seven states still had these laws until very recently, though they were seldom enforced. In China, some 15 million people with 'mental incapacity' have been compulsorily sterilized under a law that was enacted in 1995. This is an abuse of their human rights and, as the *Guardian* reported in 1997, is a particular outrage since it is known that many of these women have developed their condition from iodine deficiency in their environment.

Recently it has been reported that in Scandinavia and France, mentally defective women were compulsorily sterilized up to the 1980s. This all took place despite the findings of a study carried out for the Wood Committee in 1929 which showed that only 7.6 per cent of patients of one particular asylum had defective parents.

Disabled people are seen as a burden, and at times of economic stress this view intensifies. The Nazis, when they came to power in Germany in 1933, introduced a law for the Prevention of Hereditary Diseases which led to the forced sterilization of more than 300,000 people. Under the Third Reich, propaganda films were made to show how we were a burden on the state. We were the 'useless eaters', and we should be got rid of. In the beginning, voluntary euthanasia was advocated to end the suffering of 'the incurable', but this ultimately evolved into mass murder. In November 2003 the German Government acknowledged that two hundred and forty thousand physically and mentally disabled people were murdered in 1939/40 at the hands of the doctors of the Third Reich in six so-called clinics, which were staffed by many of those who went on to run the concentration camps where 6 million Jews were exterminated (Burleigh, 1994).

With cut-backs in the welfare state, the eugenicist argument is currently undergoing a revival in Britain. A recent poll on GMTV revealed that 86 per cent of people who rang in thought that a doctor was right to abort two disabled children. In Holland and Tasmania laws have been introduced to allow voluntary euthanasia. This is indicative of the way in which, through history, people have been socialized to view disabled people. The medical ethics committees are allowing the Genome Project to map the seat of all genetic disorders. Soon science will have the capability to eradicate many forms of impairment.

This brief excursus through the history of disabled people should cause us to ask if normality and uniformity are so important or is it difference that makes life interesting? The medicalization of impairment ignores the social context. In 1972 in the UK a child with Down's syndrome (an extra chromosome) would be deemed ineducable. Today, many such children who have attended mainstream schools are able to sit seven or eight GCSEs and are accepted by their peers. What would their lives be like if prejudice and discrimination were to be eradicated? Yet the medical profession insists on genetically screening all pregnant women over thirty for Down's syndrome with a view to termination if it is identified.

The struggle for human dignity

The oppression of disabled people, over the years, has not gone uncontested. On the contrary, many disabled people have consistently struggled for human dignity and for inclusion in mainstream society. The National League for the Blind and Disabled and the British Deaf Association, for example, were both run by disabled people and, from the 1890s, campaigned for rights. In the 1920s, when unions of disabled veterans were formed all over Britain, sit-ins and occupations were held in an attempt to force the introduction of legislation for disabled people's rights. In the 1920s and 1930s, there were hundreds of thousands of First World War veterans with no rights at all in the UK. Even those young people incarcerated in institutions for the blind or deaf had a culture of resistance; for example, when sign language was banned deaf pupils managed to develop their own pigeon sign language.[4]

In 1944 the Disabled Persons Act was passed. This included a quota system, whereby 3 per cent of the jobs in any given business had to be allotted to disabled people. This was to accommodate injured war veterans, and was abolished by the Disability Discrimination Act of 1995. It remains to be seen if this weak Act (see above) is any more effective in getting disabled people into work.

In the 1970s war veterans in the USA started the disability movement there and successfully campaigned until they achieved full civil rights legislation in the Disabilities Act of 1991 (Dreiger, 1989).[5] In the 1970s in the UK the Union of Physically Impaired Against Segregation was formed. This was initiated by Paul Hunt, who lived in a Cheshire home which he called the new workhouse. He wrote a letter to the *Guardian* (20 September 1972) calling on severely physically impaired people to form a new consumer group to put forward their views. This and a number of other organizations run by disabled people and formed in the 1970s amalgamated into the British Council of Organizations of Disabled People (BCODP). The Council, which supports the 'social model' of disability, now represents some 300,000 disabled people who all control their own organizations. The BCODP also linked a number of the local Centres for Independent Living and Local Coalitions of Disabled People (Campbell and Oliver, 1996). These organizations campaigned for full civil rights legislation. Fifteen attempts were made from 1980 to 1995 to get a Civil Rights Bill through Parliament in the UK. Instead, all that was achieved was the 1995 Disability Discrimination Act. The Direct Action Network of disabled people expressed the frustration of millions of disabled people in a series of actions which brought London and other cities and towns to a standstill. As a result, the Labour government set up a ministerial task force to advise on the implementation of full anti-discrimination legislation based on the 'social model' of disability. Disabled people are still struggling for the rights to use public transport, to get into buildings, to go to school or college with their friends, to get a job and even to go to the cinema. In October 1998, Glenda Jackson MP announced that £500 million would be spent on making London Transport buses accessible. In 2005 more was achieved with the introduction of the Public Service Duty to promote disability equality, but much still remains to be struggled for and won, not least a European Directive and a United Nations Declaration on disabled people's rights.

Recycling old ideas in the representation of disabled people

As disabled people, we often feel that the culture we are in characterizes us in a number of false ways that make us seem different to everyone else. Stereotypes of the disabled abound. Thus, there is the 'super-crip' or the disabled person who 'triumphs over tragedy'. Have you ever noticed how often perfectly ordinary things that disabled people do become newsworthy – the blind mountain climber, the boy with cerebral palsy who walked one mile, or the deaf man who was a chess champion? These things are only seen as newsworthy because journalists have a view that disabled people usually cannot or should not be doing ordinary things. The 1996 London Marathon was advertised by Nike showing a man with no legs or arms. The caption was: 'Peter is not like ordinary people. He's done the Marathon.' This plays on two ideas: first, that we are not able to do things; and, second, that we are objects of curiosity – 'freaks' who are worthy of public attention.

We are often referred to as 'cripples'. This comes from an Old German word *kripple*, meaning to be without power. We do not like being called this. President F.D. Roosevelt, the only man to be elected President of the USA four times, had physical impairment, having had polio in both legs, and was unable to walk unaided. Yet he perfected ways of disguising it, such as never being photographed in his wheelchair. He once observed that 'the American public would never vote for a president who was a cripple'. He may well have been right.

With the development of the printing press in 1480, at a time when most people in Europe could not read, cartoons and other graphic representations became popular ways of making political and moral comments to a mass audience. The old ideas of the Greeks became recycled: humankind was created by gods who were physically perfect. Since human beings were created in the gods' own image, the less physically perfect were less worthy. Evil, moral weakness and power-lessness were depicted by caricatured disabled people. For example, in an attempt to discredit Richard III, historians portrayed him as a disabled and vengeful mass murderer. However, when his portrait which hangs in the National Portrait Gallery was X-rayed, it was discovered that the king's hump had been added sixty years after his death. Modern film-makers often make their villains disabled. Little changes.

One need only look at pirates. From Lego to Stevenson's Long John Silver or Blind Pew, or Barrie's Captain Hook in *Peter Pan*; nearly all have eye-patches, hooks and wooden legs. All these disabled pirates do not accord with historical reality. Pirates had a system of simple social security long before anyone else. They had common shares in the common purse so, if they were injured during the course of their endeavours, they would retire to a tropical island with as much money as they wanted. They were unlikely, therefore, to go on trying their luck as an impaired pirate (Greenwich Museum private exhibition, 1994). Yet in the nineteenth century a number of writers became obsessed with disabled and evil pirates. In previous centuries pirates had been socially acceptable as they plundered and built up the British Empire. For example, Daniel Defoe wrote a bestseller about a certain Captain Singleton, pirate, popular hero and, on his return, thrice Lord

Mayor of London. But pirates outlived their usefulness as privateers who expand the Empire, and after the Battle of Trafalgar the Royal Navy could do the job on its own (Rieser, 1995).

Many charity adverts are designed to create fear. Take, for example, the one depicting a girl living 'under the shadow of diabetes'. She probably did not even know she was 'in a shadow' until she found herself up on the billboards of England for three years. She was simply injecting insulin every day and that was all right. Other charity advertisements use black and white imagery to make us look pitiful (for a detailed analysis of how charities use images of disabled people to disable us, see Hevey, 1992).

There is, however, some cause for cautious optimism. The Invisible Children Conference, for example, jointly organized by Save the Children and The Alliance for Inclusive Education, was an exciting and thought-provoking day held in London on 1 March 1995 and attended by more than 150 key image-makers. The conference decided that 'disabled people should be shown as an ordinary part of life in all forms of representation, not as stereotypes or invisible'. The 1 in 8 Group, which grew out of this conference, has issued the following useful guidelines to the media. There are ten main stereotypes of disabled people: the disabled person as:

- Pitiable and pathetic: e.g. charity advertisements and telethons, concepts like *Children in Need* and characters like Tiny Tim in *A Christmas Carol* or Porgy in Gershwin's *Porgy and Bess*.
- An object of violence: e.g. films such as *Whatever Happened to Baby Jane* or *Wait until Dark* which set the style for countless TV films.
- Sinister or evil: e.g. Shakespeare's *Richard III*, Stevenson's *Treasure Island*, the films *Dr Strangelove, Dr No, Hook* or *Nightmare on Elm Street*.
- Curios or exotica: e.g. 'freak shows', images in comics, honor movies and science fiction, films such as *The Hunchback of Notre Dame* or *X-Men*.
- Super crip or triumph over tragedy: e.g. films like *Reach for the Sky*, the last item on the television news – featuring a disabled person climbing a mountain, for example.
- Laughable: e.g. films like *Mr Magoo, Hear No Evil, See No Evil* and *Time Bandits*.
- Having a chip on their shoulder: e.g. Laura in the film *The Glass Menagerie*. This is often linked to a miracle cure as in *Heidi* and *The Secret Garden*.
- A burden/outcast: e.g. as in *Beauty and the Beast* set in subterranean New York, or the Morlocks in the *X-Men*.
- Non-sexual or incapable of having a worthwhile relationship: e.g. Clifford Chatterley in *Lady Chatterley's Lover, Born on the Fourth of July*, O'Casey's 'Silver Tassie' or the film *Life Flesh*.
- Incapable of fully participating in everyday life: our absence from everyday situations, not being shown as integral and productive members of society.

(Biklen and Bogdana, 1977, amended by Rieser and Mason, 1992)

Images: the way forward from and for disabled people

- Shun one-dimensional characterizations and portray disabled people as having complex personalities and being capable of a full range of emotions.
- Avoid depicting us as always receiving; show us as equals – giving as well as receiving.
- Avoid presenting physical and mental characteristics as determining personality.
- Refrain from depicting us as objects of curiosity. Make us ordinary.
- Our impairments should not be ridiculed or made the butt of jokes.
- Avoid sensationalizing us, especially as victims or perpetrators of violence.
- Refrain from endowing us with superhuman attributes.
- Avoid *Pollyanna*-ish plots that make our attitude the problem. Show the societal barriers we face that keep us from living full lives.
- Avoid showing disabled people as non-sexual. Show us in loving relationships and expressing the same range of sexual needs and desires as non-disabled people.
- Show us as an ordinary part of life in all forms of representation.
- Most importantly, cast us, train us and write us into your scripts, programmes and publications.

(Rieser, 1995, p. 44)

Unfortunately, most children and young people still rarely meet disabled children in their schools and form their views of them mainly through the media. The inclusion of disabled people in producing and creating images and the portrayal of disabled people as 'real people' is crucial. It was felt it now is the time to achieve this.

With a very few welcome exceptions – such as the children's television serial *Grange Hill*, the BBC drama *Skallagrigg* or Channel 4's *ER*, and the films, *Four Weddings and a Funeral, Shine* and *Muriel's Wedding* – disabled characters and images are largely absent, or when they do appear they are presented in a negative and stereotypical way. Change can occur. Twenty years ago Asian, black and other minority ethnic people were in a similar position. Now the necessity for their inclusion is taken for granted. Lack of portrayal of disability in our society is not accidental. Western culture from Greek and Roman times, reinforced in Renaissance Europe, has seen 'the body beautiful' as an ideal, and those with physical or mental imperfections have been seen as being in receipt of divine retribution. Such ideas are deeply embedded in myth, legend and classical literature. Today's celluloid entertainment culture reinforces the tendency to judge people by their appearance. The 1 in 8 Group has concentrated on changing the perceptions of image-makers, particularly in film and TV. There has been some shift in the TV soaps, which now include disabled characters, but these are not usually played by disabled actors. To keep the industry aware of these issues, the 1 in 8 Group organizes an annual Raspberry Ripple Award for good and bad portrayal.[6]

More recently the British Broadcasting Corporation has commissioned a number of dramas – *Every Time You Look at Me (April 2004)*, *The Egg (2003)* and *Flesh and Blood (2002)* which include disabled characters as ordinary. As part of the European Year of Disabled People (2003) The British Film Institute and Disability Equality in Education collaborated to produce for teachers a website and a DVD examining how disabled people are shown in moving image media (www.bfi. org.uk/disablingimagery). The DVD and text containing an analysis and many activities for 8–18 year olds are also available in a book (Rieser 2004).

In the next chapter I will examine how both traditional thinking about disabled people and the 'social model' impact on the English education system, one which has grown out of the oppressive history of disabled people and 'medical model' thinking, predominant in special needs education. I will argue that inclusive education, rooted in an understanding of these diverse processes, is the way forward in eliminating both disadvantage and prejudicial attitudes.

Notes

1   Mason and Rieser (1994) is for teachers and school governors.
2   This book is written in Dutch, with an English summary.
3   In Phase 1, disabled individuals were part of a greater feudal underclass. In Phase 3, which is just beginning, disability comes to be seen solely as *social restriction*. The surplus value generated in capitalist societies, combined with modern technology, means that we can be exploited as workers by capitalism in much the same way as non-disabled people. However, it also means that we can make the case *not* to be segregated either in the world of work, or more generally in the mainstream society.
4   The book *Out of Sight* contains first-hand oral histories and photographs of life in special schools and institutions in the first half of this century (Humphries and Gordon, 1992).
5   This is a good account of the international development of the Disabled People's Movement.
6   Norden (1994) gives a fascinating account of how the image of disabled people has been developed through Hollywood, while Pointon (1997) provides a very useful handbook on how the disability movement has developed a critique and a response to the way disabled people are shown in the media. These ideas could also be useful to educationalists in the way they reproduce and interpret images of disabled people in the classroom.

References

Abberley, P. (1992) 'Counting us Out: A Discussion of the OPCS Disability Surveys', *Disability, Handicap and Society*, 7 (2), pp. 139–56
Barnes, C. (1991) *Disabled People in Britain and Discrimination*, London: Hurst
Biklen, D. and Bogdana, R. (1977) 'Media Portrayals of Disabled People: A Study of Stereotypes', *Inter-racial Book Bulletin*, 8 (6 and 7), pp. 4–9
Boulton. J.T. (1979) *The Letters of D.H. Lawrence Vol. 1 1901–1913*, Cambridge: Cambridge University Press
Burleigh, M. (1994) *Death and Deliverance: Euthanasia in Germany 1900–1945*, Cambridge: Cambridge University Press
Burt, C. (1977) *The Subnormal Mind*, Oxford: Oxford University Press

Campbell, J. and Oliver, M. (1996) *Disability Politics: Understanding our Past, Changing our Future*, London: Routledge

Carey, J. (1992) *The Intellectuals and the Masses: Pride and Prejudice amongst the Literary Intelligentsia, 1880–1939*, London: Faber & Faber

Coleridge, P. (1993) *Disability, Liberation and Development*, Oxford: Oxfam

Copeland, I. (1997) 'Pseudo-science and Dividing Practices: A Genealogy of the First Educational Provision for Pupils with Learning Difficulties', *Disability and Society* 12 (5), pp. 709–22

Crow, L. (1996) 'Including all our Lives: Renewing the Social Model of Disability', in Barnes, C. and Mercer, G. (eds), *Exploring the Divide: Illness and Disability*, Leeds: The Disability Press

Davis, A. (1989) *From Where I Sit: Living with disability in an Able Bodied World* London: Triangle

Disability Awareness in Action (1995) 'Overcoming Obstacles to the Integration of Disabled People', UNESCO sponsored document for the World Summit on Social Development, Copenhagen, March 1995

Dreiger, D. (1989) *The Last Civil Rights Movement*, London: Hurst

Dugdale, R.L. (1895) *The Jukes: A Study in Crime, Pauperism, Disease and Heredity*, New York

Finkelstein, V. (1980) *Attitudes and Disabled People: Issues for Discussion*, New York: World Rehabilitation Fund

Ford, B. (1981) 'Attitudes towards Disabled Persons: An Historical Perspective', *Australian Rehabilitation Review*, 5, pp. 45–9

Galton, F. (1883) *Enquiries into Human Faculty*, New York

Galton, F. (1909) *Essays in Eugenics*, London: London Eugenics Society

Garland, R. (1995) *The Eye of the Beholder: Deformity and Disability in the Graeco-Roman World*, London: Duckworth

Goddard, H.H. (1913) *The Kallikak Family: A Study in the Heredity of Feeble-mindedness*, New York: Macmillan

Groce, N. (1985) *Everyone Here Spoke Sign*, London: Harvard University Press

Gwaltney, J. (1970) *The Thrice Shy: Cultural Accommodation to Blindness and Other Disasters in a Mexican Community*, London and New York: Columbia University Press

Haffter, C. (1968) 'The Changeling: History and Psychodynamics of Attitude to Handicapped Children in European Folklore', *Journal of Behavioural Studies*, 4

Hanks, J. and Hanks, L. (1948) 'The Physically Handicapped in Non-Occidental Societies', *Journal of Social Issues*, 4 (4)

Hevey, D. (1992) *The Creatures Time Forgot: Photography and Disability Imagery*, London: Routledge

Humphries, S. and Gordon, P. (1992) *Out of Sight: The Experience of Disability 1900–1950*, Plymouth: Channel 4 Books

Hurt, J. (1988) *Outside the Mainstream: A History of Special Education*, London: Batsford

Martin, J., Metzler, H. and Elliot, D. (1988) *OPCS Report 1: The Prevalence of Disability among Adults*, London: HMSO

Mason, M. and Rieser, R. (1994) *Altogether Better*, London: Comic Relief

Morris, J. (1991) *Pride against Prejudice*, London: Women's Press

Morris, J. (1993) *Independent Lives: Community Care and Disabled People*, London: Macmillan

Morris, J. and White, A. (1988) *OPCS Surveys of Disability in Great Britain Report 2,*

The Financial Circumstances of Disabled Adults Living in Private Households, London: HMSO

Morris, P. (1969) *Put Away*, London: Routledge

Neugebauer, R. (1996) 'Mental Handicap in Medieval and Early Modern England: Criteria, Measurement and Care', in Wright, D. and Digby, A. (eds), *From Idiocy to Mental Deficiency: Historical Perspectives on People with Learning Disabilities*, London: Routledge

Norden, M.F. (1994) *The Cinema of Isolation: A History of Physical Disability in the Movies*, New Brunswick, NJ: Rutgers University Press

OPCS (1988) *Surveys of Disability in Great Britain*, London: HMSO

Oliver, M. (1990) *The Politics of Disablement*, London: Macmillan

Oliver, M. (1996) *Understanding Disability from Theory to Practice*, London: Macmillan

1 in 8 Group (1995) 'Disability in the Media Broadsheet' 78

Pointon, A. with Davies, C. (1997) *Framed: Interrogating Disability in the Media*, London: British Film Institute Publishing

Rieser, R. (ed.) (1995) 'Invisible Children: Report of the Joint Conference on Children, Images and Disability', London: Save the Children

Rieser, R. (2004) *Disabling Imagery? A Teaching Guide to Disability and Moving Image Media*, London: Disability Equality in Education (www.diseed.org.uk)

Rieser, R. and Mason, M. (1990/1992) *Disability Equality in the Classroom: A Human Rights Issue*, London: DEE

Rose, A. (1997) 'Who Causes the Blind to See?: Disability and Quality of Religious Life', *Disability and Society*, 12 (3), pp. 395–405

Ryan, J. with Thomas, F. (1987) *The Politics of Mental Handicap*, London: Free Association Books

Shakespeare, T. (1992) 'Renewing the Social Model', *Coalition*, September, pp. 40–2

Shakespeare, T. and Watson. N. (1997) 'Defending the Social Model', *Disability and Society*, 12 (2), pp. 293–300

Sly, F., Duxbury, R. and Tilsley, C. (1995) *Labour Force Survey*, London: DfEE

Smith, A. and Twomey, B. (2002) 'Labour market experience of people with disabilities', *Labour Market Trends*, August (www.statistics.gov.uk/articles/labour_market_trends/-Peoplewithdisabilities-aug2002.pdf)

Stone, D. (1985) *The Disabled State*, London: Macmillan

Toth-Ubbens, M. (1987) *Lost Image of Miserable Beggars: Lepers, Paupers, Guex*, Lochem-Gent: Uitg.Mij. De Tijdstroom

8   Inclusive education or special educational needs

Meeting the challenge of disability discrimination in schools

Richard Rieser

Introduction

When I first had Kim he was my son.

A year later he was epileptic and developmentally delayed. At eighteen months he had special needs and he was a special child. He had a mild to moderate learning difficulty. He was mentally handicapped.

I was told not to think about his future.

I struggled with all this.

By the time he was four he had special educational needs. He was a statemented child. He was dyspraxic, epileptic, developmentally delayed and had complex communication problems.

Two years later, aged six, he was severely epileptic (EP), cerebral palsied (CP) and had complex learning difficulties.

At eight he had severe intractable epilepsy with associated communication problems. He was showing a marked developmental regression.

He had severe learning difficulties.

At nine he came out of segregated schooling and he slowly became my son again. Never again will he be anything else but Kim – a son, a brother, a friend, a pupil, a teacher, a person.

> (*Kim* by Pippa Murray, in Murray and Penman, 1996)

The great majority of children with special educational needs (SEN) will, as adults, contribute economically; all will contribute as members of society. Schools have to prepare all children for these roles. That is a strong reason for educating children with SEN, as far as possible, with their peers. Where all children are included as equal partners in the school community, the benefits are felt by all. That is why we are committed to comprehensive and enforceable civil rights for disabled people. Our aspirations as a nation must be for all our people.

So wrote David Blunkett, Secretary of State for Education and Employment, in his foreword to the government Green Paper *Excellence for All Children: Meeting Special Educational Needs* (DfEE, 1997, p. 4). Blunkett is himself a disabled person who attended a special school for the blind and left without any formal qualifications. He had to attend evening classes, while working full time, to gain the necessary qualifications to go to university. The UK government's commitment to developing inclusive education is, in principle, clear. However, it lacks an understanding of how deeply 'medical model' thinking (see Chapter 7 of this volume) permeates the world of education. Unfortunately this commitment was already weakened by 1998 in the Action Plan (DfEE, 1998). In addition the government is easily deflected by those wishing to maintain the status quo of segregated provision. For example, in the Special Schools Working Group Report (DfES, 2003), the government sees a continuing and important role for special schools – in other words, segregated provision. Nevertheless, the expectation of the forthcoming period in education is that an increasingly wide diversity of pupils will be educated alongside their peers in mainstream classrooms.

If inclusive education is to be effective, teachers have to adopt 'social model' thinking about disabled people (see Chapter 7 of this volume). They must analyse the growing documentation of good practice, but they should also be aware of the barriers which prevent inclusion. These include physical barriers, communication barriers, social barriers, attitudinal barriers, educational barriers and institutional barriers. By physical barriers I mean the separate special school system and inaccessible school buildings and equipment; communication barriers are to do with lack of appropriate signing, Brailling and augmented communication, a lack of the use of plain jargon-free language, or of appropriate computers and other aids. Social barriers are separate classes or units, or 'discrete' courses within mainstream provision, which can lead to isolation and a lack of non-disabled friends. Attitudinal barriers include ignoring, bullying and devaluing us; denying the history, experience or culture of disabled people. Educational barriers consist of inadequate and inappropriate staffing levels, training or material resources within mainstream schools to address the real teaching and learning needs of all. Institutional barriers are the rules, regulations and procedures, including inappropriate testing, targets and examinations, that discriminate against disabled people. Finally, emotional barriers are to do with low self-esteem, lack of empowerment and the denial of the chance to develop worthwhile reciprocal relationships.

The term 'disabled' includes people with: physical impairments, sensory impairments (deaf people, blind people); chronic illness or health issues, including HIV and AIDS; all degrees of learning difficulties, including specific learning difficulties such as dyslexia and speech and language impairments; and impairment based on emotional and behavioural difficulties. It also includes people with hidden impairments such as epilepsy, diabetes, sickle-cell anaemia; children labelled as 'delicate'; people who identify as 'disfigured'; people of diminutive stature and people with mental distress. All are excluded by barriers, though not all have impairments.

The fixed continuum of provision

In Chapter 7 I examined society's historical response to difference and how, in the early part of the twentieth century, as a result of eugenicist thinking, segregation and separation of adults and children with physical and mental impairments became the norm. I also argued that people became identified by their impairment and were thus the target of professional interventions under 'medical model' approaches, which, for the sake of efficiency, were provided in specialized settings. These processes have led to a geographically discrete and fixed continuum of provision in most local education authorities (LEAs). In many parts of the country a child is assessed independently of their local school and community. From this assessment they will be placed where their 'need' can best be met, often in a school for that type of need away from their peers, segregated with other children with that particular need or impairment (see Figure 8.1).

This continuum of provision is very often located in the schools and institutions that were expressly set up in the past to segregate young disabled people from their

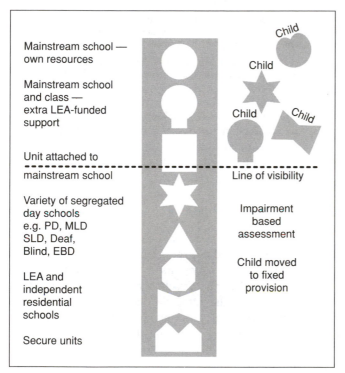

▲ In the fixed continuum the disabled child is slotted and moved according to an impairment based assessment

Figure 8.1 The fixed continuum of provision

Source: Mason and Rieser, 1994.

Table 8.1 Number of children in special schools in England and Wales, 1897–1998

Date	Number of children
1897	4,739
1909	17,600
1914	28,511
1919	34,478
1929	49,487
1939	59,768
1947	40,252*
1955	51,558*
1965	70,334*
1967	78,256*
1977	135,261*+
1987	107,126*+
1998	106,426*+
2001	104,900**
2005	104,790**

Notes:
*   hospital schools not included; + includes severe learning difficulty
**   10/30 DfES Special Education Statistical Bulletin includes maintained and non-maintained
     special schools and pupils in pupil referral units with a statement. England only.

Source: Cole, 1989, based on Chief Medical Officer, Ministry of Education, DfEE circular 9/13 1998
for England, only includes statemented children in maintained and non-maintained independent
schools and PRUs and special schools.

communities. A brief examination of the factors that led to a separate special
school system will be useful to understand the social forces that led to the separation of children with more severe impairments (Mason and Rieser, 1994; Cole,
1989). Despite the good intentions of legislators, this has remained remarkably
stable in the last twenty years (see Table 8.1).

The origin of special schools

Following the Forster Education Act of 1870, School Boards were set up to provide
elementary education for all. The Act did not specifically include provision for
disabled children. For the next fifteen to twenty years, most disabled children were
in units attached to elementary schools, or not at school at all. Elementary classes
were large and instruction was based on the 'Official Code' with rote learning and
memory tests. Teachers were paid by results. Large numbers of children made little
or no progress and the scale and complexity of learning difficulty and impairment
in the population became apparent for the first time. Some progress was made in
providing specialist tuition for blind and deaf children in the aforementioned units.
For example, by 1890 in Scotland and by 1893 in England and Wales, all blind
children aged between five and sixteen and all deaf children between seven and
sixteen were sent to school as of right. Much of this provision was made by
extending existing elementary schools. No such rights to education applied to the
much larger group of 'physically and mentally defective' children. In 1913, the

Mental Deficiency Act was passed. Consistent with eugenicist thinking, this required LEAs to ascertain and certify which children aged seven to sixteen in their area were 'educable defectives' and which were 'ineducable defectives'. In 1914 and 1918, respectively, rights to education were provided for those considered 'educable mental and physical defectives'. However, prior to this, many LEAs had made some such provision. In 1921, under strong eugenicist pressure, five categories of disablement were identified: blind, deaf, mental defective, physical defective and epileptic. Children thus labelled were certified and provided for only in separate schools or certified classes.

Following the increasing popularity of IQ testing in the 1920s and 1930s, the Spens Report recommended a tripartite system. The 1944 Education Act established secondary schools for all, but segregated into grammar, secondary modern and technical. Entry at 11-plus was based in part on IQ tests. Selection by ability prompted selection by 'disability' and the growth of special schools, the number of children in which rose sharply when eleven categories of children based on impairment were introduced. These were blind, partially sighted, deaf, partially deaf, delicate, diabetic, educationally sub-normal, epileptic, maladjusted, physically handicapped and those with speech defects. Regulations prescribed that blind, deaf, epileptic, physically handicapped and aphasic children were seriously 'disabled' and *must* be educated in special schools.

It was hoped that the majority of other categories would receive their education in ordinary schools. However, as a result of overcrowding, prejudice, misinterpretations of the legislation and teacher resistance this did not take place. In fact, it was not until the 1950s that large numbers of new special schools were opened. This continued throughout the 1960s and 1970s. Throughout this period, as new demands were made on teachers, nearly always without additional resources or training, the pressure to exclude more children became greater. In 1965, Circular 10/65 was introduced with the intention of abolishing selection at 11-plus and of instituting a system of comprehensive education, the aim being to cater for the needs of all children regardless of gender, 'race', class or ability. Ironically, this led to a further rise in the number of children in special schools, as a result of a fear over declining standards. In addition, economic cuts meant that the majority of comprehensives stuck to streaming rather than mixed-ability teaching and never catered for the full ability range. This is because effective mixed-ability teaching requires more preparation and planning time, and staffing cuts made this difficult. Even so, over the next thirty years, comprehensives proved to be the most effective way of educating the whole cohort, and where there was mixed ability there was overall the greatest exam success (Benn and Chitty, 1997).

In 1970, in England and Wales, the last 60,000 children who had been considered ineducable under the terms of the 1913 Mental Deficiency Act secured the right to education, but with the label 'Educationally Sub-Normal (severe)' (later 'Severe Learning Difficulty') attached to them. Some 400 new special schools were created largely out of the old junior training centres, which were where 'ineducable children' previously received training. Similar moves took place in Scotland in 1974.

The 1976 Education Act was intended to provide schooling for all categories of disabled children in mainstream schools. The then Secretary of State decided not to introduce it, however, owing to resistance from special schools and some LEAs, and the economic cost.

The 1981 Education Act, following the 1978 Warnock Report, again stressed the need for children with special educational needs to be educated in mainstream schools where possible, and introduced the principle of integration. However, no extra resources were made available, and despite some significant moves in some parts of the country, and some excellent examples of good practice, the proportion of the segregated school population has not declined significantly (1.41 per cent in 1977, 1.35 per cent in 1988 and 1.29 per cent in 1997, 1.27 per cent in 2003). In addition, owing to local variations in LEA policies, there is an eightfold difference in your chances of going to a mainstream school if you have a statement of special educational need depending on where you live (Norwich, 1997). This has increased to a twenty-four fold difference in 2003 with only 0.1 per cent of Newham pupils attending special schools and 2.4 per cent of children in Brighton and Hove attending special schools. (DfES, 2004a, p. 34)

The good practice in some areas has been matched by an increase in the percentage of pupils in special schools in other areas, particularly in the period from 1988 to 1991. There is little doubt that the 1988 Education Reform Act has increased the pressure in some schools to segregate disabled children, especially when schools have not already established good integration policies and allocated resources accordingly. Publication of test results is making many schools more selective about their intakes. This has affected non-statemented children with special educational needs, as there is no additional funding earmarked for them and they are not recorded in published results. Statemented children who have earmarked resources attached to them are a more attractive proposition to locally managed budgets, allocated by inflexible, cost-cutting formulae.

The Audit Commission (2002, p. 2) examined how the 1981 and 1996 special Education Acts were working. It reported that schools were struggling They found it a struggle to balance pressures on schools to raise attainment and to become more inclusive; that national targets had not reflected the good work done with many pupils with special educational needs. There was still a major need to help all children fulfil their potential and these children's interests needed to be reflected in every part of the education system. The report was entitled 'Special Educational Needs: A Mainstream Issue'. The government's response was a new strategy 'Removing Barriers to Achievement' which lays great emphasis of improving the capacity of mainstream schools to effectively include a wider range of students. As the DfES put it, '[w]e are committed to removing the barriers to learning that many children encounter in school' (DfES, 2004b, p. 28).

But the impact of discrimination in education goes much deeper. As Colin Barnes (1991, p. 28) put it after having completed a survey of government reports on education for the Disability Movement:

Institutional discrimination against disabled people is ingrained throughout the present education system. The data shows that most of the educational provision for disabled children and students remains basically segregative, is dominated by traditionally medically influenced attitudes and commands a low priority as a whole. As a result, rather than equipping disabled children and young people with appropriate skills and opportunities to live a full and active life, it largely conditions them to accepting much devalued social roles and in so doing condemns them to a lifetime of dependence and subordination.

Unfortunately, both the 1993 and 1996 Education Acts kept the 'get-out' clauses of the 1981 Act, with respect to special needs provision. These clauses, which have so often been used to compel disabled children, against their and their parents'/ carers' wishes, to attend special schools (Mason, 1998), stipulate 'that educating the child in a school which is not a special school is compatible with:

a   His [*sic*] receiving the special educational provision which his learning difficulty calls for,
b   The provision of efficient education for the children with whom he is educated, and
c   The efficient use of resources.

The SEN and Disability Act 2001 removed clauses (a) and (c) in general from Section 316 of the 1996 Act, but left these get out clauses intact in Schedule 27. So although the government's intention was to give more choice of mainstream school placement to disabled children and their parents this is not proving to be the case. The SEN Disability Tribunal is still, in some cases, upholding Local Education Authority views on placement in special schools against the wishes of parents who want a mainstream place.

It is clear that it has much more to do with attitudes and commitment than anything else. It is also clear that where integration has been planned and resourced, and where all staff have developed it as a whole school policy, it is much more successful (Hegarty and Pocklington, 1981; Booth *et al.*, 1992; Booth and Ainscow, 1998; Sebba and Schadev, 1997).

The Special Educational Needs and Disability Act 2001 is in force following a lengthy review process. However, the fundamental point is that this legislation does not guarantee the right to an education in the mainstream, if you want it. It is still concerned with assessing the individual, rather than assessing to what extent schools have removed the barriers to inclusion, inherited from the past. So long as these stipulations remain, disabled children will always be threatened with being compelled to go to a special school when the political climate shifts, when there are insufficient resources, or if the school has failed to meet their needs. There is a wider symbolic problem. As long as there are institutions called special schools, mainstream schools and teachers will not feel they have to change their buildings, ethos or teaching and learning strategies to accommodate disabled children. All of

Table 8.2 Unequal opportunities growing up disabled

	A Disabled	B Non-disabled
Living with parents	92%	86%
Gone on holiday with friends	25%	52%
Had a spare-time job	22%	32%
Looked after siblings	34%	57%
Had own key	51%	76%
Paid work	35%	67%
Had a boy/girlfriend	30%	40%
Difficulty making friends	35%	20%
Satisfactory network of friends	57%	74%
Self-esteem score	7.3[+]	8.5*
Internal locus of control	8.8	9.3*

Notes:
Group A: 400 disabled people on OPCS category 1–10; Group B: 726 non-disabled people; all respondents aged 13–22.
+ Self-esteem score of those in special schools, 6.2; those in mainstream, 7.5.
* Response score to 12 questions – 6 agree and 6 disagree.

Source: Hirst and Baldwin, 1994.

Table 8.3 Difference in GCSE and GNVQ results for year 11 students in state special and all schools for England 2001–4

Year	School type	Grade 5 A*–C	5 A*–G	1 A*–G	No passes
2001	All Schools	50%	88.9%	94.5%	5.5%
	Special school	0.6%	6.5%	29.3%	70.7%
2002	All schools	51.5%	88.9%	94.6%	5.4%
	Special school	0.6%	5.0%	37.2%	62.8%
2003	All schools	52.6%	88.6%	94.6%	5.4%
	Special school	0.9%	5.4%	32%	68%
2004	All schools	53.4%	86.4%	95.8%	4.2%
	Special schools	0.4%	4.8%	59%**	41%

Note:
** in 2004 includes entry level qualification in 2004 which is at a significantly lower level.

Source: UK Education Statistics DfES (www.dfes.gov.uk/statisticsGCSE-GNVQ attempts+ achievement)
Special schools include community and foundation special schools, pupil referal units and hospital Schools.

us involved with education must engage in the ongoing task of changing deep-seated attitudes and discriminatory behaviour if we are to create an inclusive future in which all will benefit.

Segregated education has not been good for disabled people. Hirst and Baldwin (1994) carried out a major comparative survey of the lives of young disabled and non-disabled people (aged thirteen to twenty-two) which showed stark differences in lifestyle. Most telling was an index of self-esteem which clearly showed that those who attended special schools had a significantly lower score than disabled people who attended mainstream schools, and their scores were also significantly below those of non-disabled people.

A recent Ofsted Report (Oct, 2004) found that the legislative framework had had little effect on the proportion of pupils with SEN in mainstream schools, or on the range of needs for which mainstream schools cater. There has been an increase in the number of pupils placed in pupil referral units and independent special schools. A minority of mainstream schools meet special needs very well with high expectations, effective whole school planning seen through by committed managers, close attention on the part of skilled teachers and support staff and rigorous evaluation remain the key to success. Over half the schools visited had no access plans despite being legally bound to have them from April 2003.

Yet, government statistics show at least 588,000 disabled pupils in primary (6.7 per cent of all pupils) and secondary (6.2 per cent of all pupils) and special schools. But only 15.4 per cent of disabled pupils attended maintained and non-maintained special schools. So clearly a large majority of disabled pupils are attending mainstream schools, but are not receiving inclusion, but some inadequate form of integration.

However disabled pupils attending mainstream schools still do much better than disabled pupils attending special schools and for the first time using the national pupil data base it was possible to establish this. A government commissioned research 'Inclusion and Pupil Achievement' (Dyson *et al.*, 2004, p. 39), shows that LEAs with high rates of inclusion in mainstream schools did no worse than low including LEAs in national tests. As to the difference between individuals they also showed that: at KS4 in 2002 average point score was 38.55. (The average point score is the total of GCSE or GNVQ exams with 8 for a single subject grade A* and 1 for a single subject grade G.); for non-statemented pupils with special educational needs, in mainstream, the mean score was 21.85; for statemented pupils in mainstream the mean points score was 16.99 and for pupils in special schools the mean points score was 2.4 points – or seven times below the score for statemented mainstream pupils.

In addition, Gary Thomas (1996) analysed GCSE results by type of school and found that 70 per cent of special schools do not enter any pupils for GCSE. He went on to show that 93 per cent of mainstream Year 11 students get at least one A*–G grade, whereas only 16 per cent of Year 11 students in special schools get at least one A*–G grade. This is particularly shocking if one considers the largest group of pupils in special schools are labelled as having 'Moderate Learning Difficulty' (nearly 55,000), and that in mainstream schools they would all be entered for GCSE.

The language we use

The inheritance of the past conditions current attitudes, policies and practice towards disabled children and young people in society and within education. This is nowhere more clearly demonstrated and symbolized than in the language used. Take, for example, the negative connotations associated with 'cripple' (without power) 'sufferer', 'invalid' and 'handicapped' (commonly used as a noun to describe children, when it is actually a verb meaning imposed disadvantage from beyond the person).

We wish to be known as 'disabled people' in recognition of the common oppression we face regardless of our specific impairment. People with learning difficulties reject 'mental handicap', wishing to be known as the former. We reject the inhumanity and 'medical model' thinking involved in labelling and identifying people by their impairing condition. Calling someone a 'Down's' or 'spina bifida' child makes the child no more than their condition. Using 'the blind', 'the deaf' or 'the disabled' to describe us diminishes us. We wish to be known as blind people, deaf people or disabled people. If it is necessary to identify a particular impairment, one should say, for example, 'child [or person] with Down's syndrome'.

Within education, impairing condition labels such as 'epileptic' and 'diabetic' and evaluative labels such as 'educationally sub-normal' or 'physically handicapped' have been replaced by labels based on bands of need and derived from Warnock, for example, 'MLD' ('mild learning difficulty') or 'SLD' ('severe learning difficulty'). Inevitably, since children are assessed to fit these categories of need, they become known by their label, and their destination, which tends to be specific separate provision.

In 1991 the Department for Education produced five categories of staffing provision, linked to impairment. These are now increasingly widely used and children are becoming labelled, for example, as 'PMLD' ('profound and multiple learning difficulties') – the most severe category of need with the best staffing ratio. This has reinforced the idea of a continuum of fixed provision in separate schools. We must reject the legacy of the past that has excluded us. We have to recognize that all children and adults have a right to be included in mainstream education and society as a fundamental human right (Mason and Rieser, 1994; Rieser and Mason, 1990/1992).

A constellation of services supporting inclusion

In the fixed continuum of provision, the disabled child is slotted in and moved around according to an impairment-based assessment (see Figure 8.1 above). In contrast, the constellation of services provides what the child and the class teacher need in mainstream schools. This includes a variety of services, resources and specialists who bring their expertise to the child rather than vice versa. This conception allows for the development of inclusive schools (see Figure 8.2). It also provides much greater flexibility but, because it is new and unknown, it is seen by many professionals as threatening. These two figures show the transition we wish to achieve from an education service structured on the 'medical model' to one based on the 'social model'.

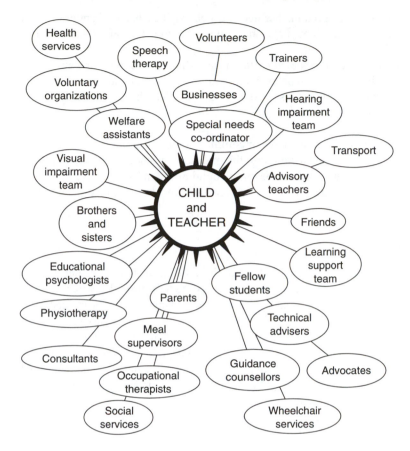

▲ The constellation of services provides what the child and the class teacher need in ordinary schools, from a variety of services, resources and specialists. This conception allows for the development of inclusive schools.

Figure 8.2 The constellation of services

Source: Mason and Rieser, 1994.

Integration and inclusion

Integration

Integration is a matter of location and there are at least four variants:

• Periodic integration: children from special schools are bussed into a mainstream school at a regular time each week for 'integration', or an 'integration event' is organized.

- Geographical integration: disabled children may be educated in units or school on the same campus or site as their non-disabled peers, but do not mix, even socially.
- Social integration: disabled children may share meals, playtime and assemblies with non-disabled peers, but are not taught with them.
- Functional integration: disabled and non-disabled children are taught in the same class.

What all forms of integration have in common is the assumption of some form of assimilation of the disabled child into the mainstream school. The school remains largely unchanged and the focus is on the child fitting in. As we have seen, if the child is unable to do this, the law can be used to direct her/him to a special school or unit.

Inclusion

Inclusion, on the other hand, is about a child's right to belong to her/his local mainstream school, to be valued for who s/he is and to be provided with all support s/he needs to thrive. Since mainstream schools are generally not organized in this way, it requires planned restructuring of the whole school. This restructuring should be seen as an extension of the school's equal opportunities policy and practice. It requires a commitment from the whole staff, the governors, parents/carers and pupils/students. Inclusion is not a static state like integration. It is a continuing process involving a major change in school ethos and is about building a school community that accepts and values difference.

In order to become inclusive, schools should adopt a 'social model of disability'. They must identify the barriers within the school's environment, teaching and learning strategies, attitudes, organization and management that prevent the full participation of disabled children and, as such, are part of the social oppression of disabled people. Functional integration is a precondition for the development of inclusion and disability equality. It does not, in itself, achieve it. The Index for Inclusion (Booth and Ainscow, 2002) was sent by the government to every school in England, Wales and Scotland. There is now an early years and play version (Booth and Ainscow, 2004) and it has been translated into seventeen languages and is being used in more than seventy countries. The index enables schools to hold a mirror up to themselves, identify barriers and find out how inclusive they are in ethos and or culture, in policies and practice. Ownership of the process of inclusion by the school is essential.

Inclusion depends on the extent to which all children get what they need to grow and develop, and how open the teacher and the children in the class are to learn and respect each and every child's experience. This sounds idealistic, but the alternative is to continue to reproduce the status quo, with its built-in discrimination against disabled children. Inclusion fundamentally challenges the traditional approach which regards impairment and disabled people as marginal, or an 'afterthought', instead of recognizing that impairment and disablement are a common experience of humanity and should be a central issue in the planning and delivery of a human service such as education.

Mike Oliver (Oliver, 1992), an educationalist and a leading member of the Disability Movement, drew out the differences between integration and inclusion in a paper he gave during National Integration Week in May 1992:

Old Integration is:	'New' Integration or Inclusion is:
a state	a process
non-problematic	problematic
a professional and administrative approach	politics
changes in school organization	change in school ethos
teachers acquire skills	teachers acquire commitment
curriculum delivery must change	curriculum content must change
legal rights	moral and political rights
acceptance and tolerance of children with special education	valuation and celebration of disabled children and children with learning difficulty
normality	difference
Integration can be delivered	Inclusion must be struggled for

Inclusive education should be the guiding principle. We should be working towards a system and an ethos where mainstream schools should accommodate all children regardless of their physical, intellectual, social, emotional, linguistic or other conditions.

Central to inclusive education is the involvement of disabled people in the consultation, planning and implementation of it. Examples already exist of the successful inclusion of children with every type and severity of impairment in mainstream schools in the UK. Many changes in school organization and practice have been necessary to make this happen, but from all such changes the non-disabled majority of children have benefited.

The best way to initiate whole school change is to have a training day delivered by disabled disability equality trainers with experience of the education system (see www.diseed.org.uk for advice on such a highly valued network). The school should then set up a representative working group to either use the checklist below or use the index for inclusion and regularly report back to staff and the board of management or governors.

Pupils/students need to be involved in this process through whole class discussion, assemblies and pupil/student councils. Parents/carers of disabled children are often disempowered by professional interventions which have threatened or broken their relationship with their disabled child. Parents for Inclusion are developing training to address this issue. The LEA, Social Services and Health Service need to provide the support and additional resources to the school to help overcome the barriers to inclusion.

The inclusion process is part of school improvement and developing more effective comprehensive schooling for all. Goals need to be built into the School Development Plan to be met over a five- or ten-year time-scale and their achievement must be monitored.

The inclusion of profoundly deaf pupils and students requires particular thought and attention. The eugenicist origins of 'special education' and the ensuing impact on current day segregation and integration had a particular impact on the education of deaf people particularly those who use sign language. In Milan in 1880 educationalists from 21 countries met and decided to outlaw the education and instruction of deaf people through sign language and develop instruction through the oral method. It was feared that the thriving deaf culture which had developed in the previous 90 years from the development of sign language now posed a threat to the gene-pool of hearing people (Facchini, 1983). This led to enforced education of deaf children through the oral method which led to them having a literacy level of half of that of their hearing peers. The deaf community has rightly fought hard for deaf children to be educated in their first language – sign language.

Many deaf children are still forced to learn without sign language. This has often meant that recently schools for the deaf and deaf clubs are the only places where sign language is readily available (Ladd, 2003). There are now models of inclusion where deaf children are included with simultaneous interpreting–English/BSL, sufficient number of deaf students to form a BSL using peer group, deaf BSL using adult instructors to develop their sign language and the hearing pupils learning sign language to communicate with their peers. This successfully occurs, for example, at Selwyn Primary or Lister Secondary School in Newham or Cottingley Primary School in Leeds and leads to deaf pupils having the best of the hearing and deaf worlds. At present this means resourcing some mainstream schools. However, given the educational history of most deaf people it is quite right that they insist on education through sign language. Oralism still seeks to educate deaf children through high tech hearing aids and cochlear implants, but the deaf community argue they miss out on both deaf language and culture, and still do not understand all that is being said. It is up to mainstream schools to meet the challenge of including deaf pupils by the means outlined above.

What follows are some of the necessary changes that schools, teachers, governors, non-teaching staff, parents/carers and pupils/students have to undertake to become inclusive.

A whole school policy on disability equality and inclusion

a   Access audit of the school environment. Carry out a full access audit of your building. Involve pupils/students. Cost and set targets of major and minor works to be included in the school development plan. Involve the governors in pressing the LEA for access works. Money is available through the Schools Access Initiative.

b   Audit access to the learning environment. Audit software and hardware suitable for supporting learning difficulties. Maintain up-to-date information on adaptations, example, signing, Brailling, vocalizing, voice recognition, touch screen, laptops, switching. Make lessons multi-media. Make sure visuals can be described or subtitled if necessary.

c   Ensure disability issues are in the curriculum. When planning a curriculum unit, topic or module think of including a disability dimension. Build up resources and literature that are non-discriminatory and include disabled people in a non-patronizing way (see guidelines in Chapter 7 of this volume). Promote the 'social model' of disability. All Equal All Different (Rieser, 2004) is one such resource pack for Early Years and KS1.

d   Disabled people are positively portrayed. Ensure all children have access to positive images of disabled adults and children in non-stereotyped activities and roles. Make sure the school has a range of picture or reading books that do this (see selected reading list at the end of this chapter). Involve disabled adults from the community in activities and lessons.

e   Diversify the curriculum. When planning the curriculum, use a wide variety of approaches to draw on different strengths, learning styles – auditory, visual or akinesthetic – and aptitudes of the pupils/students. Build up a resource bank of ideas and lessons allowing time for joint planning and review. Check teaching and learning strategies and targets are appropriate for the needs of all children in the class.

f   Develop collaborative learning and peer tutoring. The pupils/students comprise the biggest learning resource in any school. Involve them in pairing with children of different abilities and groups. All children benefit from these approaches.

g   Effective team approach for learning support and curriculum planning. Ensure that learning support is effectively co-ordinated throughout the school and in each classroom. Allow time for joint planning in the school day, involving teachers and learning support assistants. Develop the skills and confidence of the learning support assistants to carry out different roles in the classroom with groups of children.

h   British Sign Language. When a school includes deaf children, make use of British Sign Language translators and teachers. Offer deaf children the chance to work with native signers. Offer hearing children the chance to study sign language as part of the curriculum. Give a positive value to different forms of communication. For deaf and partially hearing children, it is important to understand their need for induction loops, lip reading and good room acoustics.

i   Accessible communication with parents/carers. Recognize that not everyone communicates by written or spoken English. Audit the communication needs within the school and of parents and provide notices, reports, information and directions in the relevant format, for example, large print, Braille, tape, videos in British Sign Language, computer disk and pictograms, and use symbols for people with learning disabilities.

j Be critical of disablist language. Examine language used in teaching and by other pupils. Much of it is disablist and impairment derived. Develop a critical reappraisal through disability equality training, assemblies and in class.

k Challenge impairment-derived abuse, name-calling and bullying as part of the school behaviour policy. Introduce effective policy to prevent abuse, name-calling and bullying because of physical, mental or sensory differences. Make this part of your school anti-bullying policy.

l Involve all pupils in developing behaviour policy. Policies devised with pupil/student involvement and based on principles of self-regulation and mutual respect are the most effective. Cultivate developmental discipline. Sometimes it is necessary for adults to take a lead in setting up circles of friends and buddy systems. All children should remain on roll even if for some time they are out of class. Devise systems where distressed children can take 'time-out' and talk to sympathetic adults. Have access to counselling and psychiatry.

m Develop a whole school ethos on accepting difference. Use events like assemblies, plays and sports days to demonstrate this, as well as in day-to-day functioning.

n Develop empowerment and self-representation of disabled pupils/students. Set up structures through which disabled pupils/students can express their views, develop self-esteem, and have some influence on school policies. Involve disabled adults in this process. Develop training in self-advocacy. Find ways of ensuring disabled students are represented on the School Council.

o Physical Education. Ensure PE and sporting activities involve all pupils/students, develop collaboration and encourage all pupils to improve their personal performance. Use adaptation and creative imagination to succeed in this.

p Transport and school trips policy. Make sure this includes all. Ensure that transport to and from the school for disabled pupils fits in with the school day and cater for attendance at after-school activities. Allow the disabled child's friends and siblings to use transport to break down isolation. Ensure no pupil is excluded from a trip or visit because their access or other needs are not met. This means careful advance planning and pre-visits. Ensure you don't use risk assessment to exclude pupils who think laterally to find solutions.

q Have an increasing inclusion ethos in the school development plan. The school should examine every aspect of its activity for barriers to inclusion identify temporary and longer term solutions, describe how these will be achieved, who will be responsible, how they will be funded, how their impact of student achievement will be measured, and incorporate these into the school development planning process.

r Include outside specialist support. Plan the work of speech, physio- and occupational therapists in a co-ordinated way which best supports pupils'/students' curriculum needs and reduces disruption to their learning and social needs.

s Policy on administering medication and personal assistance. Devise a policy on administering routine medication which is easy for pupils/students to use and develop systems that maintain their dignity on personal-hygiene issues. Have a system for handling medical emergencies which is easy for everyone to use.

t Maintain equipment. Ensure that specialist equipment is properly maintained, stored and replaced when necessary. Mobility aids, for example, wheelchairs and walking frames, should be regularly checked and staff trained in their proper use.

u Increase the employment of disabled staff. The Disability Discrimination Act now applies to employment in most schools. Revise the equal opportunity employment policy to increase the employment of disabled teaching and non-teaching staff. There is Access to Work money available for disabled employees from Placing, Assessing and Counselling Teams (PACT) officers at Job Centres. All children need disabled adult role models.

v Disability equality training and ongoing INSET for staff and governors. Organize a programme of in-service training for teachers, support staff and governors to help them move towards inclusion and disability equality. Ensure all staff are involved in and understand the process of inclusion.

w Governing body representation. Appoint a governor to have a brief for special educational needs, with the whole governing body involved in developing inclusion policy. Try to get disabled governors.

x Consultation with and involvement of parents/carers. Ensure there are effective arrangements for involving parents/carers in all parts of their child's school life, including any decisions that have to be made. These arrangements should involve counselling and support in helping a child towards independence. With their permission, maintain information about parents/carers who are themselves disabled, so that their access and other needs can be met.

Moving towards inclusion

In many schools the largest barriers to including pupils/students with needs that have not previously been catered for at the school are the fears and attitudes of the staff. These can best be addressed by putting disablement into an equal opportunities framework and by having whole staff disability equality sessions which should be led by disabled disability equality trainers (Disability Equality in Education offer such training – see References). This should be followed by an audit of the barriers in the school, the development of an action plan to minimize the barriers and incorporation of the plan into the school's SEN policy (CSIE, 1996; Booth and Ainscow 2002).

Sometimes particular information about children's impairments is required and this can be most usefully obtained from the children themselves or their parents. They are experts on their impairments.

Sometimes medically based professionals such as occupational therapists, physiotherapists and speech therapists can be useful in providing certain procedures or specialist equipment and practices. But it should always be remembered that the child is at school to learn alongside his or her peers and wherever possible this support should be given in class and in the least disruptive way. Often these other adults can benefit groups of children in the class.

There will often be learning support assistants in the class, usually to support particular children. The more they can be involved in joint planning, the more able they are to make a positive contribution to the learning and teaching in the class, not just for their particular pupil. The class or subject teacher has to take a lead in co-ordinating the activities of all these adults and making their activities part of the educational activity in the class. The SENCO (special educational needs co-ordinator) can play a vital role in developing such working partnerships.

For inclusion to work best requires a child-centred pedagogy in well-structured mixed-ability classrooms. There are many pressures from Ofsted, the government and the league tables to set and stream. But these are moves that undermine an inclusive ethos and can often replicate segregative practices within one institution, leading in the longer term to a drop in overall standards. A mixture of teaching styles can meet these competing pressures: whole class teaching with peer tutoring; collaborative groups; individual or paired work; and joint teaching with another class. The more flexible the teaching style, the more likely to include a wider variety of pupil/student needs.

Many teachers say they are in principle in favour of inclusion, but it requires a massive increase in resources to be possible. It must be remembered that one-seventh of all education budgets is spent on special educational needs. There is a need for increased capital investment in the school building stock to make it accessible, and, thanks to the Within Reach Campaign organized by SCOPE and the NUT, this is beginning to happen. But the major problem is that the majority of SEN spending is in the wrong place – some 1,200 special schools for 100,000 children. LEA development plans will have to identify over the coming period how these resources can be reallocated to mainstream schools in a planned way to enhance inclusion. The important point here is that LEAs should agree to ring-fence all resources and posts to special educational needs as they transfer them to the mainstream. LEAs must also set up adequate monitoring and advisory teacher posts to ensure that the resources put into mainstream schools are being used to further inclusion and meet the needs of children with SEN.

The London Borough of Newham (Jordan and Goodey, 1996) provides a useful indicator of how such moves towards inclusion can occur in a poor, multi-cultural, inner-city area. In 1984 a group of parents of disabled children ran for and were elected on to the council with the express wish of seeing the ending of segregated special education. They achieved their aim in a council policy which recognized the rights of children, whatever their needs, to learn together. The borough's latest policy has a goal of making it possible 'for every child, whatever special educational needs you may have, to attend their neighbourhood school'. Between 1984 and 1998 the number of special schools in the borough was reduced from eight to one and the number of children segregated in special education dropped from 913 to 206. Parents/carers are becoming increasingly confident in the ability of their neighbourhood school to meet diverse needs and teachers have signed an agreement on inclusive education.

This was achieved in an educational and political climate that was hostile to this process. Resourced schools were set up to meet certain needs in mainstream schools response to parental/carer concerns. These are now planned to be phased out as Newham moves to inclusive neighbourhood schools. The process from the start envisaged radically changing mainstream schools rather than fitting children with SEN into the existing system. An independent report commented that having to cater for children with serious learning difficulties helped schools make better provision for all pupils (Rouse and Florian, 1996). This was borne out between 1997 and 2003. Newham schools had the biggest improvement nationally in the GCSE results of all students in grades A–G. Many children labelled as having severe learning difficulties are now passing exams. In addition, the numbers of exclusions have been falling while they have been rising in most other parts of the country. The LEA has now appointed four monitoring officers proactively to address this process of developing inclusion from integration.

It will help to understand the inclusion process to give a thumbnail sketch of two inclusive schools.

The first is one of seventeen resourced mainstream schools in Newham. It is a purpose-built inclusive school with funding for thirty-six statemented children with severe and profound learning difficulties. In addition, there are six other statemented children. Free meals are provided for 59.6 per cent of the children and the school has a multicultural intake. There are four wings: Nursery and Reception, with 120 pupils; Years 1 and 2, with 120; Years 3 and 4, with 120; and Years 5 and 6, with 96 pupils. The additional teaching staff are organized in teams with the class teachers to give six teachers in each wing. In Key Stage 1 there are also six support staff who work as part of the team. The children choose when and what they will do each day, though they must do reading, writing and maths. They keep their own diaries and these are used as the IEP (individual education plan) for statemented children. In each wing there is a practical room, a reading room, a writing room, a finding-out room for science, geography and history and a quiet room. There are no breaks but all children do a PE activity every day, including various sports and physiotherapy. The lunchtime is a continuous sitting and there are many clubs then. The children all seem engaged in learning and are very pleasant to each other, while the support staff are deployed across the teams to meet particular needs. All staff 'change' children and administer medicines if parental permission is given. Each team has a team leader. In the wings one teacher is responsible for one part of the curriculum for the week for all 120 children. In Years 5 and 6, this is for half a term. The additional resourcing allows for shaping teams to meet the needs of all the children. The school has eight extra teachers and fourteen extra support staff, giving a staff of fifty. There is now an excellent account of school change with respect to teaching and learning for inclusion written by staff and pupils at the school (Alderson, 1999).

The second school is a comprehensive high school with 1,100 Year 8 to Year 11 pupils, with ten forms of entry. It is an additionally resourced mainstream school for thirty-six physically disabled students. They have a head of learning development, 8.4 full-time teachers, 1 part-time (two days a week) teacher, 8 learning assistants and a clerical assistant. There is a learning development room where staff from the department work and it is open to any student to come to ask for help at lunchtime or after school. Next door is a physio/resource/changing/toilet/shower suite. In addition to the thirty-six students for the resourced provision, the learning development department leads on the identified learning needs of the 247 students on the special needs register. The building has been adapted so all rooms are accessible. The school has developed collaborative/partnership teaching in which departments make bids to work with teachers from the learning development department for a term or a year. The purpose of this is to develop a shared understanding of all the arrangements and practice involved in working together, joint planning and evaluation. Time is essential for this process. This is achieved by timetabling learning development teachers and subject teachers to have non-contact periods at the same time, and these are ring-fenced so they are never asked to cover. The collaboration includes shared aims, the joint preparation and presentation of resources and shared responsibility for group discipline, marking and report writing. I visited a science, music and art class and saw the inclusive practice in process. Having disabled students in the class seemed natural to all the students. The teaching staff all seemed happy with the arrangements and talked of their benefit to everyone and how the department's flexibility gave them all the support they needed.

Thomas *et al.* (1998) have analysed the Somerset Inclusion Project, which drew its inspiration from a special school in Canada (Shaw, 1990). The Somerset Project centred on the Princess Margaret School for Physically Disabled Pupils. In 1992 it was a day and boarding special school. However, on closing in 1997, it had managed to include the vast majority of its pupils successfully in mainstream schools. Ninety staff were retrained and relocated to support the children in the mainstream. The study gives many insights into the management of change, not least because one of its authors, Dave Walker, was the headteacher of Princess Margaret and effectively oversaw a process which was to leave him without a job.

In conclusion the authors state that:

> with vision and careful planning special schools can successfully change their work in such a way to enable their mainstream partners to include children even with serious disabilities. One of our clearest findings has been that while many mainstream staff were highly sceptical about the inclusion project before it started, they had changed their views entirely after several months of seeing it in practice and were fulsome in their support of inclusion.
>
> (Thomas *et al.*, 1998, p. 198)

Conclusion

While it certainly helps to have a government or an LEA that is sympathetic to it, inclusion is fundamentally a school-based process. Mel Ainscow (1994, 1995, 1998) has argued that inclusion is part of the process of developing school effectiveness. 'Moving' schools, those that are open to change, which are usually non-hierarchical but with strong leadership, are much more able to develop inclusive practice. 'Stuck' schools, on the other hand, have hierarchical structures, poor leadership and lack of involvement of staff in change, and are much less likely to be able to undergo the restructuring that is necessary to become inclusive. Certainly the variance in inclusive practice between similar schools would support this. Teachers deciding what type of school they want to work in would do well to remember this distinction.

The thinking of the disability movement, the development of the 'social model' and the voice of disabled people who have experienced segregated and integrated education are essential in the development of inclusion. *The Salamanca Statement and Framework for Action on Special Needs Education* (UNESCO, 1994) recognizes this crucial role: 'encourage and facilitate the participation of parents, communities and organizations of disabled people in the planning and decision making processes concerning the provision for special educational needs'.

Inclusion is a process of school change that benefits not only disabled people but the entire school community. Eventually society will experience a reduction in prejudice and discrimination against disabled people as difference becomes part of everyone's experience and disabled people become part of the community in their own right. As we go to press, inclusive education has been adopted as the norm in Article 24 of the United Nations Draft Declaration on the Rights of People with Disabilities, a new international rights convention.

References

Ainscow, M. (1994) *Special Needs in the Classroom: A Teacher Education Guide*, London: Jessica Kingsley

Ainscow, M. (1995) 'Education for all: Making it Happen', *Support for Learning*, 10 (4), pp. 147–57

Ainscow, M. (1998) 'Reaching out to all Learners: Opportunities and Possibilities', keynote presentation at North of England Education Conference, Bradford

Alderson, P. (1999) *Learning and Inclusion: The Cleeves School Experience*, London: David Fulton

Audit Commission (2002) 'Special Educational Needs: A Mainstream Issue', London, Audit Commission LAR2894 www-audit commission.gov.uk

Barnes, C. (1991) *Disabled People in Britain and Discrimination*, London: Hurst

Benn, C. and Chitty, C. (1997) *Thirty Years on: Is Comprehensive Education Alive and Well or Struggling to Survive*, London: Penguin

Booth, T. and Ainscow, M. (1998) *From Them to Us: An International Study on Inclusive Education*, London: Routledge

Booth, T. and Ainscow, M. (2002) *Index for Inclusion: Developing Learning and Participation in Schools*, Bristol: Centre for Studies on Inclusion

Booth, T. and Ainscow, M. (2004) *Index for Inclusion: Developing Learning, Participation and Play in Early Years and Childcare*, Bristol: CSIE, www.inclusion.org.uk

Booth, T., Swann, W., Masterton, M. and Potts, P. (1992) 'Diversity in Education' and 'Curricular for Diversity in Education', *Learning for All*, London: Routledge

Centre for Studies of Inclusive Education (1996) *Developing an Inclusive Policy for Your School*, Bristol: CSIE

Cole, T. (1989) *Apart or a Part?: Integration and the Growth of British Special Education*, Milton Keynes: Open University Press

DfEE (1997) *Excellence for all Children: Meeting Special Educational Needs*, London: HMSO

DfEE (1998) *An Action Programme for Special Educational Needs*, London: HMSO

DfES (2003) 'The Report of the Special Schools Working Party', London

DfES (2004a) 'Removing Barriers to Achievement: The Government's Strategy for SEN', DfES /0117/2004, London

DfES (2004b) 'Statistics of Education: Schools in England', 2004 Edition

Dyson, A., Farrell, P., Hutcheson, G. and Polat, F., (2004) 'Inclusion and Pupil Achievement' Department for Education and Skills', London (DfES RR578)

Facchini, Massimo (1985) 'An historical reconstruction of events leading to the congress of Milan in 1880', in William C. Stokoe, and Virginia Volterra (eds) *SLR' 83: Proceedings of the third International Symposium on Sign Language Research*, Rome, June 22–26 1983, Rome/SiverSpring: CNR/Linstok Press, pp. 356–62

Hegarty, S. and Pocklington, K. (1981) *Educating Pupils with Special Needs in Ordinary Schools*, Windsor: NFER

Hirst, A. and Baldwin, S. (1994) *Unequal Opportunities Growing up Disabled*, London: HMSO

Jordan, L. and Goodey, C. (1996) *Human Rights and School Change: The Newham Story*, Bristol: CSIE

Ladd, P. (2003) *Understanding Deaf Culture: In Search of Deafhood*, Bristol: Multilingual Matters

Mason, M. (1998) *Forced apart: The Case for Ending Compulsory Segregation in Education*, London: Alliance for Inclusive Education

Mason, M. and Rieser, R. (1994) *Altogether Better*, London: Comic Relief

Murray, P. and Penman, J. (1996) *Let Our Children Be: A Collective of Stories*, Sheffield: Parents with Attitude

Norwich, B. (1997) *A Trend towards Inclusion: Statistics on Special School Placement and Pupils with Statements in Ordinary Schools England 1992–96*, Bristol: CSIE

Ofsted (2004) 'Special Educational Needs and Disability: Towards Inclusive Schools', London

Oliver, M. (1992) 'Talk given to Greater London Association of Disabled People', Integration Week, May 1992, Bristol: CSIE

Rieser, R. (2004) *All Equal All Different: A Unique Resource to Develop Disability Equality in Early Years and Key Stage 1*, London: Disability Equality in Education, www.diseed.org.uk

Rieser, R. and Mason, M. (1990/1992) *Disability Equality in the Classroom: A Human Rights Issue*, London: Disability Equality in Education

Rouse, M. and Florian, L. (1996) 'Effective Inclusive Schools: A Study in Two Countries', *Cambridge Journal of Education*, 26 (1), pp. 71–80

Sebba, J. with Sachdev, D. (1997) *What Works in Inclusive Education?*, Essex: Barnardos

Shaw, L. (1990) *Each Belongs: Integrated Education in Canada*, Bristol: CSIE

Thomas, G. (1996) *Exam Performance in Special Schools*, Bristol: CSIE

Thomas, G., Walker, D. and Webb, J. (1998) *The Making of the Inclusive School*, London: Routledge

UNESCO (1994) *The Salamanca Statement and Framework for Action on Special Needs Education*, Paris: UNESCO

Selection of recommended inclusive children's books

3–8 years

Bunnett, Rochelle, *Friends at School*, Star Bright Books. Letterbox*. Beautifully photographed images capture warmth of an inclusive classroom as children play together.

Dowling, Dorothy and Dowling, Jack, *Learning Together ABC: A Fingerspelling Alphabet with Signs for Deaf and Hearing Children*, Sheffield: 18 Blackstock Drive.

Foreman, Michael, *Seal Surfer*, Anderson Press. Letterbox. As the seasons change we follow a special relationship between a disabled boy, his grandfather and a seal.

Hearn, Emily, *Race You Franny, Good Morning Franny, Franny and the Music Girl*, Women's Press of Canada. Third book: Letterbox. Adventures of a wheelchair-using girl.

Hill, Eric, *Spot Goes to School*, National Deaf Children's Society. Sign Language book.

Larkin, Patricia, *Dad and Me in the Morning*, Albert Whitman. Letterbox. Lovely book about a deaf boy and his dad, signing, lip reading and squeezing hands as they share a dawn walk.

Merrifield, Margaret, *Come Sit by Me*, Women's Press of Canada. Letterbox. HIV/AIDS.

Naidoo, Beverley, *Letang's New Friend, Trouble for Letang and Julie, Letang and Julie Save the Day*, Longman. Second book: Letterbox. Letang, just arrived from Botswana, befriends wheelchair-using Julie.

Sakai, Kimiko, *Sachiko Means Happiness*, Children's Book Press, Letterbox. Sachiko's acceptance of her grandmother's Alzheimer's with warm and gentle illustrations.

Wilkins, Verna, *Boots for a Bridesmaid*, Tamarind. Letterbox. Story of Nicky and her wheelchair-using mum.

Wilkins, Vera, *Are We There Yet?*, Tamarind. Letterbox. A family day out at a theme park with Max, Amy and wheelchair-using Dad.

9–14 years

Brown, Christy, *Down all the Days, My Left Foot*, Pan (over thirteens).

Harris, R.H., *Let's Talk about Sex*, Walker Books.

Keith, Lois, *A Different Life*, Live Wire/Women's Press. Excellent novel about a fifteen-year-old girl adjusting to not being able to walk and how she learns to be strong (over twelves).

Keith, Lois, *Mustn't Grumble*, Women's Press. Excellent book in which thirty-six disabled women write about their lives (over thirteens).

Stemp, Jane, *Waterbound*, Hodder Headline. An excellent book written by a disabled author, *Waterbound* is the story of a time in the future when eugenics has triumphed [.] or has it? The discovery of disabled siblings beneath the city leads to a revolution (over tens).

The above books and many others are available from Disability Equality in Education Unit GL, Leroy House, 436 Essex Road, London N1 3QP, Tel: 44 (0) 207 359 2855, e-mail: info@diseed.org.uk or see the DEE website (www.diseed. org.uk). DEE also provides training for inclusion to meet your needs.

9 'Multitude' or 'class'

Constituencies of resistance, sources of hope

Tom Hickey

The commencement of the second millennium is an exciting time. Across the world, people from an immense variety of backgrounds are refusing, in increasing numbers, to accept that a world dominated by corporations and by imperialist wars and occupations is the only world that is possible. In what was once called 'the Third World', people are rejecting squalor, deprivation and poverty as inevitable conditions of their lives; they are using the new power they have found from employment in the urban, commercial and industrial sectors to make their voices heard. In the developed world of Western Europe and North America there is a new mood of resistance to welfare cuts, privatisation, casualisation, insecurity and worsening wages and conditions and pensions. In rich and poor countries alike, people are refusing to accept environmental despoliation as a condition of economic development, and are prioritising their health and the sustainability of their communities over corporate profitability. Whether protesting against the neo-liberal agendas of the World Trade Organisation and the International Monetary Fund, or demonstrating in millions across the world against the imperial adventures of the US and Britain in Iraq and elsewhere, the oppressed of the world are, for the first time in decades, rediscovering their role as the agents of history. These struggles are against war and imperialism, against the neo-liberal agenda being imposed on the world by the World Bank, the IMF and the World Trade Organisation, and against the pro-market policies being adopted by national governments across the world.

The new millennium opened with the renewal of Western imperialism as a grand design. The most dramatic example was, of course, the invasion and occupation of Iraq, and the attempt to install a puppet government there. Although the official reason given by US and UK governments was the threat of Iraq's 'weapons of mass destruction', many people believe that the immediate objective was the removal of a dictator and a regime that had once been the allies of the US but had since become uncontrollable. They believe that the aim was to create a region in thrall to US military power, to secure its strategically important oil resources for the West, and to signal to the rest of the world that no challenge to US supremacy would be countenanced whether in North Korea, in Iran or from the economic dynamism of a rapidly growing China. The principles and policies required in the interests of a free market, capitalist world order would be imposed globally, and by force if necessary.[1] This was to be a genuinely global imperialism, and a 'war without boundaries'.[2]

The millennium was also ushered in by the first manifestation of opposition to the neo-liberal agenda of the international organisations – the Seattle protest in November 1999. This was the beginning of the movement against corporate globalisation. The movement that says 'No!' to the neo-liberal intent to turn every aspect of human life, and every feature of the natural world, into commodities to be bought and sold and profited by. The Seattle protest was against the poverty and inequality that were perceived to have been caused by the intensifying global reach of capital and the market.[3] It paralysed the scheduled meetings of the assembled dignitaries, and led to the partial abandonment of the proceedings. It also raised awareness about the existence of a movement against neo-liberalism. Across the globe, in both developed and underdeveloped societies, images of armour-clad 'Robocop' riot police, wielding CS gas guns and stun grenades, confronting protesters armed with whistles and banners, transformed perceptions. The dominant view, propagated in news and current affairs, and in much of the academy, and reflected in the style and subject matter and foci of the products of mass culture, was no longer tenable. This view held that, with the collapse of Stalinism and Social Democracy in the 1980s and 1990s, there was no feasible alternative to liberal capitalism as a social and economic system, and no viable alternative to free market, neo-liberal policies not only in trade and commerce nationally and internationally, but equally in education, healthcare, welfare, sanitation, and development.[4] Here was evidence that this view was not being passively received and accepted. Here too was evidence, in the violent reaction against the protest, that governments and their representatives harboured a deep unease that their citizenries would not heed the message. It was as if the images of Seattle under siege announced a new war between the powerful and the marginalised, between the rich and the poor, between the beneficiaries of a liberal economic order and its casualties. In the years that immediately followed Seattle, this movement not only proved its resilience but gradually cohered around the slogans that expressed the common interests uniting the oppressed in rich and poor countries: 'Our world is not for sale!', 'Another world is possible!', and 'You are G8; we are 6 billion!'

From these beginnings, the movement grew in strength and sophistication. The protests traversed the globe and all five continents. In the depths of a January winter, 250,000 protested in Vienna. In April, 30,000; the protest was against the IMF/World Bank meeting in Washington. In June, in Windsor, Ontario, it was against the Organisation of American States, and 60,000 protested against McDonalds in Millau, in France. In July, in Okinawa, the target was the G8, and in Philadelphia the protests were around the presidential nomination. In August there were 20,000 protesting in Los Angeles; in September 20,000 against the Asia-Pacific Summit of the World Economic Forum in Melbourne, and 20,000 against the IMF/World Bank in Prague. In November, there were demonstrations in Seoul, South Korea, and in December 100,000 in Nice, in France. In April 2001, 80,000 protested in Quebec against the Free Trade Area of the Americas, and in

May, across the globe, May Day was reclaimed for the movement as a day of resistance and celebration. In July, there were three days of protest by hundreds of thousands of people against the G8 summit in Genoa, Italy. Even the attack on the Twin Towers, the Pentagon and the White House, on 11 September 2001, which many pundits thought might derail the movement, had little long term effect as the invitation to guilt by false association was refused. The protests were loosely organised by a variety of nationally based coalitions which co-ordinated arrangements using e-mail and internet sites as well as the more traditional methods of meetings and word of mouth.[5] In a short space of time, this movement against corporate globalisation became, as one analyst has put it, 'the most phenomenally successful engine of mass mobilisation in history'.[6]

These negative protests against neo-liberalism were rapidly supplemented by a second and novel phenomenon in the political arena. Commencing in Porto Alegre, Brazil, in 2001, with 1,000 delegates from 100 countries, began a series of 'Social Forums'. These were then replicated in a variety of European countries (in Florence in 2002; in Paris in 2003, in London in 2004), and then with 100,000 participants, and 20,700 delegates representing 156 countries in Porto Alegre again in 2003. From there, the World Social Forum went to Cairo in 2003, and to Mumbai in India in 2004, then back to Porto Alegre on an expanded scale in 2005. At these gatherings, militants, activists, political groups, journalists and intellectuals congregated. They gathered to consider not simply the effects of the protests but also the content of a positive agenda for the movement (George and Bircham, 2001). No barrier of distance, language, culture or political tradition was allowed to prevent the dialogue, despite the absence of elaborate transport, accommodation, finance or simultaneous translation services. Thousands travelled both within and between continents to participate.

The movement and its forums were further promoted and strengthened by their involvement in the anti-war movement. At the first European Social Forum, in Florence in November 2002, a million people demonstrated against the threatened war on Iraq. On the 15 February 2003, there followed the unprecedented day of international protest against the looming war. Between 1.5 and 2 million were on the streets of London alone. It has been estimated that, in the first three months of 2003, 35 million people protested against the war internationally in some 3,000 demonstrations. It was evident that the world had become, with the end of the Cold War, a more unstable and threatening and violent place economically and militarily. Equally, it had become a more engaged, promising, and exciting place as well.

This new reality of a world in turmoil is not just a reality of different groups of the oppressed struggling for their own self-interests, or against the obvious and immediate causes of their misfortunes. It is also a world in which there is a contest over how best to understand the world, and how to interpret the struggles that are taking place in it. There are evident links and common causes between, and involved in, all of these struggles. It is not obvious, however, how best to describe or name these causes. Yet if the causes cannot be identified, named and explained it will be impossible for the struggles against them to be well directed – these struggles will miss their target because the movements will not know precisely what that target is. If the links and commonalities are not identified, it will be impossible to frame a strategy that has the chance of victory. This is, in part, what the series of World Social Forums, and their regional offshoots, are about. First, who or what is the enemy, and what is the nature of the task? Is the enemy the set of neo-liberal policies pursued by national governments and parties, and by the international organisations? Is it, instead, the inherited and unfair distribution of wealth and poverty of resources between a rich North and a poor South, and the heedless 'consumer culture' of the developed world? Alternatively, is 'the enemy' best understood as the particular system of production and distribution known as capitalism – the capitalist mode of production?

Even if these causes are mutually implicated, they are nevertheless distinct – and importantly so. If the main problem is the dominant neo-liberal, market friendly policy programme then the whole of the economic and social system does *not* have to be changed to overcome that problem. On the other hand, if the problem is the system itself then changing the policies pursued within it will not yield a solution at all but will, at best, obscure the extent and difficulty of the task.

Closely associated with this question is the issue of where the friends and allies of the global protest movement are to be found. How are the interests and aspirations of European or North American workers related to those of fishing communities in East Asia, or landless labourers in South Asia, or shanty town dwellers in Africa, or the unemployed of Central or South America, or the home-less victims of Israeli incursions in Gaza or the West Bank? How are the variety of social and ideological oppressions to be related to these economic conditions? Are the different forms and intensities of oppression suffered by women, for example, from one society to the next simply different expressions of one universal oppression based on sex and its different gender inflections in different cultures, or are some of these differences distinctions in kind? What, moreover, are the sources of these material differences in circumstances and ideological differences in expectations between men and women? Are there common causes that can be identified both for the economic exploitation of social groups and for the patterns of gender and other oppressions?

And what of the anti-war and anti-imperialist movement? What is its relation-ship to the global protests against neo-liberalism? If you were against the US and British war on Iraq, does that mean that you were (or should also be) against the policies of the WTO, and against the privatisations pursued by George Bush's administration in the US and Tony Blair's administration in the UK? Are there three movements (anti-neo-liberal, anti-war and anti-capitalist), or is there only one? If there is one global protest movement then what kind of movement is it, or should it be?[7]

This is a debate which is a central concern of the movement against corporate globalisation. Much of the debate at the fifth World Social Forum in Porto Alegre, Brazil, in 2005 was concerned with it, as will be the European Social Forum in Athens in 2006. There are those who see the purpose of global mobilisations simply to be pressuring governments and international organisations into altering the neo-liberal thrust of policy, and returning to the Keynesian, state-managed capitalism of the mid-twentieth century. The main body of those who associate themselves with the global protests, however, are struggling to resolve what the exact objectives and analysis of an anti-capitalist movement should be in the twenty-first century. Directly expressive of this debate, and addressing most of its key strategic concerns, are the differences in analysis and strategy that emerge from two recent and pivotal texts. They are Alex Callinicos' *An Anti-Capitalist Manifesto*, and Michael Hardt and Antonio Negri's *Empire*.[8] The former is an explicit attempt to update Marx's *Communist Manifesto* for the circumstances of the twenty-first century; the latter is an implicit attempt to do the same thing, an argument about the ways in which the system has changed fundamentally since the nineteenth century, and the consequences of those changes for radical analysis and strategy. This chapter presents the argument of both, and then considers them in relation to the original analysis developed by Marx, the approach that is, in effect, their negative and positive reference points respectively.

Hardt and Negri offer a new conception through which to understand global capitalism: 'Empire'. The essence of this argument is fourfold. First, as a result of the intensified process of globalisation at the end of the twentieth century, the capitalist system has imposed its order everywhere, and has liberated itself from dependence on the nation state. The nation state has thus been displaced as the political and geographical organising unit for capital accumulation; the counterpart to this is that capital has become 'deterritorialised'. The shape and configuration of this new global system of capitalism is no longer defined by the relations between nation states but by the interests and initiatives of global capital in the form of the major global corporations. This globalisation is not simply a process of market deregulation but a proliferation of supranational regulation infusing and suffusing all aspects of life.[9] Second, and one of the corollaries of this change, the dependence of capital accumulation in the late nineteenth and twentieth centuries on the political and military dominance of the underdeveloped world in the form of colonialism and imperialism has been overcome. The advantages for the capitalist system of colonial underdevelopment as its exploited 'outside' have now (as a result of a process in train since the end of the Second World War) been internalised through the creation of a single world economy. All parts of the global system, developed and underdeveloped economically, rich and poor, traditional and modern culturally, are incorporated and included, and subjected to the unitary logic of capital. There is no longer any 'outside' to the system. Third, this diffusion of the power of capital, and the severing of its ties with the nation state, has dissolved any focus or centre to the structure of power. Power has now become diffused throughout Empire. Its core cannot be identified and isolated either politically and institutionally, or geographically. This flux of power is independent of space or place. Thus Empire is not the name or conception of a thing, an object, or even a discrete process, but rather a state of being which incorporates and implicates everything and everyone.

The resistant counterpart of capital accumulation in the system has traditionally been identified (since the late nineteenth century) as the working class – Marx's 'proletariat'. This identity and location for a challenge to the system has now changed, according to Hardt and Negri. The discontents of the system have changed as much as have its organising principles. The reality of the working class, as both victim of the process of capital accumulation, and as potentially powerful agent of social change, has now been dissolved by a more amorphous body – 'the multitude'. This is the fourth leg of their thesis. The multitude is just as exploited by capital as was the proletariat but is not the same kind of potentially self-conscious entity with easily identified commonalities of circumstance and common interests. It is not defined by the nature of its work or the precise relation it has to capital. Nor do the nature of its exploitation, or the detail of its employment contracts, delimit it. It is a concept that embraces all who work (or are impoverished by being denied that opportunity). Moreover, they argue, the nature and the conditions of labour have changed over the past period. Labour is more mobile both functionally and geographically, and this mobility is itself a celebration of nomadic flexibility. It is more highly educated and informed, and has become communicatively enabled by new technologies and fascinations. It is more creative and spontaneous than its previous incarnations. It is in this that its power lies. The multitude may be organisationally diffuse (thus disorganised or unorganisable) but it is powerful in virtue of the dependence of Empire on its ingenuity and creativity. This mutuality of dependence is organic. In this sense, the multitude is inside and part of Empire. It may be in an antagonistic relationship to the structure or processes of Empire, and may have identifiably distinct interests from it, but it does not look on Empire from the outside. The multitude contains the potential for the transcendence of Empire but it does not relate to it in the manner that the proletariat was both capital's alterity and its potential negation.

In their more recent book Hardt and Negri develop the notion of the multitude, particularly in relation to the challenge for democracy that Empire represents.[10] The multitude is neither proletariat nor those fragmentary elements of a dispossessed and variegated population which emerged from dated Postmodernist treatments of contemporary society.[11] It is rather a networked citizenry whose creative labour produces the resources on which a viable democracy of the future will depend. This potential is sharply contrasted with the condition of continuous war, the permanent and general 'state of exception', with which the unwinnable (and hence permanent) war on terror has furnished the US government. Here war, as permanent 'police activity', that is 'global and interminable', supplementing the regulatory order of the IMF, the UN, the WTO and the World Bank, is contrasted with the democratic resources of hope possessed by the multitude. The world of the multitude is one of decentralisation, centre-less networks, the production of 'the common' as a new shared space beyond scarcity, and in which the biopower and biopolitics of immaterial labour (engaged in knowledge generation and transmission) is dominant, and furnishes the most important weapon against Empire.

The Hardt and Negri thesis offers itself as an analysis of the system, and of the role of the class struggle within it, and one that is intended as an alternative to that offered by classical Marxism. It is an analysis in which the concept of class has been revised.[12] No longer is 'class' technically defined in terms of the relationship of a group to the means of production, as in classical Marxism. It now embraces all those who work, and all those who are adversely affected by the system, and who periodically recognise and express their animosity towards it. The radical agency with the potential to transform the system is no longer 'the working class' but 'the multitude'. It is 'all those who work under the rule of capital and thus potentially . . . the class of those who refuse the rule of capital'. In this analysis, it is not so much that the multitude must make a revolution in order to overcome the alienation imposed on labour and human existence by the capitalist system. Rather it is the case that the transformation in the conditions of being and the realisation of freedom are being achieved by the multitude *under* the rule of capital through the exercise of creativity, cooperation and self-mobilisation. The multitude's 'right . . . to self-control and autonomous self-production' are presented as actualities rather than potentialities. Thus, it would appear, organisation is unnecessary and even counter-productive, politics as a terrain of incompatible and competing interests is a misunderstanding, and perceiving the struggle for human liberation as one that must be against the power of the capitalist state, against bourgeois ideology and against imperialism, is a misconception. These were the appropriate grid references for a map of capitalism in its youth. They are no longer relevant for a map of the new terrain of Empire.

Callinicos' project in *An Anti-capitalist Manifesto* is different. Like Hardt and Negri, he is concerned to make the case for 'the replacement of global capitalism', and sets out a strategy for how this might be achieved. Following Marx's analysis, he records how the system imposes pain, anxiety and distress on all those subject to its domination, and how these consequences are exacerbated by the economic crises into which it descends periodically as the rivalry of competing capitals forces them to overproduce. Damaging to the humans who are subject to it, and destructive of its own wealth as asset values crash in its crises, the rule of capital also has a devastating impact on the environment. Careless of issues of sustainability, in denial over the greenhouse effect, and cavalier in championing the potential pollution and destruction of genetic modification, the representatives of capital pursue policies exclusively directed to the process of capital accumulation. Central to understanding this policy direction, however, is appreciating that it is a world of separate, competing capitals, and that these remain organised primarily on a national basis, with the protection afforded by their nation states. Thus it is that the competition between capitals sometimes becomes military competition between states, and can lead to imperialism and imperialist war. Here the reader begins to see the ways in which this analysis diverges from that of Hardt and Negri. In Callinicos' representation of the system, we are not in Hardt and Negri's 'smooth space' or 'no space'; we are in a definite and identifiable space with a topography characterised by interlocked and hostile blocks of capital whose arrangement underpins a terrain of interlocked nation states that compete, politically and strategically, on behalf of their national capitals. Wars, invasions and occupations, and the competitive military spending and arms production of rival states between wars, are not manifestations of irrational, atavistic, pre-modern drives but are integrally linked to the competitive nature of the capital accumulation process.

The alternative to this system that threatens the wellbeing and ultimately the survival of humanity is, for Callinicos, socialism. While refusing the invitation to speculate on the detail of how such a system would operate, he does present the core principles on which its organization would need to be based if it were to overcome the failures of capitalism. These are, he argues, justice, efficiency, democracy and sustainability. Central to the problem of how to achieve this transition is the identification of a social agency with the interest in attaining that goal, and with the capacity to achieve it. It is for this reason that, in defending classical Marxism as the liberatory programme for the twenty-first century, he places the working class at the centre of his strategy for social change.

Callinicos' continued concern to focus on the working class arises precisely from the conjunction between the collective power to change the world and the collective interest in, and motivation to, change it that Marx was the first to identify in his discovery of the proletariat. He believes that this power and motivation remain despite a long period of defeats and retreats by the workers' movement, and despite the changing nature of working class occupations in the advanced and longer established industrial countries. The questions are: why did Marx argue this case originally, and does the argument still have purchase today?

Marx: 'class' and historical materialism

Historical Materialism was the first systematic attempt to identify *structures* that constrain human behaviour, and determine the circumstances in which humans *become* the social beings that they are. As such, it was a radical break with tradition as both philosophy and social theory. It was a break from the natural rights tradition (from Plato and Aristotle to Aquinas) in which social regulations and codes are rationally binding on human behaviour in virtue of an absolute, and presupposed, human nature and idea of what was Good. It was a break from the empiricist tradition (Locke and Hume), which had treated knowledge as derivable only from observation, and from social contract theory (Hobbes and Locke), which took membership of a society to be evidence of the implicit consent of the governed to the authority of the sovereign power. It was a break from the romantic philosophical tradition that had invested humans with an *inner* power both to determine the Good, and to construct laws that met its requirements (Kant), or which treated all phenomena and events as part of an integrated, organic totality that was unfolding according to the plan of an objective (i.e. natural) reason (Fichte, Schelling, Hegel). Historical Materialism, by contrast, was materialist in that humans were treated as material beings who had to satisfy their basic needs for survival and reproduction as a species before they could do anything else. It was historical in that the possibilities for social and economic organization in the present were always set (in the sense both of 'restricted' and 'made possible') by the circumstances that had been inherited from the past.[13]

The young Marx, concerned with the issue of human freedom and emancipation, believed himself to have discovered in the proletariat not only a social group with its own *interest* in the overthrow of the political and economic order, but also a group whose structural position in modern society provided its members with the *power* to do so. It was the first exploited class in human history to have this potential. It was also a social group which was unable to liberate itself from exploitation without liberating the whole of humanity from its various oppressions. In the early 1840s, both Marx and Frederick Engels turned their attention to the class structure of nineteenth-century European capitalism, and the struggles between the contending classes to which it gave rise. This focus was to enable them to develop a theory of history, Historical Materialism, whose central distinctive feature was the identification of class struggles as the social dynamic throughout human history. The concept of class used by these authors, and by their followers today, cannot be understood independently of this theory of which it is a part.

For Marx and Engels, as they argued in *The Manifesto of the Communist Party*, 'the history of all hitherto existing society is the history of class struggle'. By this, they did not mean that there were no other interesting or significant features of past and existing societies that were significant for their histories. Their claim was that in order to understand any of these other features adequately, and to grasp why whole societies developed for a period and then decayed and were replaced by successors, required appreciating them in the knowledge of their central feature. That feature was the struggle between the direct producers of wealth, on the one hand, and the minority of rulers whose existence depended on the appropriation of part of that wealth, on the other. Indeed, it was the precise way in which the ruling minority extracted a surplus from the work of the direct producers and appropriated it for its own use, the mechanism of 'exploitation', that constituted the defining property of each type of human society. Slave societies differed from feudal societies, and these from capitalist societies, not simply by the degree of deprivation and degradation of the direct producers but by the mode of surplus extraction. In slave societies, this was achieved through constituting the producers as *the property* of the master, and hence also all that is produced by them. In feudal societies, it was achieved by the enforcement of traditional *legal rights and duties* entitling the lord to a share of peasant production. In capitalist societies, it depended on contracting with workers, as legally free agents, that they will *exchange in the market* their power to work for a period in return for an agreed wage. They then create goods in that period which would be the property of the capitalist, and whose value exceeded that of the wages that the producers would be paid.

Marx's model of society and history had three key features. First, the claim that it is the economic structure (i.e. the social relations of production, or which class has direct control of the means of production) that is the real foundation of society, and hence that 'it is the mode of production of material life (which) conditions the social, political and intellectual life process in general'. Second, that there have been in human history a sequence of different modes of production, each characterised by a distinctive method of taking a surplus from the wealth produced by the efforts of the direct producers, of which the capitalist mode is merely the latest but not the last, despite its appearance of permanence and naturalness. Third, that the class relations in any given mode of production (the 'relations' of production) would bear a definite relationship to the level of development of the techniques used to produce (the 'forces' of production). This was a dramatic and exciting vista on the human condition, whose scope and ambition has never been, and may never be, matched.[14]

All societies that evolved beyond a primitive stage, they argued, generated a class of rulers who would extract from the labour of the producing class as much as possible of what was surplus to the survival needs of the producers. The exact nature of this process of surplus extraction, and the character of the producing and exploiting classes involved in it, would depend on the way in which access to (i.e. ownership or effective control of) the means of production (tools and raw materials – the 'instruments' and 'objects' of human labour) was distributed between classes. This distribution of the means of production – which class owns or controls them – constituted what Marx called the 'relations of production'. Marx defined classes then in terms of their relationship to the means of production. In the capitalist mode of production, the bourgeoisie has exclusive ownership or control of the means of production, from which the proletariat has been excluded.[15] This contrasts with pre-capitalist, feudal society where, though exploited by a feudal ruling class, the peasantry as the class of direct producers did have direct access or legal entitlement to work the land and to own seed-corn, plough and draught animals, their 'objects and instruments of labour'.

Throughout the different types of human society thus defined, ruling classes exist on the basis of their capacity to extract and appropriate a surplus from the direct producers. This was the process that Marx referred to as 'exploitation'. In this technical usage, the term did not mean, as it tends to be used today, the *excessive* benefit derived by the most ruthless employer. In this technical sense, *all* employers in a capitalist system are exploiters since all profit, however large or small, constitutes the successful extraction of surplus from the direct producers. They remain exploiters even when running their operations at a commercial loss since their role and position is predicated on profit seeking. In such a case, they are merely *unsuccessful* exploiters. Through their accumulation of wealth, and the power attached to it, ruling classes develop the ability to enshrine their position in cultural tradition, in dominant belief systems and in legal constraints, thereby justifying the *enforcement* of their appropriation rights should that prove necessary. It was the behaviour of these contending classes in the different societies in human history (masters versus slaves, lords versus peasants, capitalists versus workers), each pursuing its own interest, that constituted 'class struggle' – the struggle over the distribution of the social surplus between the classes.

Attempts to intensify surplus extraction were, of course, resisted by the producing class, sometimes in open conflict, more often in resentment and sullen resignation and protest. Not until the development of the capitalist mode of production, however, and the emergence of the modern proletariat as the directly producing class, was there the opportunity for the producers to resist the process as such. In pre-capitalist societies, class divisions were typically obscured by social position and social status, by legal rights and obligations, by the weight of tradition and custom, and by the hierarchy of orders and ranks to which they gave rise. It was only with capitalism that the visibility of class divisions came to the fore.

Only with the emergence of this system could those who were objectively members of the classes which Marx's theory had identified more easily identify for themselves the commonality of their positions. Only as capitalism further developed did the increasing polarization of society into the two main classes, bourgeoisie and proletariat, enable each to see its class interests more clearly.

Capitalism is a social system that had thus produced a class with an *interest* in its overthrow. By concentrating this class in workplaces that facilitated the association of its members, and inducing mutuality and interdependence by its continuous pressure for further division of labour, it had also created a class with the potential *political power* to achieve that overthrow. The system had, in Marx's words, produced its own gravedigger. Only with the development of capitalism, moreover, was there an increasing socialisation (interdependence) of otherwise geographically dispersed and functionally discreet human activities. Only with capitalism did human productive techniques (both knowledge and technology) reach a level at which their capacity to satisfy the evolving needs of humanity no longer required the exploitation of the majority of mankind by others of the species. This was the sense in which Marx held the capitalist mode of production to be simultaneously the best and the worst thing to have happened to humanity. He celebrated the historical role of the social system while being its most trenchant critic.

This did not mean that class interests were always, or even normally, perceived with clarity. Those workers who did band together in mutual self-defence did so, most often, only on a temporary basis, or in defence of a sub-class, sectional interest – as employees of *this* company, as workers from *that* industry, as engineers or as nurses or as teachers. The recognition of a common position, and of shared interests as employees in a particular firm or industry, did not typically translate into a generalised consciousness of class. When it did so, it would be the result of the educative effect of prolonged struggle, of the formation of class-based political organisations, of an intractable political and economic crisis of the capitalist order. It was these that *could*, but would not automatically, give rise to an awareness of the historic role of the proletariat. In other words, *generalised* class consciousness would not be the norm, but rather the exception, and would be the prelude to social revolution.

It was for this reason that Marx distinguished between the notion of a class 'in itself' (i.e. those subject to the same objective economic and social conditions, and occupying the same structural position in relation to the process of exploitation) and a class 'for itself' (i.e. knowing the common interests of the whole, and identifying with it). Outside periods of social revolution, only a small minority of the subordinate class or classes would be possessed of the latter knowledge. The majority, under the influence of the dominant ideology of the society (the ideas encouraged and funded to conduce to the interests of the ruling class), would be subject to a 'false consciousness' about its true position. While 'class', for Marx, was on the one hand a relational and objective concept (classes exist *analytically* in so far as they endure common circumstances, and hence have identifiable interests incompatible with those of other classes), it also had an important subjective element. This subjective element was pivotal: for Marx, classes only exist *in reality* when they have some level of self-consciousness as classes, and begin *to act* in pursuit of their class interests.[16]

Each succeeding type of society in history, defined and differentiated from each other by their distinctive relations of production, had its own cultural artefacts and traditions, its own legal order, its own political institutions and processes, and its own set of dominant ideas about what is right, good and proper. These cultural, legal, political and ideological processes had their own histories, of course, so that the precise legal duties and obligations in feudal France did not match those in feudal England, and the exact features of the political institutions today in the capitalist United States do not replicate the detail of those in capitalist India. As instances of slave or feudal or capitalist modes of production, however, all of these societies needed their non-economic aspects to share one feature and acquit themselves of one primordial role, whatever their national traditions and peculiarities – to be compatible with, and to facilitate the development of, the relations of production. There was, Marx claimed, using an architectural metaphor, a requirement for correspondence under normal circumstances between these 'superstructural' features of any type of society or mode of production and its economic 'base'.

Whatever the peculiarities of national culture and politics, a supportive relationship between them and the sphere of production was identified by the model as a requirement for social stability. Capitalist relations of production had a requirement, at least in a weak sense, for a legal and political and ideological superstructure compatible with them, one that would facilitate rather than 'fetter' the reproduction and further development of capital. Compatibility was not inevitable, however, and normal circumstances did not always obtain. Neither human society nor its history had the character of inanimate machines or biological organisms in which each part of the whole was mechanically or naturally related to each other by its definite function. Superstructural levels *could* evolve in ways that were incompatible with, or sub-optimal for, the dominant relations of production because they were, after all, the consequences of human decisions and human action. Human beings often make mistakes, or act in ignorance of the consequences of their behaviour. Such functional failures of the superstructure would then tend to impair the efficient operation of the economic base, giving rise to a tension or contradiction that could only be resolved by a change in one or the other. Feudal laws hampered the development of capitalist relations of production until social revolutions of the eighteenth and nineteenth centuries swept them away. Centuries later, capitalist productive dynamism has created the technological, social and economic conditions necessary for an egalitarian and properly human social order (communism) but the fruition of that possibility required and requires the culture, laws and institutions of liberalism which defend the private ownership of productive assets to be similarly swept away.

Class struggle is treated in Marx's model as *endemic* to the capitalist system. It is ineradicable and perpetual, though it does not always, or even typically, take the form of open conflict or expressed hostility. It arises ineluctably from the tension generated by the zero-sum game between wage income and profits to capital. The objective interests of the bourgeoisie and the proletariat are incompatible, and therefore generate not a tendency to permanent hostility and open warfare but a permanent tendency toward them. The system is thus prone to economic class conflict, and, given the cyclical instability of its economy, subject to periodic political and economic crises. It is at these moments that the possibility exists for social revolution. Crises provide the opportunity for transition from the oppressive and exploitative, competitive and alienating conditions of the order of capital to a realm of human freedom in which humanity as a whole, through a radically democratic structure, engages collectively in satisfying its needs, ordering its priorities, and constructing new needs and aspirations to strive for, and challenges to overcome.

Marx and the class structure: mapping past, present and future

Marx's description of the class structure of nineteenth-century capitalism (the stage of capitalism's adolescence in Europe) was, naturally, only accurate in detail for its period. The continuing relevance, or otherwise, of the model depends on its fundamental categorisations and relational properties rather than on these details. So how has the structure of developed capitalist society changed in the last century and a half?

Between the bourgeoisie and the proletariat lay, Marx argued in the nineteenth century, an intermediate layer of those who neither exploited wage labour, nor were exploited as wage labour. These were self-employed artisans, own account traders, much of the professions, etc. They were neither workers nor capitalists, not on principle or out of choice but because such was the nature of employment opportunities at that stage in the development of capitalism. Marx referred to this group as the 'petty bourgeoisie'. His expectation was that, with the further development of the mode of production, this intermediate layer would diminish in importance, some graduating into the ranks of the bourgeoisie proper but most being proletarianised as the ambit of capital expanded to draw more skills into the direct process of extracting surplus value. Within the proletariat, he also distinguished between those who were formally and regularly employed and those in the 'lumpen proletariat'. The lumpen proletariat consisted of those outside regular employment, and at the margins of society, forced by the lack of opportunities to exist in a twilight world of bare subsistence, migrating in and out of petty criminality, and unable to develop a sense of belonging, of class consciousness, and of class solidarity. Politically, Marx argued, the tendency would be for the two chief classes, bourgeoisie and proletariat, to develop parties and programmes serving their distinct interests. While attracted to the liberal and individualist ideology and rhetoric of the bourgeois parties in normal circumstances, both the petty bourgeoisie and the lumpen proletariat could be drawn towards the socialist programme of the proletariat at times of economic or social crisis, when the dominant political ideas seemed to offer no solution.

Changes in the balance of occupations, in their rewards and statuses, and in their functions in the last hundred years means that a Marxian class map at the end of the twentieth century differs interestingly from Marx's nineteenth-century map. Most notably, it contains the category of a 'new middle class'. This consists of employees in what have been described as 'contradictory class locations' – those who are paid a wage or salary by capital but who, by virtue of the nature of their occupations, are not part of the proletariat.[17] This group can usefully be sub-divided into those who work as middle or junior managers for capital, and those who retain a large degree of autonomy (i.e. who operate largely independently of direct managerial supervision) because of the kind of work that they do. Managers supervise and direct the labour force, and determine the detailed deployment of *given* resources. This distinguishes them from the senior executives who make strategic determination of *the level* of those resources, and who are, in conse-quence, members of the capitalist class. Autonomous employees, by contrast, do not direct labour or administer budgets and resources. Into this category, for example, fall university lecturers, senior company accountants, hospital doctors, research engineers and scientists, senior social workers, etc. In both cases, livings are earned by the selling of labour power for a wage or a salary but, unlike members of the proletariat, those in this new middle class do control either the labour of others, or the deployment of their own. Different aspects of their employment conditions are shared with different classes: they are wage labourers by remuneration, but possessed usually of all the petty-bourgeois vanities by virtue of their possession of some control over the labour process. They also tend to share the attitudes and aspirations of the petty bourgeoisie, and its fluctuating political allegiances.

The proletariat, in this contemporary map, continues to possess its traditional characteristics and properties. Its objective interests are incompatible with those of the owners of capital. It is internally differentiated by deep divisions of educational background (from minimal to higher level), skill attainment, income and cultural interests, and by divisions of gender, ethnicity and nationality. It is, however, occasionally forced by circumstances to transcend these divisions when the reality of its common interests takes precedence over its typically section-alist consciousness. In these respects, it is no different from the proletariat of the nineteenth century.

Confusions, however, abound. What Marxists refer to as the 'lumpen proletariat' is often described today by non-Marxists as an 'underclass'. The difference is significant. In the first place, the 'underclass' designation excludes its members from the proletariat. It also implies that all other classes share a common feature (being 'included' in society) that distinguishes them from the long-term or period-ically unemployed (who are said to be 'excluded'). Thus, members of the bourgeoisie, of the new middle class, and of the proletariat are all treated as one social grouping, with interests that differ from those of the 'underclass'. This view is captured by the descriptive slogan, 'A two-thirds, one-third society', and in Britain is institutionalised by the British government's 'Social Exclusion Unit'. By contrast, Marxists argue that this is an empirically false and theoretically misleading characterisation. First, the interests of a marginalised group vary directly not indirectly with the level of struggle and the success of the proletariat as a whole. The struggle of the better organised sections of the working class benefit all in raising the general level of wages, by defending the number of jobs, and by influencing government welfare policy. Second, there is no reason in principle why workers on short-term contracts and other forms of casual employment should not be drawn into the organised working class. Indeed, they may have a very special interest in becoming part of it. Third, much social commentary generates a systematically distorted picture of advanced societies by conflating two different groups: those who are marginalised and demeaned by unemployment and casual labour, and those who are only seeking part-time employment or a series of temporary contracts. Most of those included as part of a marginalised 'underclass' are, in this sense, no more marginalised than other members of the working class. The size of the truly marginal section of society is, as a consequence of this conflation, systematically over-estimated. Fourth, the deep divisions of incompatible class interests within the 'two-thirds of society' (between the proletariat, the new middle class, and the bourgeoisie) are ignored by this analysis.

If the size of the marginalised sector of society is over-estimated by much contemporary analysis, the size of the working class is under-estimated. 'White collar' employees in all sectors are often excluded from the category, and treated as if they are part of the middle class. A similar theoretical fate befalls all those in the service sector in other empirical and theoretical studies. Thus, the senior civil servant in charge of a department of government and the manager of one of its offices, on the one hand, and all of the secretaries and clerks and minor officials engaged in largely routine tasks for less than the average wage, on the other hand, are both treated as if they are members of the same class in virtue of the *non-manual* character of their work. Similarly, cleaners, cooks, nurses, radiographers and junior hospital doctors will find themselves excluded from the proletariat, and sharing a class category with the managers and strategic administrators of the quasi-privatised hospital trust, or the health authority, in virtue of sharing the same sectoral location for the expenditure of their efforts.

The practical political consequences of these theoretical differences cannot be over-emphasised. The description and analysis of social trends offered by contemporary sociology depicts a working class in numerical decline, and suffering a loss of social and political cohesion, as a result of economic de-industrialisation and of fragmenting and diverging interests within the working class. If such were the case then not only is Marx's account of the historical evolution of human societies seriously flawed, his characterisation of the proletariat as a class with a historic mission is, and must always have been, mistaken. It was never, and could not have been, the agency of human emancipation. If flawed as a political project, the effect of this purported trend has no less an impact on Marx's class analysis as an explanatory model. With the character and dynamics of the 'economic base' no longer determinable in terms of class relations of production, other aspects of society could hardly be explained by reference to it.

It is, however, a contested trend. The Marxist observes that the purported trend is only 'identified' on the basis of a definition of the concept of class derived from the status hierarchy of different occupations, i.e. the working class is only in numerical decline if it is defined to include only manual occupations, or 'productive' as opposed to service sector labour. Alternatively, if it is treated as wage labour, and even with the new middle class excluded, it remains the large majority of the population in advanced societies, and constitutes a numerically *growing* class as a proportion of the world's population once the development of capitalism in underdeveloped societies, and their integration into the global capitalist economy, are considered.[18] Moreover, the existence of sharp divisions (of income levels, political allegiances, and social attitudes) within the working class can only be interpreted as evidence for a process of class fragmentation if one presumes the existence of a 'golden age' of political and social cohesion. Historically, there was no such period. The proletariat, argues the Marxist, has always suffered from such sectional divisions. The real issue, she argues, is whether Marx was correct in claiming that the proletariat shared common *objective* interests, and in predicting periodic and cyclical economic and political crises in which these interests *could* take precedence over sectional interests in determining class consciousness. If so, then the sociologists' trend is false, and is part of a tendentious theoretical argument. It is itself part of bourgeois ideology.

Marx: interpretation and critique

Marxism is also condemned for being an 'economism', and for providing a 'class reductionist' analysis of social phenomena. By 'economism' is meant the explanation of a society's operation or its features by reference to the requirements of its economic processes. This is considered by critics to be illegitimate as an explanation because it ignores the political or social or ideological or cultural determinants of the social phenomenon being studied. What is strange about the criticism is that, though addressed *to* Marxism, it does not seem to address Marxism. Marx never constructed his explanations of historical features of societies or social events as naïve reductions to their economic effects on production. He was insistent on the need for detailed political and historical and cultural analysis, and was himself a rigorous exponent of that method. It was in response to crude 'economic reductionism' that he once declared, in a letter to a friend, that if that was Marxism then 'I am not a Marxist!' Nonetheless, it was a consequence of his model that while cultural and political practices and institutions had their own histories, which needed detailed study in themselves to be understood, this autonomy was only partial. All such social phenomena could only exist in so far as the conditions for social reproduction had been satisfied; and all such political and cultural features of a society would themselves have an effect on the efficiency of material production. To trace those relationships between the economic base and features of the superstructure was not to exhaust *everything* that needed to be included in an explanation of them. It *was* to provide an ineliminable feature of any adequate explanation.

'Class reductionism' is closely related to 'economism'. Marx is accused of 'reducing' all the features of human social experience to the mere appearances or reflexes of the class division of society. Thus, it is argued, for example, that the oppression of women is explained by Marxists in terms of its function for the reproduction of capital, and consequently the specificities of that oppression are ignored or minimised. In a seemingly innocent inversion of the normal application of the word, these critics affirm that Marxism 'privileges' class. Once subjected to analysis, however, this turns out to be no more than an objection to Marx's use of the model he thinks appropriate for social explanation. It must be assumed that this criticism is not directed at the process of reducing the complex world to key variables that can be modelled. If that were the criticism, it would be an objection to *all* scientific endeavour in both the natural or the social worlds. Hence, it can only be an objection to the use of *class* analysis, and not an objection to 'reduction', as such.

Marx and Marxists did and do explain oppression by reference to its operation in a particular society, and in capitalism that means the contribution of oppressions to the reproduction of capital. In the case of sexist behaviour and institutions (as in the case also of homophobia), the mechanism connecting these oppressive features with the requirements of capital is the role of the family in the reproduction of the labour force. That is an indirect connection, however. The Marxist does not argue that personal and institutional prejudices are reproduced in peoples' heads and in their customary behaviour by the unmediated needs of the economy. Culture is the agency for the transmission of these values and reflexes, but this is not a culture which exists in a material vacuum. It is a culture whose conditions for existence are provided by material production.

It is for this reason that a historical materialist account of female oppression, for example, is *incompatible* with a feminist account to the extent that the latter relies on patriarchy theory. Theories of patriarchy explain social development by reference to male interest in the maintenance of female oppression, and this interest is treated as a transcendent feature of human experience, constant across different types of society. Historical materialism explains social development by reference to the requirements of surplus extraction by the ruling class from the labour of the direct producers. All forms of oppression are explained in relation to that. Thus, the oppression of women will take different forms in different societies, and in no society will the nature and impact of oppression be the same for all women irrespective of their class.[19] With women from different class backgrounds experiencing oppression in radically different ways, and targeting different objectives as part of its eradication, the generic and undifferentiated category 'women' does not identify an effective agency of social change. Moreover, argues the Marxist, though many working class men may enjoy the effects of an unequal division of domestic labour which has survived from the nineteenth century, the main beneficiary of oppressive practices and ideas is capital, not men. Oppressions, in dividing the working class, operate to secure the reproduction of capital; they construct social conflict between men and women, or black and white, or skilled and unskilled, thereby tending to dissolve the conflict between capital and labour.

It is in this sense that the Marxist argues that the *whole* of the working class suffers from oppression, and has an objective interest in opposing it. It is for this reason that the contemporary Marxist argues that it remains the proletariat that is the only agent of change that combines the potential power to effect social change with an objective interest in doing so.

Verdicts

Given this corrective to the standard misunderstandings of the Marxist concept of 'class', where are we now in adjudicating between different theories and strategies for today's movement? Hardt and Negri offer us a utopian, even ecstatic, manifesto. It is an appeal to the possibilities of the future but with little regard to the constraints of the present, or for the strategic and tactical challenges of political transition. Or so it has been argued.[20] Callinicos, by contrast, is precisely concerned with the relationship between tactics and strategy for the movement, and by the dependence of both on a vision of the future that is rooted in an analysis of the present state of things. This is the manner in which the difference between them first appear. Yet it is not, on reflection, clear that Hardt and Negri do fail to locate the immanence of tomorrow's promise in the conditions of today. They precisely argue that the present is partly defined by the development of a hyper-globalisation that has 'deterritorialised' capital and relegated the importance of the nation state. Further, they argue that technological development has moved the centre of gravity of labour away from industries and services, and towards the immaterial objects of communication and information. This is what they believe has created an affective and potentially networked challenge to the rule of capital/Empire, one that celebrates difference and diversity, is non-hierarchical, does not need structured organisation, and whose multiform and multitudinous nature makes it increasingly irrepressible and unsuppressionable.[21] It is thus not their 'bad utopianism' that constitutes their difference with classical Marxism but rather their reconceptualisation of the 'class' which has radical potential. For them the radical agency of change is not the relatively narrowly defined proletariat of Marxism but the multitude. The latter is more embracive than the latter, and contains it. Moreover, as with Marx's identification of the proletariat, their discovery of the multitude is the naming of an entity that only exists *in potentia*. Proletariat and multitude alike only have *real* existence when they act as entities that are conscious of themselves and of their hostility to their enemy. Both, in other words, have to be brought into existence.

Thus, the difference separating these prognoses for the system and the opposition that it provokes is not so much a matter of realism versus utopianism but of analytical power and practical effect. Which of the two captures best the conditions of contemporary capitalism, and which offers the more effective guide to action? Both are invocations, advocations and rallying cries. Both offer strikingly similar short-tem programmes for the movement.[22] The choice between them largely depends on the assessment of the relevance of the classical Marxist model in contemporary world conditions. Has it been displaced as an explanatory tool by contemporary developments, and, if so, are those developments better captured in the ideas of 'Empire' and 'multitude'?

For educators, moreover, it should be clear that neither the concept 'working class' nor that of 'multitude' could simply be a designation for those who might have been subjected to environmental deprivation, or for those who should be treated as victims. In both cases, it is not simply alienation that is being identified as the condition of those falling under the concept but *empowerment* as well. It is the accuracy of the accounts of those empowerments that is at issue. In every classroom in the state school system, and even in the privileged recesses of private education, the large majority of school students will be sensitive to the new movements and struggles that are renewing the world as a site of promise and possibility. This debate about the nature of the movements and the source of their potential should be a key moment in the preparation of engaged citizens and critical intelligences.

Notes

1 See Ali (2002), Achcar (2002), McNally (2002), Callinicos (2003), Harvey (2004).
2 Meiksins Wood (2001), quoted in McNally, ibid.
3 See Danaher and Burbach, 2000; Danaher, 2001; Went, 2000; Stiglitz, 2002.
4 For the arch expression of this pessimism and resignation, see Giddens (1998); for a critique and antidote see Callinicos (2000).
5 For a brief synopsis of the movement, see Hickey and Rupprecht, 2005; for a detailed treatment and identification of its constituent elements, see George and Bircham, 2001.
6 Callinicos, 2005.
7 Equally, it can be asked whether the 'anti-war' movement should automatically be considered 'anti-imperialist' since many who were opposed to the war (particularly, perhaps, in Britain and the US) did not see it as an imperialist adventure but rather as a disproportionate or counterproductive reaction to the 'threat' that the Saddam regime was claimed to represent.
8 Callinicos (2002), Hardt and Negri (2000).
9 See Balakrishnan (2001) for an incisive review.
10 Hardt and Negri (2004).
11 For Postmodernist treatments of class, and the social fragmentations that were claimed to have undermined its analytical and political relevance as a concept, see Bauman (1992, 1993), Good and Velody (1998), Maheu (1995), Laclau and Mouffe (1985), Seidman and Wagner (1992); for critiques, see Callinicos (1991) and Harvey (1989).
12 They do not claim that the working class no longer exists, nor that it is shrinking as a proportion of the population. Their claim is that 'industrial labour has been displaced from its hegemonic position over other forms of labour by immaterial labour' (Hardt and Negri, 2004, p. 223). See also Barbalet (1986).
13 Appreciating its position in the intellectual tradition is not just useful for an understanding of the genesis of Historical Materialism, it is indispensable in making a properly reflective assessment of it. It is so because a rejection of some form of historical materialism thus defined (if not precisely Marx's version with H and M) entails either a commitment to some modern version of the three traditions he rejected, or to an incoherent postmodern relativism.
14 For an elaborate and extended contemporary exposition, interpretation and defence of it, see Cohen (1978); and for criticisms of this particular elaboration from a Marxist

perspective, see Callinicos (1979). For a Weberian critique of Historical Materialism, see Giddens (1981); for responses see Wright (1983, 1989), and Callinicos (1989); for Giddens' retorts, see Giddens (1985, 1989). For a postmodernist critique, see Laclau and Mouffe (1985); for a response see Geras (1990). For a sophisticated reconsideration of Marx's scientific project and the philosophical critique that underlay it, see Bensaid (2002).

15　That the exact features of a capitalist class or a working class do not, in reality, match these pure, ideal forms is not a shortcoming of the theory or of its concepts. That the working class includes those who have sources of income other than wages (e.g. rental income from a lodger, dividends from some shares in a privatised utility, clandestine receipts from 'moonlighting' as a petty bourgeois cabbie or jobbing plumber in the evenings) does not threaten the coherence of the theoretical concept 'working class'. Marx himself noted that the emergence of the joint stock company in the nineteenth century had begun a process that would progressively remove capitalist production from the direct control of individual capitalists, and would have been unsurprised to learn that today's major shareholders are pension funds, some of which, as mutual funds, are under the *nominal* ownership and control of the workers who pay into them.

16　For the clearest original expression of this view, see Marx (1977, 1978).

17　For the development of the concept, see Wright (1978); for the elaboration of the argument here, see Callinicos and Harman (1989).

18　For contemporary estimates, see Callinicos and Harman, op.cit.

19　The issue is complicated by the fact that there are those who, in describing themselves as 'socialist feminists', do *not* subscribe to patriarchy theory but rather use a historical and materialist analysis.

20　See, inter alia, Balakrishnan, op.cit.

21　'. . . biopolitical weapons will probably be more similar to those proposed by Lysistrata to overcome the Athenian men's decision to go to war than those put in circulation by idealogues and politicians today. It is not unreasonable to hope that in a biopolitical future . . . war will no longer be possible, and the intensity of the cooperation and communication between singularities (workers and/or citizens) will destroy its possibility. A one-week global biopolitical strike would block any war' (Hardt and Negri, 2004, p.347).

22　Hardt and Negri offer two in Empire: the guarantee of a basic income for all and the abolition of all immigration controls. Callinicos argues for cancellation of Third World debt, the Tobin Tax, a shorter working week, redistributive taxation, and the abolition of immigration controls. In both cases, these are transitional demands – they can be defended rationally, and are expressive of contemporary moral sentiment, yet they are undeliverable within the capitalist mode of production. Particularly in relation to migration and its control by nation states, the arguments concerning the irrationality and the immorality of border controls that damage economic growth in economies suffering from labour shortages, and systematically discriminate against refugees, the poor and the non-European migrant, are well represented. See Harris (2002), Harding (2000) and Stalker (2001).

References

Achcar, G. *The Clash of Barbarisms: September 11th and the making of the New World Disorder*, MR 2002

Ali, T. *The Clash of Fundamentalisms: Crusades, Jihads and Modernity*, Verso 2002

Balakrishnan, G. 'Virgilian Visions', *New Left Review* 5, 2002

Barbalet, J. 'Limitations of Class Theory and the Disappearance of Status: The Problem of the New Middle Class', *Sociology*, v.20, n.4, pp. 557–75

Bauman, Z. *Intimations of Postmodernity*, Routledge 1992

Bauman, Z. *Postmodern Ethics*, Blackwell 1993

Bensaïd, D. *Marx for Our Times: Adventures and Misadventures of a Critique*, Verso 2002, trns. Gregory Elliott

Callinicos, A. *Is there a Future for Marxism?*, Macmillan 1979

Callinicos, A. 'Anthony Giddens: A Contemporary Critique' in *idem*. (ed.) *Marxist Theory*, OUP 1989

Callinicos, A. *Against Postmodernism: a Marxist Critique*, Polity 1991

Callinicos, A. *Against the Third Way*, Polity 2000

Callinicos, A. *An Anti-Capitalist Manifesto*, Polity, 2002

Callinicos, A. *The New Mandarins of American Power*, Polity 2003

Callinicos, A. 'The challenge for the left . . .', *Socialist Worker*, 22 January 2005

Callinicos, A. and C. Harman *The Changing Working Class: Essays on Class Structure Today*, Bookmarks 1989

Cohen, G. *Karl Marx's Theory of History: A Defence*, OUP 1978

Danaher, K. and S. Burbach (eds) *Globalise This! The Battle Against the World Trade Organisation and Corporate Rule*, Common Courage Press 2000

Danaher, K. *Democratising the Global Economy*, Common Courage Press 2002

George, S. and E. Bircham (eds) *Anti-capitalism: A Guide to the Movement*, Bookmarks 2001

Geras, N. *Discourses of Extremity: Radical Ethics and Post-Marxist Extravaganzas*, Verso 1990

German, L. 'Theories of Patriarchy', *International Socialism*, 12, Spring 1981

Giddens, A. 'Marx's Correct Views on Everything', *Theory and Society*, 14, 1985

Giddens, A. 'A Reply to My Critics', in D. Held and Thompson, *Social Theory of Modern Societies, Anthony Giddens and his Critics*, CUP 1989

Giddens, A. *The Third Way: Renewal of Social Democracy*, Polity 1998

Good, J. and I. Velody (eds.) *The Politics of Postmodernity*, CUP 1998

Good, J., L. McDowell and P. Saree, Sage 1989

Harding, J. *The Uninvited: Refugees at the Rich Man's Gate*, Profile 2000

Hardt, M. and T. Negri *Empire*, Harvard, 2000

Hardt, M. and T. Negri *Multitude: War and Democracy in the Age of Empire*, Penguin 2004

Harman, C. 'Base and Superstructure', *International Socialism*, 32, Spring 1986

Harris, N. *Thinking the Unthinkable: the Immigration Myth Exposed*, Tauris 2002

Harvey, D. *The Condition of Postmodernity: An Enquiry into the Origins of Cultural Change*, Blackwell 1989

Harvey, D. *The New Imperialism*, OUP 2004

Hickey, T. and A. Rupprecht 'Anti-globalisation movement' in Prem Poddar and David Johnson, (eds.) *A Historical Companion to Postcolonial Thought in English*, New York; Columbia University Press, 2005.

Laclau, E. and C. Mouffe, *Hegemony and Socialist Strategy: Towards a Radical Democratic Politics*, Verso 1985

Maheu, L. (ed.) *Social Movements and Social Classes: the Future of Collective Action*, Sage 1995

Marx, K. 'The Eighteenth Brumaire of Louis Bonaparte', in Marx *Selected Writings*, OUP 1977

Marx, K. 'The Class Struggles in France', in Marx and Engels *Selected Works*, vol.1, Progress 1978

McNally, D. *Another World is Possible: Globalisation and Anti-capitalism*, Arbeiter Ring, 2002

Meiksins Wood, E. 'War Without Boundaries', *Canadian Dimension*, Nov/Dec, 2001

Seidman, S. and D. Wagner *Postmodernism and Social Theory: The Debate Over General Theory*, Blackwell 1992

Stalker, P. *The No Nonsense Guide to International Migration*, Verso 2001

Stiglitz, J. *Globalisation and its Discontents*, Allen Lane 2002

Went, R. *Globalisation: Neoliberal Challenges, Radical Responses*, Pluto 2000

Wright, E.O. 'Giddens' Critique of Marxism', *New Left Review*, 138, 1983, pp. 11–35

Wright, E.O. *Class, Crisis and the State*, Verso 1978

Wright, E.O. 'Models of historical trajectory: an assessment of Giddens' critique of Marxism', in D. Held and J. Thompson *Social Theory of Modern Societies: Anthony Giddens and his critics*, CUP 1989

10 Social class and schooling

Differentiation or democracy?

Richard Hatcher

> The gap between the best and worst performers in our system actually widens as they go through education; and it is both significantly wider and more closely related to socio-economic status in this country than elsewhere.
>
> (DfES 2004, *Five Year Strategy for Children and Learners*,
> Chapter 1, para 23)

If you want to know how well a child will do at school, ask how much its parents earn. The fact remains, after more than 50 years of the welfare state and several decades of comprehensive education, that family wealth is the single best predictor of success in the school system. Of course some children from well-off homes don't do well at school and some children from poor backgrounds succeed, but the overall pattern is clear: social class, defined in terms of socio-economic status, correlates closely with attainment at school. In this chapter I explore the extent of social class inequality in society and school, the cultural and political processes which reproduce patterns of educational inequality, and ways in which schools might interrupt them.

Economic inequality

Economic inequality is very substantial in Britain and it is increasing. The richest 10 per cent get nearly 28 per cent of total income, while the poorest 10 per cent get just under 3 per cent, according to the Institute for Fiscal Studies (Denny and Elliott, 2004). Inequality is greater at the end of Labour's second term of office than it was under Margaret Thatcher. The Gini coefficient, a measure of inequality, has increased from an average of 29 points under Thatcher to 35 points in 2001–2 under Blair (Waugh, 2003). Figures from the Inland Revenue on the distribution of marketable wealth (which includes rent and dividends) show that the richest 1 per cent of the population had 20 per cent of the nation's wealth in 1996 and 23 per cent in 2001, after the first four years of the Labour government. The poorest half of the population had 7 per cent in 1996 and 5 per cent in 2001 (Foot, 2003). In spite of overall improvements in income, health and housing, people without qualifications are more excluded from society and live in greater relative poverty than 50 years ago, according to the report *Changing Britain, Changing Lives* (Ferri *et al.*, 2003), which compared cohorts of adults born in 1946 and 1970.

Child poverty

Of particular relevance to school is the extent of child poverty. There was a high level of child poverty under the Conservative governments of Thatcher and Major. In the mid-1990s Britain was third from bottom in a list of industrialised countries, ahead only of Italy and the US. Today one in four children are in families which fall below the poverty line (defined as families living on less than 60 per cent of average income). The British figure of 24 per cent compares to an average of 8 per cent in the four best countries in Europe (Stewart, 2005a). Patterns of class inequality intersect with those of ethnicity: the figure is significantly higher for Pakistani and Bangladeshi children (75 per cent) and Black/Black British children (46 per cent) (Phillips, 2005).

The Labour government's target has been to reduce child poverty by one quarter in 2004, one million children. The proportion of children in poverty fell from 34 per cent in the year when Labour took office (1996/7) to 28 per cent in 2002/3. The purchasing power of the poor has risen significantly, but the proportion in relative poverty is still far higher than in 1979, at the end of the previous Labour government's term of office (Stewart, 2005a). A study published by the Joseph Rowntree Foundation (Sutherland, Sefton and Piachaud, 2003) shows that the government is on course to achieve this target (confirmed by Hills and Stewart, 2005) but that if it is to meet its long-term target of halving child poverty by 2010 it would need to substantially increase redistribution of wealth towards the poorest families. Two things inhibit this redistribution. One is the market. There is a contradiction at the heart of government policy between its attempts to reduce poverty by a range of anti-poverty measures and its commitment to the market, which functions to increase inequality. The national minimum wage has made little impact on inequality because of high pay rises at the top. Pensions and benefits for the poor have risen much less than the income of high earners, which remains relatively low taxed. The second obstacle to the Labour government adopting the more radically redistributive measures necessary to further reduce child poverty is its reluctance for electoral reasons to risk alienating middle-class support.

Class inequality in education

These massive differences in the economic status of families have massive consequences for the education of their children, which the government acknowledges in its *Five Year Strategy for Children and Learners* (DfES 2004):

> 20 [. . .] Those from higher socio-economic groups do significantly better at each stage of our system than those from lower ones – indeed [. . .] socio-economic group is a stronger predictor of attainment than early ability.

21   In general, though, those that do well early do even better later in life, while those that do not perform well fall further behind; and the chances of breaking out of this cycle of underachievement reduce with age.

22   Those who do better than average at age 7 are more than twice as likely to get qualifications at degree level by the age of 25 than those who performed poorly at 7. Results for 11 year-olds show an even starker picture – over 85 percent of 11 year-olds that do not reach the expected level for their age will not get five good GCSEs at age 16. Throughout secondary school, the pattern of attainment becomes increasingly fixed – 95 percent of those who fail to reach the expected level at the age of 14 will not get five good GCSEs. This pattern persists in the adult workforce, with highly qualified workers receiving more training and investment than less qualified workers.

23   This is not simply a case of the system recognising and labelling learners' innate levels of ability. The gap between the best and worst performers in our system actually widens as they go through education; and it is both significantly wider and more closely related to socio-economic status in this country than elsewhere.

(DfES 2004, Chapter 1)

This conclusion is based on a number of recent research studies. School level data shows that in the median mainstream secondary school in England 44 per cent of pupils achieved 5 or more grade A*–C GCSE passes. In schools with between 35 per cent and 50 per cent of pupils eligible for free school meals (FSM), the usual indicator of family socio-economic status, the figure was 24 per cent. In schools with over 50 per cent FSM, the figure was 18 per cent. A similar comparison of SATs test results at Key Stage 2, the end of primary school, shows a median figure of 69 per cent achieving Level 4 in English, which drops to 54 per cent in schools with 35–50 per cent FSM (Power *et al.*, 2002). According to a report on *Education and Child Poverty* published in March 2003 by the End Child Poverty campaign, this class gap in attainment is evident at just under 2 years of age and widens during school, until at 15 pupils from poorer homes are one-third as likely to get 5 A*–C GCSEs as those from better-off families. The attainment gap between pupils on free school meals and other pupils doubles between the ages of 7 and 14. At age 7, 80 per cent of FSM pupils gained the expected level in maths compared to 93 per cent of non-FSM pupils. By age 14 in 2003 46 per cent of FSM pupils achieved level 5 compared to 75 per cent of non-FSM pupils (End Child Poverty, 2003). Most recently McKnight *et al.* (2005) conclude that 'recent research has shown that the association between income and attainment has increased, with children from higher income backgrounds experiencing greater increases in attainment relative to children from lower income backgrounds', so that 'young children with similar levels of competence diverge as they progress through school according to their socio-economic background' (p49).

The class differences at school level continue into higher education. The HEFCE report *Young Participation in Higher Education* (HEFCE, 2005) shows that young people from the most well-off wards are up to six times more likely to go to university than those from the poorest. (Unfortunately there is no data available on the relationship between the social composition of A Level and advanced GNVQ students and their grades and university applications, so it is not possible to specify to what extent the class difference in admissions are due to lower attainment as against self-selection factors such as fear of debt, social identity issues and different career aspirations.) In recent decades the individual economic return on higher education has increased, tending to perpetuate these class differences in later working life. The wage premium for men with degrees compared to those with no qualifications was 48 per cent in 1980 and 72 per cent in 1995, though it may have stopped rising now (Sefton and Sutherland, 2005). In their report *Changing Britain, Changing Lives*, Ferri *et al.* (2003) compared cohorts of adults born in 1946 and 1970. Family income for those with degrees was 30 per cent higher than for those with no qualifications in the cohort born in 1946, but for the 1970 cohort the figure was almost 50 per cent.

New Labour education policy and social class

How has New Labour addressed the issue of social class inequality in the school system? The first point to note is that the recognition of the impact of social class on attainment in the *Five Year Strategy for Children and Learners* (DfES, 2004) is unusually frank. It has previously tended to be minimised within the government's 'school improvement' agenda in order to focus on what teachers can do to raise standards regardless of the social composition of the school. In 1997, New Labour's first year of office, David Blunkett, the Secretary of State for Education, said 'Poverty is no excuse for failure. We have many examples of teachers, pupils and schools who are succeeding against the odds in deprived rural and urban areas' (quoted in Gold, 2003, p. 22). More recently, in January 2003, David Miliband, the schools minister, repeated the claim that poverty cannot be an excuse for low attainment: 'The evidence is clear . . . that schools serving similar types of pupils achieve dramatically different results' (quoted in Gold, 2003, p. 22). It is true that there are differences in attainment among schools with similar intakes, but the much larger differences which the government is referring to are largely the result of significant advantages some schools have over others. According to a survey carried out by the *Times Educational Supplement*, most poor schools performed about the same. Of the high-performers, most had some special intake advantage, such as being all girls or selecting on religious grounds, or had extra funding from specialist status (Gold, 2003).

The government's overall aim has been to raise standards of pupil attainment. But raising standards does not necessarily reduce inequality. On the contrary, as the government itself recognises, overall standards have risen, including those of lower-achieving pupils, while the class inequality gap has not only remained but widened. We need therefore to look at those policies specifically aimed at reducing it.

A particular priority has been the early years (Stewart, 2005b). In 1998 the government launched the National Childcare Strategy. An increase in maternity benefits has allowed more low-income children to spend more time with their mother in the first 6 months. Nursery places have been expanded: by 2004 all 3 and 4 year olds were guaranteed a part-time place. The Sure Start project for children age 0–4 has targeted additional resources on the most deprived 20 per cent of wards. It has proved popular with parents and there is some evidence of success. The 2004 budget committed an increase in spending by 2007/8 of £699m on children's centres and disadvantaged two-year olds. Nevertheless the amount allocated to pre-school provision remains a very low percentage of GDP compared to many other countries.

Excellence in cities

The major government policy aimed at tackling low education achievement in socially deprived schools has been Excellence in Cities. EiC was launched in 1999 and by 2004 it had been extended to one in three of all state secondary schools, with significant resourcing of about £350m a year. It has seven main elements: learning mentors, learning support units, the 'Gifted and talented' programme, city learning centres for IT, 'leading edge' schools and specialist schools, and action zones where clusters of schools work together.

How successful has EiC been? According to an Ofsted report on EiC published in June 2003, the percentage of young people achieving 5 or more A*–C grades (or equivalent) rose at the same rate as the national average in the four years from 1998 to 2001, and faster than the national average in 2002 (Shaw, 2003). (However, it should be noted that many EiC schools have achieved dramatic gains in their scores by entering large numbers of pupils for GNVQs in subjects which each counted as the equivalent of four GCSEs.) The results in KS3 maths and English tests have improved faster in EiC areas than nationally in the past four years. But the report notes that EiC is not the only reason for improvement. According to David Bell, the chief inspector for schools,

> There are rapid improvements in some schools but this is offset by disappointing progress, or even decline, of others. You've got to be realistic about what such schemes can achieve ... they can have a positive impact on pupil attainment [. . .] But there is still a substantial gap in achievement [between] excellence in cities and education action zones and pupils across the country.
>
> (Quoted in Woodward, 2003)

McKnight *et al.* (2005) point out that the class gap in school leaving examinations is the same in 2003 as it was in 1989. In other words, the reduction in class inequality which has been achieved has succeeded in recovering the ground which was lost as a result of the particularly divisive policies of the Thatcher government. It seems likely that further reductions will prove to be more difficult to achieve, in the context of continuing high economic inequality, without significantly more radical measures in education.

However, the overall direction of Labour's reform programme for schooling is to reinforce patterns of class inequality rather than to reduce them. This process of class reproduction takes place at every level from that of the structure of the school system to the individual classroom. Its underlying principle is differentiation, which acts as a mechanism of social class selection: in effect a process of negative discrimination. It is exemplified most recently in the principal aim of Labour's *Five Year Strategy for Children and Learners* (DfES, 2004), to 'promote personalisation and choice'.

Choice and the admissions market

At the systemic level the principle of differentiation is embodied in a key theme of government education policy: 'choice and diversity'. Labour has exacerbated the existing historical divisions within the British school system by attacking the notion of the comprehensive school (itself only partly achieved) and promoting different types of state schools. Parents are able to exercise some choice about which school to send their children to, and this combines with government-sponsored diversity of provision to perpetuate patterns of social class inequality which favour middle class families because middle class parents have the social capital to be able to 'play the system' more successfully (Ball, 2003).

The government's claim that 'diversity and choice' are the best way both to raise standards and to reduce inequality contradicts recent evidence from the PISA study comparing school student attainment in a number of countries (OECD/Unesco, 2003). The UK performs well overall but has one of the largest attainment gaps between rich and poor students in the developed world. The PISA report shows that comprehensive school systems are more effective at reducing inequality. It praises Finland, which performed best in the study, for its comprehensive system and for giving teachers a high degree of responsibility and autonomy. Andreas Schleicher, head of the OECD's educational indicators and analysis division, says there are no advantages to selection. 'The trade-off between quality and equity does not exist in reality'. This finding contradicts the Labour government's policies of diversity of types of schools coupled with selection by parental choice and, overtly or covertly, by schools themselves, which tends to create an even more hierarchical school system and to reinforce patterns of social segregation (Slater, 2003). Yet the government's new education minister, Ruth Kelly, used her first speech to appeal to middle class voters by promising to extend parental choice (Taylor and Smithers, 2005).

This is the context in which the effect of the Academies programme, which is aimed at socially deprived areas, needs to be judged. Initial results show that most academies have significantly improved their GCSE results (Blair, 2004). What has not been analysed is whether this is at the expense of neighbouring schools. Are these lavishly funded new schools disproportionately attracting the most proactive and educationally supportive parents, and are they disproportionately avoiding taking pupils with behavioural and learning difficulties? In any case, academies cannot represent a generalised solution to the problem of social inequality in school because they have exceptionally privileged status and funding and there will only be 200 of them in England.

Personalisation and categorisation

The function of differentiation as a mechanism of social class selection is also exemplified by another key government policy, personalised learning. First launched by Tony Blair at the 2003 Labour Party Conference, it was defined by David Miliband that year as 'an education system where assessment, curriculum, teaching style, and out of hours provision are all designed to discover and nurture the unique talents of every single pupil . . .' (quoted in M. Johnson, 2004). In 2004 the DfES published a pamphlet by Charles Leadbetter entitled *Learning about Personalisation: How Can We Put the Learner at the Heart of the Education System?* and sent it to all Schools (Leadbetter, 2004). Personalised learning is one of the key themes of Labour's *Five Year Strategy for Children and Learners* (DfES, 2004). At first sight, this might seem to be an uncontentious policy, but a closer look shows that what Labour means by personalised learning is a crude categorisation of pupils' abilities as the basis for social selection into different job-related pathways.

According to Miliband, '. . . the most effective teaching depends on really knowing the needs, strengths and weaknesses of individual pupils. So the biggest driver for change and gain is use of data on pupil achievement to design learning experiences that really stretch individual pupils . . . (quoted in M. Johnson, 2004). But 'pupil data' generated by a regime of tests and targets does not provide the basis for really knowing pupils. As the authors of the book *Learning Without Limits* (Hart *et al.*, 2004) say, 'Tasks can be successfully matched at an appropriate level of demand for young people of different abilities or levels of attainment without any genuine connection being achieved between young people's hearts and minds and the tasks they are asked to undertake' (p. 182). Government policy concep-tualises children's learning in terms of scores, levels and targets, and this has had a profound effect on how teachers conceptualise the abilities of children. This is the theme of Hart and her co-authors:

> the act of categorising young people by ability reifies differences and hardens hierarchies, so that we start to think of those in the different categories as different kinds of learners with different minds, different characteristics and very different needs.
>
> (Hart *et al.*, 2004, p. 29).

It is a way of thinking exemplified by the government's promotion of the spurious concept of 'gifted and talented'. Assessment has become central to the teacher's role, and its primary purpose is selection, not the diagnosis of learning needs. It is a logic of selection by failure, not success for all.

One important way in which the fixed ability template affects teachers' thinking is that it creates a disposition to accept as normal, indeed inevitable, the limited achievement of a significant proportion of the school population

(Hart *et al.* 2004, pp. 28–9).

Government policy has been to encourage teachers to make different provision for different pupils on the basis of their perceived ability. As Hart *et al.* (2004, p. 10) note, 'a major focus of reform initiatives has been to endorse differentiation by ability as an essential feature of good practice' (p. 10). It has promoted the organisation of pupil groups by 'ability', both between and within classes, in secondary and primary schools. Differentiation of pupils by perceived ability, shaped largely by social class, results in a differentiated curriculum. Teachers adapt their teaching to their perceptions of the child, and notions of fixed ability result in less intellectually demanding teaching which discriminates against working class pupils, locking them into a cycle of increasing inequality of attainment. The consequence is that the majority of working class children and young people receive an intellectually diluted education, a sort of cultural minimum wage. More than 30 years ago Keddie (1971) noted that teachers organise teaching for middle class pupils in terms of the logic of the subject and for working class pupils in terms of their expectations of these pupils as unable to cope with an academic curriculum. Hart *et al.* (2004, p. 35) refer to research by Hacker *et al.* (1991), who identified

> . . . noticeable changes in the 'type' of instruction that teachers gave when they moved from teaching a high-ability to a low-ability class. In high-ability classes, there was an emphasis on acquiring concepts, learning principles, applying concepts to problem-solving activities and working independently. In contrast, teacher–pupil interactions in low-ability classes concentrated on the transmission of factual information through statements made by the teacher.

Differentiation is a process of social selection by means of negative discrimination – giving less to those who have less. The negative discrimination of ability grouping is reinforced by the pressure on schools to meet government-driven pupil performance targets by focusing resources on those pupils most 'profitable' for the school in terms of test results, who are disproportionately from better-off families (Gillborn and Youdell, 2000).

From age 14 differentiation becomes overt social segregation, within and between schools, when any pretence of a common curriculum ends and foreign languages, the arts and humanities become optional. It is mainly schools in working class areas which will abandon these subjects, while they remain an indicator of academic success in middle class schools (Ward, 2002). For the majority of working class students the diet is a basic core – exemplified by Tomlinson's proposed school-leaving tests in functional English, maths and information technology – and vocational training. First came the decision to allow

FE colleges to take students from 14 part-time, again mainly working class. The latest government plan, to be published in a White Paper in 2005, is that 14-year-old students can go to FE college full time, or take up a trade such as plumbing under a 'young apprenticeship' scheme on a split week basis between college, school and work – all justified in the name of personalised learning. And David Bell, the chief inspector, is proposing to call for new vocational schools for 14–16 year olds. It will tend to perpetuate the separation of pupils from different social classes into 'academic' and 'vocational' pathways through school which lead to different opportunities after school in terms of employment and higher education destinations (Ainley, 2003). And this is exactly what Charles Clarke advocates in his foreword to the *Five Year Strategy*: 'as young people begin to train for work, a system that recognises individual aptitudes and provides as many tailored paths to employment as there are people and jobs'.

Charles Leadbetter (2004), in his DfES pamphlet, is correct to stress that 'The biggest challenge to the personalized learning agenda is its implications for inequality.' He warns that differences in provision, and choice, will benefit the middle class at the expense of the working class unless there is substantial state action to compensate. He reveals here a fundamental misunderstanding of the 'personalisation and choice' agenda. This agenda is a deliberate strategy to make education conform to the needs of employers under the cloak of the apparently user-friendly language of 'personalised learning' and parental choice. The aim is the abandonment of any pretence of education providing high quality access for all to a common culture of knowledge, which is regarded both as unnecessary for increasingly dualised labour market needs and undesirably expensive. The dualised labour market dictates a dualised curriculum comprising a narrow and diluted common core of basic competences and a broader subject curriculum which is marginalised in the primary school (though for middle class children the impoverished school curriculum is supplemented by the 'curriculum of the home', not to mention private tutors) and in the secondary school becomes the province of the largely middle class higher achievers. Selection for the labour market inevitably becomes social class selection because the compensatory measures Labour is introducing, best exemplified by its policies for pre-school provision, are far too weak to bridge the huge and widening class gap in education, especially when the overall thrust of Labour's education policies is to reinforce it.

The school and the production of human capital

The state school system does not just function to reproduce the advantages of the middle class over the working class. It has a more fundamental purpose, which is to help to reproduce the conditions of existence of capitalist society as a whole. In this context the principal function of the school is to produce the sorts of future workers which the economy needs, its 'human capital'. Labour's rationale for its education reforms makes it clear that the most important, and overriding, function of the education system is its contribution to economic competitiveness (see for example the White Paper *Schools: Achieving Success*, DfES, 2001). From this perspective, the dominant class interests which drive education policy are not those of the middle class, although they benefit from it at the expense of the working class, but those of the dominant class itself, the employers, the rich, the ruling class.

Labour's 'human capital' argument is that economic competitiveness in the new knowledge economy depends on a highly educated labour force. This is a dangerous half-truth. Certainly the economy requires a layer of highly educated workers, but it also requires a substantial layer of less-qualified workers for low-skilled jobs, many of them in the expanding service sector, and a pool of unemployed and semi-employed who can be moved into and out of the labour force as needed. A school system geared to these stratified labour needs inevitably reproduces educational inequality, not counters it.

In addition to Labour's conception of the aims of education, its electoral interests as a political party militate against tackling class inequality in education. It has to convince the dominant class that its policies will meet their economic needs for an appropriately skilled, stratified and socialised workforce. But it also has to win enough votes to remain in power. New Labour built itself by occupying the 'middle ground' in British politics and attracting middle class votes away from the Conservatives. It is determined to retain that support by avoiding egalitarian reforms which might undermine the privileged position of middle class families in the education system.

There is one other aspect of Labour's education policies which impacts on class inequality. The combination of the micro-management of teachers' work and the intensification of their workload has greatly reduced teachers' ability to develop innovative curriculum initiatives and teaching methods to tackle class inequality (in contrast with the flourishing of creative anti-racist and anti-sexist initiatives in the 1970s and 1980s, up to the 1988 Education Act).

Class as a social relationship

It is possible to draw the conclusion that the weight of social class inequality in society is so great that schools can do nothing much to counter it. Many teachers and educationists have rejected this sociological fatalism and have sought to develop more radical alternatives. The starting point is a reconceptualisation of the concept of social class. Up to now I have used it in the sense of socio-economic status. Family income and occupation are the most common ways in which class is defined in relation to school. Class is seen as a location within a stratified and hierarchical social structure of distribution of jobs and income. It is certainly true that this correlates closely with educational attainment, but it is not helpful in explaining why this correlation exists.

I want to draw here on the work of Ellen Meiksins Wood (1995) in her book *Democracy against Capitalism*. She argues that there are two ways of thinking about class in society – as a structural location or as a social relation. The first treats class as a form of stratification which factors out relationships of power and exploitation between classes. The second presupposes that relations of production distribute people into class situations, that these situations entail essential antagonisms and conflicts of interest, and that they therefore create conditions of struggle. Class formations and the discovery of class consciousness grow out of the process of struggle, as people 'experience' and 'handle' their class situations (Wood, 1995, p. 80).

School is one crucial social institution within which class relationships work themselves out. The work of Bob Connell, an Australian educationalist, and his colleagues is particularly helpful. In their book *Making the Difference: Schools, Families and Social Division* (Connell et al., 1982), they argue that we must change the terms of the discussion from a focus on inequalities of social class in terms of location to a focus on class as a 'complex association of activity, situation, and structure' (p. 146).

> Educational inequality isn't a matter of factor piling upon factor, and cannot be understood by a kind of arithmetic of advantage and disadvantage . . . Of course some people have more money, more education, than others. But equally plainly there is a larger reality all around and underneath those differences – the social relations and practices in which they arise. Notions like 'inequality' are not much use when we try to grasp how people enter those relations what they do to them, where they come from, and how they might be changed.
>
> (p. 193)

For Connell and his co-authors, the core of the social relationships of schooling is the relationship between the student and knowledge. This is the key idea which I want to develop. They argue that social class positions people, including school students in different relationships to school knowledge. (I will omit the upper class, because their children tend not to attend state schools, but the argument applies *a fortiori* to them.) Middle class families are more likely to embody and transmit to their children the sorts of cultural capital which are validated by the school.

Middle class families are more likely to provide the sort of cultural experiences, ranging from shared reading activities to music tuition and involvement in clubs and other activities outside the home, which have significant benefits in terms of success at school. Middle class parents, almost by definition, have themselves succeeded in the education system and provide role models for their children of the causal link between school success and career success. Middle class parents are more likely to possess instrumental knowledge about how to succeed in the education system: knowledge about how to choose a school; knowledge about how to negotiate with teachers, in order perhaps to secure a place for one's child in a higher set; knowledge about how to effectively support the child's homework or assessed coursework; knowledge about curriculum choices and their likely subsequent benefits; knowledge about how to apply to university and choose an appropriate course. In short, it is the knowledge, communication skills and confidence which middle class parents tend to have and use to maximise their positional advantage in education.

Class differences in relationships to language have a particular importance. School success depends on the ability to understand and use 'academic' forms of language. The spoken language of the home may be linguistically similar in register to that of the school, facilitating learning, or linguistically distant. Reading and writing are the fundamental skills which determine subsequent school success. It is not simply mastery of the technical skills, it is also the meaning of reading and writing for the child. Homes where children have few books and seldom see their parents reading or writing tend to generate a different orientation to literacy, a different cultural predisposition, from ones where reading and writing, in particular the sorts of texts which demand language skills similar to those required for school success, are everyday activities. Middle class children have more of the linguistic capital which is valorised by the school, because the oral language of the middle class family is more influenced by the written form.

Empirical evidence is provided by an analysis of the 2001 PISA data by Nash (2003). PISA, the Programme for International Student Assessment, measured how well 15 year olds performed in English, maths and science in 43 countries. It found a high correlation between family socio-economic status and the number of books in the home, and between family SES and the child's reading attainment. Family SES and reading attainment both correlate closely with pupils' job aspirations.

Class relationships to school knowledge

Different class relationships to school knowledge has been the theme explored by Bernard Charlot, a French sociologist of education, in a number of books (Charlot, 1997). In *Ecole et savoir dans les banlieus . . . et ailleurs* (Charlot *et al.*, 1992), Charlot and his colleagues describe their large-scale ethnographic study of students at secondary and primary schools in both poor and relatively affluent districts of Paris. On the basis of their empirical research they argue that differences in academic achievement are associated with different relationships to knowledge on the part of the student, and that academic achievement in school is dependent on developing a particular relationship to knowledge. They distinguish three epistemological processes which define relations to learning in school.

- In the first, knowledge is defined in terms of the learning situation in which the student is involved, and the student role is defined in terms of coping with that task.
- In the second, knowledge is seen as objectivised: abstracted from the learning task, decontextualised and external to the learner. The role of the student is seen as to appropriate it.
- In the third, the learner is engaged in a process not only of objectifying and appropriating knowledge but entering into it, interpreting it and relating it to the self in a process of consciously reflexive self-education.

The first process is typical of low-achieving students. It is a relationship to school rather than a relationship to knowledge. The other two processes, especially the third, are associated with higher academic attainment. These processes are highly class-differentiated. Working class students tended to see learning much more in terms solely of the completion of tasks than as the entering into universes of knowledge. Many of them were motivated to succeed at school in order to get a good job, but they did not conceptualise this link between school and future destinations as mediated by intellectual work in the way that most middle class students did. Middle class students tended to give meaning and value to intellectual work both for intrinsic reasons – as interesting and enjoyable in itself – and for extrinsic ones – as the means to higher education and a good job.

Charlot's argument has important consequences for teaching. First, it poses entry into intellectual universes as the key to academic success. Second, it poses, as the necessary condition of this relationship to knowledge, its meaning for the student. Without that, neither the presentation of an intellectually demanding curriculum nor hard work by the learner is enough. The student can work hard but ineffectively in terms of academic success. Charlot and his colleagues argue that teachers can help students to construct a meaningful relationship to knowledge and thus achieve greater academic success, but that teachers have often adopted one of two opposite, and ineffective, approaches. One is to present knowledge through an academic curriculum which has little meaning for working class students, since it doesn't connect with their experiences and identities. The other is to make the curriculum 'relevant' to working class students, but at the expense of diluting its intellectual demands. Charlot and his colleagues argue that teachers often use strategies with working class students which are intended to facilitate learning, but which actually serve to exclude them from the entry into abstract systems of knowledge which is necessary for academic success. They give examples: the focus on the local and the personal which tends to restrict students to the immediate context; the fragmentation of knowledge into small simple steps with little intellectual challenge, the slippage towards the affective at the expense of the cognitive.

Working class pupils can succeed

For Charlot and his colleagues the challenge for the school is to bring the intellectual world and the world of the child or young person together in a meaningful way. Can this be achieved for working class pupils? Or is it that the working class doesn't have enough cultural resources to succeed at school? If so, class society inevitably produces the class school. Hart *et al.* (2004) reject this pessimistic and determinist view and offer an alternative based on the principle that all children have the capacity to learn, even in a profoundly economically unequal society. The core idea is not 'ability' but 'transformability', the potential to transform learning capacity. I want to draw on and develop three of the themes of their approach: the centrality of concepts and the written language to intellectual development, the notion of common learning made accessible by 'connectedness' – teachers developing individual pedagogic relationships with them – and making school knowledge fully meaningful for working class students by integrating it with, and thus helping create, the knowledge they use to understand and act in the world.

Concepts and the written language

The 'value of an intellectual life', the importance of 'seeking to induct young people into the life of the mind' (Hart *et al.*, 2004, p.176) is central to *Learning Without Limits*. Pupils need to 'focus on the concepts, the big ideas, that will increase their capacity to make sense of the world' (p. 177). The evidence from the case studies in their book is supported by a study in the US which showed that teaching high school students how to 'construct conceptual models of scientific phenomena and how to monitor and reflect on their progress' led to high achievement by low achievers (White and Frederiksen, 1998, p. 5, quoted in Hart *et al* 2004, p. 34).

I want to develop this point by drawing on the work of Jean-Pierre Terrail (2004), a French sociologist of education. He argues that the problem is not to give children the desire to learn, they already have that, but to avoid discouraging them by enabling them to confront the real intellectual difficulties which school knowledge offers. The key to entry into intellectual universes is reading and writing. In fact every aspect of social life is increasingly penetrated by elaborated knowledge which can only be acquired through writing. There is no 'non-intellectual' knowledge. Language is not just a medium of communication; it mediates thinking, it enables interior discourse. Written language differs from oral language in three ways. First, it is more standardised. Second, it is more explicit, because it is divorced from context and paralinguistic signals. Writing requires decentring: the writer has to envisage the reader. And third, written text is thought objectivised, distanced, an object of reflection to be worked on. To enter into written culture is to take on this distanced reflexive relationship to language. The capacity for distancing from experience is inherent in language, because language is a conceptual medium. Words are not reflections of things. They are concepts. All children have language and therefore all children have the conceptual basis to enter into written culture. That some children have more linguistic resources does not mean that others lack the capacity to develop theirs. The advantage of some is not the incapacity of others. According to Terrail teachers often misunderstand both the conceptual demands of knowledge and the capacities of children, and consequently adopt a pedagogy of the concrete, substituting images and examples for an explicit verbal discourse informed by concepts.

Common learning and connectedness

The belief in the capacity of all children to cope with the intellectual demands of school knowledge leads to a different conception of 'differentiation'. Its starting point has been expressed by Brian Simon:

> . . . if we want to develop effective pedagogical means relevant to primary and secondary classrooms and children, we need to start from the *opposite* premises from those embraced by Plowden. Instead of pinpointing the

supposed need of each individual, we should start by identifying the needs and characteristics of children in general – those common to all.

(Simon, 1994, p. 150)

This does not mean a homogenised pedagogy that ignores differences among children. Hart and her co-authors explain that while ability-focused teachers 'attempt to match tasks to what they see as salient differences between their students',

> Teaching that seeks to foster diversity through co-agency is concerned not with match but with connection, achieving a genuine meeting of minds, purposes and concerns between teachers and young people. [. . .] Tasks and outcomes are deliberately left open, or constructed in such a way as to offer choice of various kinds, so that young people have space to make their own connections [. . .].
> . . . the teachers project themselves empathetically into young people's minds and try to imagine, in relation to any particular set of curricular concerns and intentions, what will seem accessible, worthwhile and interesting from young people's point of view.

(Hart *et al.*, 2004, p. 183)

This means that teachers need to get to know the students they teach very well. There are implications here for secondary schools, where the number of pupils who teachers teach each week makes such connectedness impossible. Personalisation is one of the principles of the Coalition of Essential Schools in the US, where no teacher in an affiliated school teaches more than 80 students – at Central Park East Secondary School in New York the limit is 40 (Meier and Schwarz, 1999). This a very different conception and practice of 'personalisation' of learning from that currently being advocated by New Labour.

The meaning of the curriculum

Another theme of the transformability paradigm is the relationship between the student and the curriculum. Hart and her co-authors speak of the necessity 'to find ways of making connections between school learning and the students' worlds, to find ways to make learning meaningful, relevant and important to them' (2004, p. 168). The student needs to be able to use 'school knowledge' to organise under-standings and actions in order to further his or her own meanings and purposes. Charlot and Figeat (1979, p. 245) stress that the key relationship is the couple 'problem-knowledge'.

> All learning must start from problem situations, that is to say situations which have a meaning for the student, which pose a problem, which demand the elaboration of ideas to resolve this problem and which lead effectively to the mastery of rigorous concepts and language.

The solution is not a diluted curriculum restricted to popular experience, but one in which 'academic' knowledge and popular experiences and meanings are interwoven and mutually and critically illuminate each other, so that 'school knowledge' infuses and informs the purposes and actions in the life-worlds of children and young people. But especially for working class students school knowledge is often experienced as alienating. As Connell (1994, p. 137) says:

> . . . the experience of teachers in disadvantaged schools has persistently led them to question the curriculum. Conventional subject matter and texts and traditional teaching methods and assessment turn out to be sources of systematic difficulty. They persistently produce boredom. Enforcing them heightens the problem of discipline, and so far as they are successfully enforced they divide pupils between an academically successful minority and an academically discredited majority.

The issue is exemplified by the disaffected school students in a research study by Riley and Rustique-Forrester (2002):

> A common feeling expressed by many of the students we talked to was that 'learning' was boring. [. . .] Almost uniformly, students found few connections between what they encountered in school and what they were experiencing, or were likely to experience, outside of it.
>
> (p. 34)

> Examples of teaching enjoyed by disaffected young people, and perceived as effective by them, included those experiences where pupils were able to connect learning to their own lives and their expectations about their futures.
>
> (p. 72)

The curriculum itself needs to be reconstructed. As Connell (1994, p. 140) says:

> Each particular way of constructing the curriculum (i.e. organizing the field of knowledge and defining how it is to be taught and learned) carries social effects. Curriculum empowers and disempowers, authorizes and de-authorizes, recognizes and mis-recognizes different social groups and their knowledge and identities.

At this point I want to introduce a new element into the argument. Thus far I have spoken of the aim of education for working class students solely in terms of success within the academic curriculum in order to reduce inequality of outcomes. This is a necessary aim but not the whole story. Connell in *Schools and Social Justice* argues for 'a broader conception of the "empowerment" of working class students as the goal.

Such a concept would embrace not only skills and knowledges required for success within the existing system but also skills and knowledges required for collective action.

(Connell, 1993, p. 104)

There is a tradition within working class education of education as a means to social emancipation which stretches back to the early nineteenth century. Richard Johnson describes the concept of 'really useful knowledge', which started out from everyday concerns and which broke down the distinctions between learning and life, and between the theoretical and the applied:

> Really useful knowledge involved, then, a range of resources for overcoming daily difficulties. It involved self-respect and self-confidence which came from seeing that your oppressions were systematic and were shared. It included practical skills, but not just those wanted by employers . . . Really useful knowledge was also a means to overcoming difficulties in the long term and more comprehensively. It taught people what social changes were necessary for real social ameliorations to occur.[1]

(R. Johnson 1983, p. 22)

Connell argues, on both social justice and epistemological grounds, for the replacement of the current mainstream hegemonic curriculum with a new common curriculum based on principles of social justice.

> The strategy seeks a way of organizing content and method which builds on the experience of the disadvantaged, but generalizes that to the whole system, rather than confining it to an enclave. The strategy thus seeks a practical reconstruction of education which will yield relative advantage to the groups currently disadvantaged.

(Connell, 1993, p. 38)

Similarly, in *Democratic Schools*, which contains four case studies of American schools, James Beane and Michael Apple (1999, p. 19) say: 'Our task is to reconstruct dominant knowledge and employ it to help, not hinder, those who are least privileged in this society'.

Meaningful knowledge in practice

We can find at least elements of a curriculum based on 'really useful knowledge' in some schools today, and see that they can provide the basis for a different relationship to knowledge by working class students which can empower them in the ways that Connell suggests. In the United States there is greater freedom to innovate, at least in some contexts, as the following brief case studies demonstrate.

A curriculum which combines being intellectually challenging and building on students' concerns and experiences in the wider society is one of the key issues in Newmann's (1996) research into 'authentic achievement', based on the School

Restructuring Study of 24 significantly restructured public schools in the United States. Newmann and his associates define 'authentic achievement' in terms of the following criteria: the construction of knowledge (rather than its reproduction); disciplined enquiry (comprising the use of a prior knowledge-base, in-depth understanding and elaborated communication); and value beyond school (that is, discourses, products and performances which have a meaning and purpose beyond the demonstration of competence to a teacher) (Wehlage *et al.*, 1996). They single out four schools as most successful because of their concern for the intellectual quality of classroom practice. I will briefly describe one of them, an innovatory multiracial school, with around one-third of the students receiving free or reduced-fee lunch, governed by teachers and parents and based on a Deweyan concept of applied learning (Doane, 1996). 'The school's curriculum was built around enquiry-oriented activities (that involved real-world application of knowledge' (Newmann, *et al.*, 1996, p. 166). Two consecutive fifth grade lessons illustrate the school's emphasis on intellectual quality. A newspaper report of the killing of 3 high school students by rival gang members led to a discussion of the reasons why young people joined gangs, possible alternatives and solutions. The students worked in groups, writing letters to the local radio station and newspaper, creating slogans, posters, songs and leaflets persuading students to be independent, collecting data on gang crimes for the school newspaper, and producing and videotaping a role-play to show to the school. 'Consistent with [the school's] commitment to Applied Learning, the lessons connected school knowledge to situations outside the classroom and included specific attempts to influence audiences beyond their own classroom' (*ibid.*, p. 167).

A similar conception underlies the case studies in Apple and Beane's book *Democratic Schools*.

> The idea of a thematic curriculum dominates these schools, not simply as an effective methodology that keeps children happy, but because this approach involves putting knowledge to use in relation to real life problems and issues. [. . .] Rather than being lists of concepts, facts and skills that students master for standardized achievement tests (and then go on to forget, by and large), knowledge is that which is intimately connected to the communities and biographies of real people. Students learn that knowledge makes a difference in people's lives, including their own.
>
> (Apple and Beane, 1999, p. 119)

One of the case studies is of an innovatory two-way bilingual elementary school governed by teachers and parents in Milwaukee, Wisconsin. Approximately two-thirds of the students are eligible for free school lunches. Bob Peterson, a teacher at the school and one of its founders, begins his description of the school with an account of 3 fifth graders on their own initiative devising a role-play based on anti-gay discrimination. In the class discussion that followed, other students related it to family experience, a recent gay rights demonstration and Martin Luther King's march for civil rights: 'the incident reminded me of the inherent links between classroom and society: how society influences the student who shows up in our classrooms for six hours a day and how broader movements for social reform affect daily classroom life' (Peterson, 1999, p. 70).

Another case study in *Democratic Schools* describes the ninth grade programme at a school of technical arts in Cambridge, Massachusetts (Rosenstock and Steinberg, 1999):

> Cambridge is the 'text' as students investigate the neighborhoods, the systems, the people, and the needs that compose an urban community.
>
> (p. 53)

> The goal of CityWorks projects is to help students understand their community and its needs, and ultimately to see themselves as people who can affect that community and create new opportunities for others who live and work there.
>
> (p. 54)

These examples demonstrate that a curriculum which brings together 'school knowledge' and the real-life experiences and concerns of students is capable of enabling them to construct a meaningful problem-solving relationship to knowledge. As Beane and Apple (1999, p. 17) say:

> A democratic curriculum invites young people to shed the passive role of knowledge consumers and assume the active role of 'meaning makers'. It recognizes that people acquire knowledge by both studying external sources and engaging in complex activities that require them to construct their own knowledge.

Conclusion

Let me end by briefly summarising the outline of my argument.

- There is substantial economic inequality in Britain and the gap is widening.
- Economic inequality correlates strongly with educational achievement in schools.
- Government education policies are not significantly reducing the inequality gap. Their organising principle is differentiation, promoting the idea of fixed class-based abilities which operates as a process of social selection.
- Differentiation in classrooms has become a process of negative discrimination against working class pupils and students, resulting in intellectually and culturally impoverished provision for them.
- It also entails disembedding meaningful school knowledge from forms and processes of transmission and acquisition which are alienating to working class students.
- Class needs to be conceptualised as a relationship, not a location.
- In school, the central relationship is between the student and knowledge.

- Different relationships to knowledge are causally related to differences in academic achievement.
- Those different relationships to knowledge are structured, but not determined, by social class cultures.
- Individual educational trajectories are socially shaped but not socially pre-determined. Working class children and young people have the capacity to succeed.
- Changing students' relationships to knowledge needs to be the organising principle of policies to raise working class achievement and reduce educational inequality.
- Central to educational success is entry into 'intellectual worlds' through reading, writing, and concept development.
- A common curriculum can be made accessible to all young people if teachers develop individual pedagogic relationships with them.
- Making school knowledge fully meaningful for working class students entails integrating it with, and thus helping to create, the knowledge the child and young person uses to understand and act in the world.
- To do this requires both bringing the experiences and concerns of the child and young person into the curriculum and reconstructing the curriculum on a basis which combines high intellectual quality with the perspectives of the socially deprived and oppressed rather than those of the privileged and powerful.
- This provides the basis both for high academic achievement within the system and wider goals of education for emancipation.

The way to tackle the deep class inequality in our school system is not the government's agenda of personalisation, choice and diversity but to adopt the radical measures needed to provide working class children and young people with the intellectual tools for entry into the culture of knowledge and full citizenship. A high quality education for all requires a broad common core curriculum until age 16. What is good for some is good for all. If a privileged enriched curriculum is right for the 5 or 10 per cent so-called 'gifted and talented', how much more is it deserved by those less advantaged? If an introduction to the 'world of work' is thought right for some at 14, it is right for all, though as part of a critical education, not as premature job training. And in that context there is of course room for an element of choice, provided it does not serve to reinforce social inequalities.

Note

1   See also Cole, 2004, for an extended analysis of the ways in which 'really useful knowledge' is applicable to the twenty-first century.

References

Ainley, P. (2003) 'Towards a seamless web or a new tertiary tripartism? The emerging shape of post-14 education and training in England', *British Journal of Educational Studies*, 51 (4) pp. 390–407.

Apple, M.W. and Beane, J.A. (1999) Lessons from democratic schools, in M.W. Apple and J.A. Beane (eds) *Democratic Schools*, Washington, DC: Association for Supervision and Curriculum Development.

Ball, S.J. (2003) *Class Strategies and the Education Market*, London: Routledge Falmer.

Beane, J.A. and Apple, M.W. (1999) The case for democratic schools, in Apple, M.W. and Beane, J.A. (eds) *Democratic Schools*, Washington, DC: Association for Supervision and Curriculum Development.

Blair, A. (2004) 'Inner-city academies celebrate their GCSE success', *The Times*, August 17, p. 17.

Charlot, B. (1997) *Rapport au savoir*, Paris: Editions Economica.

Charlot, B. and Figeat, M. (1979) *L'Ecole aux enchères*, Paris: Petite Bibliotheque Payot.

Charlot, B., Bautier, E. and Rochex, J-Y. (1992) *École et savoir dans les banlieus . . . et ailleurs*, Paris: Armand Colin.

Cole, M. (2004) 'Rethinking the future: the commodification of knowledge and the grammar of resistance', in M. Benn and C. Chitty (eds) *A Tribute to Caroline Benn: Education and Democracy*, London: Continuum.

Connell, R.W. (1993) *Schools and Social Justice*, Philadelphia: Temple University Press.

Connell, R.W. (1994) 'Poverty and education', *Harvard Educational Review*, 64 (2), pp. 125–49.

Connell, R.W., Ashenden, D.J., Kessler, S. and Dowsett, G.W. (1982) *Making the Difference: Schools, Families and Social Division*, Sydney: Allen and Unwin.

Denny, C. and Elliott, L. (2004) 'The uphill struggle against child poverty', *The Guardian* 31 March.

DfES (Department for Education And Skills) (2001) *Schools: Achieving Success*, London: HMSO.

DfES (Department for Education And Skills) (2004) *Five Year Strategy for Children and Learners*, London: HMSO, http://www.dfes.gov.uk/publications/5yearstrategy/

Doane, K.B. (1996) 'Careen and Lamar elementary schools', in F.M. Newmann, (ed.), *Authentic Achievement: Restructuring Schools for Intellectual Quality*, San Francisco: Jossey-Bass.

End Child Poverty (2003) *Education and Child Poverty*, London: End Child Poverty.

Ferri, E., Bynner, J. and Wadsworth, M. (2003) *Changing Britain, Changing Lives*, London: Institute of Education, University of London.

Foot, P. (2003) 'Adding up to much less', *The Guardian* 26 November.

Gillborn, D. and Youdell, D. (2000) *Rationing Education*, London: Routledge.

Gold, K. (2003) 'Poverty *is* an excuse', *Times Educational Supplement* 7 March, pp. 22–3.

Hacker, R.G., Rowe, M.J. and Evans, R.D. (1991) 'The influences of ability groupings for secondary science lessons upon classroom processes. Part 1: homogenous groupings (science education notes)', *School Science Review* 73 (262), pp. 125–9.

Hart, S., Dixon, A., Drummond, M.J. and McIntyre, D. (2004) *Learning without Limits*, Maidenhead: Open University Press.

HEFCE (Higher Education Funding Council for England) (2005) *Young Participation in Higher Education*. London: HEFCE.

Hills, J. and Stewart, K. (2005) A tide turned but mountains yet to climb?, in J. Hills and K. Stewart (eds) *A More Equal Society?*, Bristol: The Policy Press.

Johnson, M. (2004) *Personalised Learning – an Emperor's Outfit?*, London: IPPR. See www.ippr.org.uk

Johnson, R. (1983) 'Educational politics: the old and the new', in A.M. Wolpe and J. Donald (eds) *Is There Anyone Here from Education?*, London: Pluto Press.

Keddie, N. (1971) 'Classroom knowledge', in M. Young (ed.) *Knowledge and Control*, London: Collier-Macmillan.

Leadbetter, C. (2004) *Learning about Personalisation: How Can We Put the Learner at the Heart of the Education System?*, London: DfES. Available at: http://www.standards. dfes.gov.uk/innovation-unit/personalisation/pllearn/?version=1

McKnight, A., Glennerster, H. and Lupton, R. (2005) 'Education, education, education . . . : an assessment of Labour's success in tackling education inequalities', in J. Hills and K. Stewart (eds) *A More Equal Society?*, Bristol: The Policy Press.

Meier, D. and Schwarz, P. (1999) 'Central Park East Secondary School: the hard part is making it happen', in M.W. Apple and J.A. Beane (eds) *Democratic Schools*, Buckingham: Open University Press.

Nash, R. (2003) 'Dreaming in the real world: social class and education in New Zealand', in J. Freeman-Moir and A. Scott (eds) *Yesterday's Dreams*, Christchurch: Canterbury University Press.

Newmann, F.M. (ed.) (1996) *Authentic Achievement: Restructuring Schools for Intellectual Quality*, San Francisco: Jossey-Bass.

Newmann, F.M., King, M.B. and Secada, W.G. (1996) 'Intellectual quality', in F.M. Newmann (ed.) *Authentic Achievement: Restructuring Schools for Intellectual Quality*, San Francisco: Jossey-Bass.

OECD/Unesco (2003) 'Literacy skills for the world of tomorrow – further results from Pisa 2000', *Education and Skills* 5, pp. 1–392.

Peterson, B. (1999) 'La escuela Fratney: a journey toward democracy', in M.W. Apple and J.A. Beane (eds) *Democratic Schools*, Washington, DC: Association for Supervision and Curriculum Development.

Phillips, C. (2005) 'Ethnic inequalities under New Labour: progress or entrenchment?', in J. Hills and K. Stewart (eds) *A More Equal Society?*, Bristol: The Policy Press.

Power, S., Warren, S., Gilllborn, D., Clark, A., Thomas, S. and Coate, K. (2002) *Education in Deprived Areas: Outcomes, Inputs and Processes*, London: Institute of Education.

Riley, K. A. and Rustique-Forrester, E. (2002) *Working with Disaffected Students*, London: Paul Chapman.

Rosenstock, L. and Steinberg, A. (1999) 'Beyond the shop: reinventing vocational education', in M.W. Apple and J.A. Beane (eds) *Democratic Schools*, Washington, DC: Association for Supervision and Curriculum Development.

Sefton, T. and Sutherland, H. (2005) 'Inequality and poverty under New Labour', in J. Hills and K. Stewart (eds) *A More Equal Society?*, Bristol: The Policy Press.

Shaw, M. (2003) 'Ofsted finds little action in city zones', *Times Educational Supplement*, 6 June.

Simon, B. (1994) *The State and Educational Change*, London: Lawrence and Wishart.

Slater, J. (2003) 'Class segregation holds Britain back', *Times Educational Supplement*, 4 July.

Stewart, K. (2005a) 'Changes in poverty and inequality in the UK in international context', in J. Hills and K. Stewart (eds) *A More Equal Society?*, Bristol: The Policy Press.

Stewart, K. (2005b) 'Towards an equal start? Addressing childhood poverty and deprivation', in J. Hills and K. Stewart (eds) *A More Equal Society?*, Bristol: The Policy Press.

Sutherland, H., Sefton, T. and Piachaud, D. (2003) *Poverty in Britain: The Impact of Government Policy Since 1997*, York: Joseph Rowntree Foundation.

Taylor, M. and Smithers, R. (2005) 'Kelly woos parents with talk of choice', *The Guardian*, January 7.

Terrail, J-P. (2004) *École: l'enjeu démocratique*, Paris: La Dispute.

Ward, H. (2002) 'French: strictly for the bourgeoisie?', *Times Educational Supplement*, 22 November.

Waugh, P. (2003) 'Poverty levels have grown under Labour', *The Independent*, 12 May.

Wehlage, G.G., Newmann, F.M. and Secada, W.G. (1996) 'Standards for authentic achievement and pedagogy', in F.M. Newmann (1996) *Authentic Achievement: Restructuring Schools for Intellectual Quality*, San Francisco: Jossey-Bass.

White, B.Y. and Frederiksen, J.R. (1998) 'Inquiry, modelling and metacognition: making science accessible to all students', *Cognition and Instruction* 16 (1), pp. 3–118.

Wood, E.M. (1995) *Democracy against Capitalism*, Cambridge: Cambridge University Press.

Woodward, W. (2003) 'Aid for city pupils has mixed success', *The Guardian*, 2 June.

Index